Inside Writing

A Writer's Workbook with Readings

William Salomone
Palomar College

Stephen McDonald
Palomar College

Martin Japtok
Palomar College

D0142443

CENGAGE
Learning·

Australia • Brazil • Mexico • Singapore • United Kingdom • United States

Inside Writing: A Writer's Workbook with Readings, Form B, Seventh Edition
William Salomone, Stephen McDonald, Martin Japtok

Product Director: Annie Todd

Developmental Studies Product Manager: Annie Todd

Content Developer: Margaret Manos

Associate Content Developer: Elizabeth Rice

Product Assistant: Luria Rittenberg

Media Developer: Elizabeth Neustaetter

Intellectual Property Analyst: Ann Hoffman

Manufacturing Planner: Betsy Donaghey

Art and Design Direction, Production Management, and Composition: Cenveo® Publisher Services

Cover Image: www.gettyimages.com

For product information and technology assistance, contact us at
Cengage Learning Customer & Sales Support, 1-800-354-9706

For permission to use material from this text or product, submit all requests online at **www.cengage.com/permissions**. Further permissions questions can be emailed to **permissionrequest@cengage.com**.

Library of Congress Control Number: 2014936371

Student Edition:
ISBN: 978-1-285-44587-8

Annotated Instructor's Edition/Instructor's Annotated Edition:
ISBN: 978-1-285-45188-6

Cengage Learning
20 Channel Center Street
Boston, MA 02210
USA

Cengage Learning is a leading provider of customized learning solutions with office locations around the globe, including Singapore, the United Kingdom, Australia, Mexico, Brazil and Japan. Locate your local office at: **international.cengage.com/region.**

Cengage Learning products are represented in Canada by Nelson Education, Ltd.

For your course and learning solutions, visit **www.cengage.com.**

Purchase any of our products at your local college store or at our preferred online store **www.cengagebrain.com.**

Instructors: Please visit **login.cengage.com** and log in to access instructor-specific resources.

Printed in the United States of America.
Print Number: 01   Print Year: 2014

To Rosemary, Marlyle, and Nagadya

Contents

Chapter Five Using Punctuation and Capitalization **283**

Chapter Six   Readings for Writers 347

Preface

Inside Writing was constructed on the premise that there is really only one reason for learning the essential rules of English grammar—to become better writers. In this text, we constantly stress that all college students are writers and that the aim of any college writing course—developmental or otherwise—is to improve writing. To this purpose, *Inside Writing* has been created with clear and simple organization, a friendly, nonthreatening tone, thorough integration of grammar sections with writing sections, and unique thematic exercises.

The Reason for This Text

We are all aware of widespread disagreement about what should be presented in a first-semester developmental writing course. *Inside Writing* was written to address the resulting diversity of course content with a union of grammar and writing instruction. In it, we teach basic grammar and sentence structure, yet we also provide extensive practice in sentence combining and paragraph writing.

Moving beyond a Traditional Approach. The traditional approach to developmental writing has been to review the rules of grammar, punctuation, and usage and then to test the students' understanding of those rules through a series of chapter tests. However, as research and experience have demonstrated, there is no necessary correlation between the study of grammar and the development of competent writers. As a result, many English departments have restructured their developmental courses to focus on the process of writing, developing courses that have very little in common with each other from one campus to the next. Today, some developmental writing instructors teach the traditional exercises in grammar, others focus on journal and expressive writing, others emphasize sentence combining, and still others teach the writing of paragraphs and short essays.

Using an Integrated Approach. **Inside Writing** responds to this spectrum of course content by integrating grammar instruction and writing practice. Certainly the practice of writing is important in a first-semester developmental class. Yet the study of traditional grammar, punctuation, and usage is also important because it provides a fundamental knowledge of sentence structure—knowledge that writers need not only to revise their own writing but also to discuss their writing with others. The writing practices in this text are specifically designed to support, not merely to supplement, the grammar instruction. As soon as students have mastered a particular grammatical principle, they are asked to put their knowledge into practice in the writing sections of each chapter. This immediate reinforcement makes it more likely that students will improve their writing as well as retain the rules of grammar, usage, and mechanics.

Text Organization and Features

Inside Writing, Form B, is presented in six chapters and an appendix. Each of the first five chapters consists of five sections that cover major principles of basic grammar, sentence construction, and paragraph writing. The appendix provides a review of common ESL issues. Throughout the text, the instruction is kept as simple as possible, giving the students only the information that is absolutely essential. The sixth chapter includes reading selections to accompany the writing instruction in the first five chapters.

- Each chapter's grammar instruction is divided into three sections so that the students are not presented with too much at once.

- Each of the three grammar sections includes various practices and ends with three exercises that give the students an opportunity to apply the concepts and rules they have learned.

- Each chapter is followed by a practice test covering the material presented in the first three sections of the chapter, and the text closes with a practice final examination.

- The fourth section of each chapter presents both instruction and exercises in sentence combining, based on the specific concepts and rules covered in the three grammar sections. For example, in the chapter covering participial phrases and adjective clauses, the sentence combining section instructs the students to combine sentences by using participial phrases and adjective clauses.

- The fifth section of each chapter includes instruction in writing paragraphs and essays and a choice of several writing assignments, again designed to reinforce the grammar sections of the chapter by leading students to employ in their own writing the rules for sentence structure they have studied.

- The sixth chapter, "Readings for Writers," offers reading selections that parallel the writing instruction in each of the first five chapters.

- The appendix, "Working with ESL Issues," discusses common challenges faced by the ESL writer, including the correct use of count and noncount nouns, articles, subjects and verbs, and adjectives.

- At the end of the text, answers to the practices—but not to the exercises—are provided. These answers allow the students to check their understanding of the material as they read the text. The extensive exercises without answers permit the instructor to determine where more explanation or study is needed.

- Many of the practices and exercises develop thematic ideas or contain a variety of cultural, mythological, and historical allusions. Some exercises, for example, describe a variety of trickster heroes, detail the history of London Bridge, or tell the story of Pyramus and Thisbe. In addition, individual sentences within practices and exercises often provoke questions and discussion when they refer to characters and events from history, mythology, or contemporary culture.

This feature of *Inside Writing* encourages developmental writing students to look beyond grammar, mechanics, and punctuation. It reminds them—or it allows us as instructors to remind them—that the educated writer has command of much more than the correct use of the comma.

Connecting Concepts and Writing Practice. To emphasize further the connection between the writing assignments and the grammar exercises, the writing assignment in each chapter is modeled by three thematic exercises within the grammar sections of the chapter. For instance, in Chapter 3, Exercises 1D, 2D, and 3C are paragraphs that use examples to support a statement made in a topic sentence. The writing practice section then extends this groundwork by presenting instruction in the writing of a similar expository paragraph or essay.

In each writing assignment the students are introduced gradually to the writing process and encouraged to improve their writing through prewriting and careful revision. They are also introduced to the basic concepts of academic writing—thesis statements, topic sentences, unity, specificity, completeness, order, and coherence to communicate their own thoughts and ideas. However, the main purpose of the writing instruction is to give the students an opportunity to use their new knowledge of grammar and sentence structure to communicate their own thoughts and ideas.

Changes to This Edition

We have improved the Seventh Edition of *Inside Writing* in several areas:

- Over 50 percent of practices and exercises are new.

- New thematic exercises that function not only as a way to test the students' comprehension of grammar, punctuation, or usage principles but also as an example of the writing assignment introduced in the chapter have been added throughout the text.

- New thematic exercises have been added throughout the text. These function not only as a way to test the students' comprehension of grammar, punctuation, and usage principles but also as an example of the writing assignment introduced in the chapter.

- Exercises are included that ask students to find and bring to class from their own readings (such as magazines, newspapers, books, or websites) sentences that illustrate the concept under review.

- Six new reading selections have been added to Chapter Six, "Readings for Writers." Five of these selections have been drawn from college textbooks in the fields of environmental science and American history. Our intention is to provide our students with practice in reading and responding to the kind of material they will find in their college texts.

- The chapter "Choosing the Right Words and Spelling Them Correctly" has been removed from the text to allow instructors more time to review and complete all material in the first five chapters. It will, however, be available online for instructors to use if they wish to do so.

■ Chapter tests are now formatted so that instructors can test only the material in the chapter under study, bypassing the review questions from earlier chapters.

■ As with all previous editions, we have included allusions designed to interest both the instructor and the student. For example, in just the first section of Chapter 1 are allusions to Hester Prynne, George Washington, Siddhartha, *The Wizard of Oz,* Narcissus, Scheherazade, P.T. Barnum, Emily Dickinson, Madonna, the *Hindenburg,* Rip Van Winkle, Juneteenth, Mother Teresa, the Sphinx, Woody Guthrie, and Utopia, to name just a few.

Many instructors use these allusions as part of their classes, asking students whether they know what they refer to, or, if a joke is involved, whether they get the joke. Here's an example from page 13: "Did you enjoy your recent trip to Utopia?" Instructors can use this sentence as they would any other sentence in the practice (identifying helping verbs, main verbs, and verbals), or they can stop for a moment and ask whether anyone knows what a utopia is. A few students at this class level will have heard of the word but not many. An interesting follow-up question is to ask whether anyone knows the derivation of the word (no one will), using the opportunity to discuss word origin and meaning. Many allusions, of course, are more serious: "Charging up the hill, Pickett's men bravely faced the rifles and cannons." The point is that such allusions provide a depth of content and often a light tone that go beyond the rote recitation of practices and exercises.

An Exceptional Support Package

The Instructor's Manual provides suggestions for how to use the text, answers to the exercises, diagnostic and achievement tests, a series of five chapter tests and five alternate chapter tests, a final examination, answers to the tests and final examination, additional writing assignments, and model paragraphs. With this material, the instructor can use a traditional lecture approach, working through each chapter and then testing the students together, or the instructor can allow the students to work through the book at their own pace, dealing with the students' questions individually and giving students tests as they complete each chapter. In addition, the material omitted from this edition of the text—Chapter Six, "Choosing the Right Words and Spelling Them Correctly"—will be available online for those instructors who prefer to teach it.

This text is available in an alternate version, "Form A," for added teaching flexibility (ISBN 0-1550-4268-8).

Acknowledgments

We thank our friends and colleagues in the English Department at Palomar College, particularly those of you who have used *Inside Writing* and have so generously offered your support and suggestions.

We extend our thanks to the staff at Cengage Learning, including Annie Todd, Necco McKinley, Elizabeth Rice, Luria Rittenberg, and Tania Andrabi, and to Margaret Manos, who has so ably assisted us throughout the revision.

Finally, of course, we thank our families and friends for their patience and support as we once again worked late into the night.

William Salomone
Stephen McDonald
Martin Japtok

Naming the Parts

Let's face it. Few people find grammar a fascinating subject, and few study it of their own free will. Most people study grammar only when they are absolutely required to do so. Many seem to feel that grammar is either endlessly complicated or not important to their daily lives.

The problem is not that people fail to appreciate the importance of writing. The ability to express oneself clearly on paper is generally recognized as an important advantage. Those who can communicate their ideas and feelings effectively have a much greater chance to develop themselves, not only professionally but personally as well.

Perhaps the negative attitude toward grammar is due in part to the suspicion that studying grammar has little to do with learning how to write. This suspicion is not at all unreasonable—a knowledge of grammar by itself will not make anyone a better writer. To become a better writer, a person should study *writing* and practice it frequently. In addition, anyone wishing to become a better writer will also have to read regularly, just as anyone wishing to be a musician has to listen to music.

However, the study of writing is much easier if one understands grammar (just as becoming a musician is helped by learning something about the technical aspects of music). Certainly a person can learn to write well without knowing exactly how sentences are put together or what the various parts are called. But most competent writers do know these things because such knowledge enables them not only to develop their skills more easily but also to analyze their writing and discuss it with others.

Doctors, for example, don't necessarily have to know the names of the tools they use (stethoscope, scalpel, sutures), nor do mechanics have to know the names of their tools (wrench, screwdriver, ratchet). But it would be hard to find competent doctors or mechanics who were not thoroughly familiar with the tools of their trades, for it is much more difficult to master any important skill and also more difficult to discuss that skill without such knowledge.

The terms and concepts you encounter in this chapter are familiar to most of you, but probably not familiar enough. It is not good enough to have a vague idea of what a linking verb is or a general notion of what a prepositional phrase is. You should know *precisely* what these terms mean. This chapter and subsequent chapters present only what is basic and necessary to the study of grammar, but it is essential that you learn *all* of what is presented.

A sound understanding of grammar, like a brick wall, must be built one level at a time. You cannot miss a level and go on to the next. If you master each level as it is presented, you will find that grammar is neither as difficult nor as complicated as you may have thought. You will also find, as you work through the writing sections of the text, that by applying your knowledge of grammar you can greatly improve your writing skills.

SECTION 1

Subjects and Verbs

Of all the terms presented in this chapter, perhaps the most important are **SUBJECT** and **VERB**, for subjects and verbs are the foundation of every sentence. Sentences come in many forms, and the structures may become quite complex, but they all have one thing in common: <u>Every sentence must contain a SUBJECT and a VERB.</u> Like most grammatical rules, this one is based on simple logic. After all, without a subject you have nothing to write about, and without a verb you have nothing to say about your subject. In other words, without a subject there is nobody in the sentence who does anything, and without a verb, the subject cannot do anything.

Subjects: Nouns and Pronouns

Before you can find the subject of a sentence, you need to be able to identify nouns and pronouns because the subjects of sentences will always be nouns or pronouns (or, occasionally, other words or groups of words that function as subjects). You probably know the definition of a noun: **A noun names a person, place, thing, or idea.**

> **noun**
> A noun names a person, place, thing, or idea.

This definition works perfectly well for most nouns, especially for those that name concrete things we can *see, hear, smell, taste,* or *touch.* Using this definition, most people can identify words such as *door, road,* or *tulip* as nouns.

 EXAMPLES

        N   N   N

Paula reads her favorite **book** whenever she goes to the **beach.**

     N   N   N

My brother likes to watch **football** on **television.**

Unfortunately, when it comes to identifying <u>ideas</u> as nouns, many people have trouble. Part of this problem is that nouns name even more than ideas. They name **emotions, qualities, conditions,** and many other **abstractions or concepts.** Abstract nouns such as *fear, courage, happiness,* and *trouble* do not name persons, places, or things, but they <u>are</u> nouns.

On the following pages are a few examples of nouns, arranged by category. Add nouns of your own to each category.

Persons	*Places*	*Things*	*Ideas*
Paula	New York	spaghetti	sincerity
engineer	beach	book	anger
woman	India	sun	democracy
artist	town	bicycle	intelligence
_____	_____	_____	_____
_____	_____	_____	_____
_____	_____	_____	_____

 PRACTICE   Place an "N" above all the nouns in the following sentences.

               N   *N*   *N*

1. Jane was playing her favorite song on my iPhone.

2. Hester stared at the bright red letter on her dress.

3. Narcissus could not stop staring at his reflection in the pond.

4. The story of George Washington and the cherry tree is probably a myth.

5. Homer says that black holes are stories made up by science-fiction writers.

To help you identify all nouns, remember these points:

1. Nouns can be classified as **proper nouns** and **common nouns**. **Proper nouns** name specific persons, places, things, and ideas. The first letter in each of these nouns is capitalized (Manuelita, Missouri, Mazda, Marxism). **Common nouns** name more general categories. The first letter of a common noun is not capitalized (man, mansion, moss, marriage).

2. **A, an,** and **the** are noun markers. A noun will always follow one of these words, though not necessarily immediately. There might be other words between **a, an, the,** and the noun.

 EXAMPLES

                        N   N

The young **firefighter** was given a new **car.**

                 N   N   N   N

The final **point** of the **lecture** addressed **an inconsistency** in the last **report.**

3. If you are unsure whether or not a word is a noun, ask yourself if it could be introduced with **a, an,** or **the.**

 EXAMPLE

              N   N   N

My **granddaughter** asked for my **opinion** of her new **outfit.**

4. Words that end in **-ment, -ism, -ness, -ence, -ance,** and **-tion** are usually nouns.

EXAMPLE

                  N   N

Her **criticism** of my **performance** made me very unhappy.

 PRACTICE   Place an "N" above all the nouns in the following sentences.

                     N   N   N   N

1. The guide led the class on a tour of the caverns.

2. Siddhartha left his home and wandered into the world.

3. Homer licked his lips at the thought of a huge plate of Spam.

4. Scheherazade tried to think of another story, but her mind was a complete blank.

5. The best suggestion came from an agnostic who always sat in the back of the church.

6. A deep depression and a sense of meaninglessness settled on the wounded king.

7. When the misanthrope left the party, we all breathed a sigh of relief.

8. His philosophy of life had never included ideas like acceptance and willingness.

9. It took great courage and determination for the cowardly lion to face the wizard.

10. Our graduation was interrupted by a coyote chasing a roadrunner across the stage.

    A pronoun takes the place of a noun. The "pro" in *pronoun* comes from the Latin word meaning "for." Thus, a <u>pro</u>noun is a word that in some way stands "for a noun." Pronouns perform this task in a variety of ways. Often, a pronoun will allow you to refer to a noun without having to repeat the noun. For instance, notice how the word *John* is awkwardly repeated in the following sentence:

<u>John</u> put on <u>John's</u> coat before <u>John</u> left for <u>John's</u> job.

Pronouns allow you to avoid the repetition:

John put on <u>his</u> coat before <u>he</u> left for <u>his</u> job.

> **pronoun**
>
> A pronoun takes the place of a noun.

In later chapters we will discuss the use of pronouns and the differences among the various types. For now, you simply need to be able to recognize pronouns in a sentence. The following list includes the most common pronouns. Read over this list several times until you are familiar with these words.

Personal Pronouns

I	we	you	he	she	they	it
me	us	your	him	her	them	its
my	our	yours	his	hers	their	
mine	ours				theirs	

Indefinite Pronouns

some	everyone	anyone	someone	no one
all	everything	anything	something	nothing
many	everybody	anybody	somebody	nobody
each				
one				
none				

Reflexive/Intensive Pronouns

myself	ourselves
yourself	yourselves
himself	themselves
herself	
itself	

Relative Pronouns

who, whom, whose
which
that

Demonstrative Pronouns

that this
those
these

Interrogative Pronouns

who, whom, whose
which
what

 PRACTICE

Place an "N" above all nouns and a "Pro" above all pronouns in the following sentences.

    Pro   *N*   *N*   *Pro*

1. We enjoyed the ride on the river, but everyone kept falling out of

       N

the raft.

2. Each of us should know which little piggy went to market.

3. Ankara is the capital of Turkey, but Istanbul is its most important city.

4. Do you know what P.T. Barnum said about suckers?

5. Anything you say right now could be used against you in a court of law.

6. Does anyone understand her explanation of fractals?

7. The Super Bowl is well known for its unique advertisements, but my brother does not enjoy them.

8. The archeologists determined that many of the fragments they found belonged to an earlier period.

9. My collection of rare books does not include anything by Herman Melville or Paul Lawrence Dunbar.

10. Almost anyone who reads the poetry of Emily Dickinson will admire her description of a hummingbird.

 PRACTICE   In the following sentences, write nouns and pronouns of your own choice as indicated.

       N   N   Pro   N

1. A ___*dog*___ at the ___*picnic*___ ate ___*our*___ ___*lunch*___ .

   Pro   Pro   N   Pro

2. _____ should ask _____ to sing a _____ for _____ .

   Pro   N   N   N

3. _____ of the _____ asked for a _____ of _____ .

   Pro   N   Pro

4. _____ took the _____ that belongs to _____ ?

      N   Pro   N   Pro

5. After _____ cooked _____ _____ , _____ asked

   Pro   N   N   Pro

_____ _____ to watch the _____ with _____ .

Verbs

Once you can identify nouns and pronouns, the next step is to learn to identify verbs. Although some people have trouble recognizing these words, you should be able to identify them if you learn the following definition and the few points after it: **A verb either shows action or links the subject to another word.**

---

verb
A verb either shows action or links the subject to another word.

As you can see, this definition identifies two types of verbs. Some are "action" verbs (they tell what the subject is <u>doing</u>), and others are "linking" verbs (they tell what the subject is <u>being</u>). This distinction leads to the first point that will help you recognize verbs.

Action Verbs and Linking Verbs

<u>One way to recognize verbs is to know that some verbs can do more than simply express an action.</u> Some verbs are action verbs; others are linking verbs.

ACTION VERBS

Action verbs are usually easy to identify. Consider the following sentence:

The deer leaped gracefully over the stone wall.

If you ask yourself what the **action** of the sentence is, the answer is obviously *leaped*. Therefore, *leaped* is the verb.

 EXAMPLES OF ACTION VERBS *run, read, go, write, think, forgive, wait, laugh*

 PRACTICE   Underline the action verbs in the following sentences.

1. Madonna <u>leaned</u> on the drummer.

2. The German blimp *Hindenburg* burned after its trip to the United States.

3. Pirates and football players wear bandannas on their heads.

4. The cat searched everywhere for a better hat.

5. President Lincoln talked to General Grant in his library.

LINKING VERBS

Linking verbs are sometimes more difficult to recognize than action verbs. Look for the verb in the following sentence:

Helen is a woman of integrity.

Notice that the sentence expresses no real action. The verb *is* simply links the word *woman* to the word *Helen*.

 EXAMPLES OF LINKING VERBS forms of *be:* am, is, are, was, were, be, being, been

forms of *become, seem, look, appear, smell, taste, feel, sound, grow, remain*

Linking verbs can link three types of words to a subject.

1. They can link nouns to the subject:

   Hank <u>became</u> a hero to his team. (*Hero* is linked to *Hank*.)

2. They can link pronouns to the subject:

   Cheryl <u>was</u> someone from another planet. (*Someone* is linked to *Cheryl*.)

3. They can link adjectives (descriptive words) to the subject:

   The sky <u>was</u> cloudy all day. (*Cloudy* is linked to *sky*.)

 PRACTICE Underline the linking verbs in the following sentences.

1. The author <u>was</u> sad about the lack of success of his novel.

2. My favorite dish is pork with leeks and a side dish of fried lotus roots.

3. Rip Van Winkle felt dizzy after his long nap.

4. Our new neighbors seem rather shy and quiet.

5. My favorite colors are ash gray and charcoal gray.

Verb Tense

Another way to identify verbs is to know that they appear in different forms to show the time when the action or linking takes place. These forms are called *tenses*. The simplest tenses are present, past, and future.

Present		*Past*	
I walk	we walk	I walked	we walked
you walk	you walk	you walked	you walked
he, she, it walks	they walk	he, she, it walked	they walked

Future	
I will walk	we will walk
you will walk	you will walk
he, she, it will walk	they will walk

Note that the verb *walk* can be written as *walked* to show past tense and as *will walk* to show future tense. When a verb adds "-d" or "-ed" to form the past tense, it is called a **regular verb**.

Other verbs change their forms more drastically to show past tense. For example, the verb *eat* becomes *ate,* and *fly* becomes *flew.* Verbs like these, which do not add "-d" or "-ed" to form the past tense, are called **irregular verbs**. Irregular verbs will be discussed in Chapter Seven, which is available online. For now, to help you identify verbs, remember this point: Verbs change their forms to show tense.

 PRACTICE   In the following sentences, first underline the verb and then write the tense (present, past, or future) in the space provided.

present **1.** Aeneas <u>praises</u> Dido once a week.

_____ **2.** Odysseus wanted to go home.

_____ **3.** Mark's new papillon will sit for treats.

_____ **4.** The Johnstown Flood killed 2,200 people in 1889.

_____ **5.** Ian plays cello pieces by Jacqueline du Pré every Wednesday.

Helping Verbs and Main Verbs

A third way to identify verbs is to know that the verb of a sentence is often more than one word. The **MAIN VERB** of a sentence may be preceded by one or more **HELPING VERBS** to show time, condition, or circumstances. The helping verbs allow us the flexibility to communicate a wide variety of ideas and attitudes. For example, note how adding a helping verb changes the following sentences:

I run indicates that an action is happening or happens repeatedly.

I will run indicates that an action is not now occurring but will occur in the future.

I should run indicates an attitude toward the action.

The **COMPLETE VERB** of a sentence, then, includes a **MAIN VERB** and any **HELPING VERBS.** The complete verb can contain as many as three helping verbs.

     MV
He *writes.*

   HV   MV
He *has written.*

   HV HV   MV
He *has been writing.*

    HV   HV   HV   MV
He *might have been writing.*

You can be sure that you have identified all of the helping verbs in a complete verb simply by learning the helping verbs. There are not very many of them.

These words are **always** helping verbs:

can	may	could
will	must	would
shall	might	should

These words are sometimes helping verbs and sometimes main verbs:

Forms of *have*	Forms of *do*	Forms of *be*		
have	do	am	was	be
has	does	is	were	being
had	did	are		been

In the following examples, note that the same word can be a helping verb in one sentence and a main verb in another:

 EXAMPLES

       MV
Anna **had** thirty pairs of shoes.

       HV   MV
Thomas **had** thought about the problem for years.

       MV
She **did** well on her chemistry quiz.

       HV MV
Bob **did** go to the game after all.

       MV
The bus **was** never on time.

       HV   MV
He **was** planning to leave in the morning.

When you are trying to identify the complete verb of a sentence, remember that any helping verbs will always come before the main verb; however, other words may occur between the helping verb(s) and the main verb. For instance, you will often find words like *not, never, ever, already,* or *just* between the helping verb and the main verb. Also, in questions you will often find the subject between the helping verb and the main verb.

 EXAMPLES

   HV   S   MV
Will the telephone **company raise** its prices?

   S   HV   MV
Nobody has ever **proved** the existence of the Loch Ness Monster.

PRACTICE   In the spaces provided, identify the underlined words as main verbs (MV) or helping verbs (HV).

_MV_   **1.** Juneteenth <u>is</u> one of the most important days in African American history. _____   **2.** It <u>is</u> celebrated to commemorate the end of slavery.

_____   **3.** Supposedly, the Emancipation Proclamation <u>was</u> not read to slaves in Houston until June 19, 1863. _____   **4.** That <u>was</u> more than five months after the Proclamation was supposed to have taken effect. _____   **5.** Why the news of the Proclamation <u>did</u> not spread faster is unclear. _____   **6.** Because slaves <u>did</u> the field work, perhaps they were kept ignorant of their freedom until the crops were in. _____   **7.** It <u>has</u> also been said that the person bearing the news of the Proclamation was murdered before he could deliver the message. _____   **8.** Juneteenth (June 19) <u>has</u> a special significance to the citizens of Texas, where it is called Emancipation Day. _____   **9.** It has <u>been</u> a state holiday in Texas since 1980. _____   **10.** For years, people in many states have <u>been</u> celebrating Juneteenth as the date when slavery ended in the United States.

PRACTICE   **A.** In the following sentences, place "HV" over all helping verbs and "MV" over all main verbs.

                                           HV   *MV*

1. LaDainian Tomlinson is considering another knee operation.

2. The Sirens have caused many shipwrecks.

3. Thor was swinging his hammer in all directions.

4. Should we go then, you and I?

5. Zhou Enlai should have exerted more influence on Mao Zedong.

B. In the following sentences, write helping verbs and main verbs of your own choice as indicated.

    MV
6. Christie ___sat___ with her best friend at the movie.

             MV   MV
7. The huge meteor _____ across the sky and _____ directly for

    Palomar College.

         HV   MV   MV
8. Kwame _____ not _____ the egusi soup that I _____

    for him.

         HV   MV
9. A spider _____ slowly _____ along the wall behind my sister.

       HV   HV   MV
10. You _____ never _____ _____ your hand in the garbage

         HV   MV
    disposal when it _____ _____.

Verbals

A fourth way to identify verbs is to recognize what they are not. Some verb forms do not actually function as verbs. These are called **VERBALS.** One of the most important verbals is the **INFINITIVE,** which usually begins with the word *to* (*to write, to be, to see*). The infinitive cannot serve as the verb of a sentence because it cannot express the time of the action or linking. *I wrote* communicates a clear idea, but *I to write* does not.

Another common verbal is the "-ing" form of the verb when it occurs without a helping verb (*running, flying, being*). When an "-ing" form without a helping verb is used as an adjective, it is called a **PRESENT PARTICIPLE.** When it is used as a noun, it is called a **GERUND.**

 EXAMPLES

        MV   Verbal
I **hope to pass** this test.

    HV   MV
I **should pass** this test.

             Verbal   MV
The birds **flying** from tree to tree **chased** the cat from their nest.

             HV   MV
The birds **were flying** from tree to tree.

    Verbal MV
Jogging is good cardiovascular exercise.

    MV
I **jog** for the cardiovascular benefits of the exercise.

PRACTICE

In the following sentences, write "HV" above all helping verbs, "MV" above all main verbs, and "Verbal" above all verbals.

HV MV   Verbal

1. Paradise should be a good place to sleep late.

2. Playing with a sore ankle, the tennis player could not defeat her opponent.

3. To illustrate Meryl Streep's talent, Penelope will describe her comedic, musical, and dramatic performances.

4. The photographer had taken a picture of Mother Teresa attending a sick man.

5. The old lady stirring the broth of bat wings and spider legs might agree to give you a taste.

 PRACTICE

Place "HV" above all helping verbs and "MV" above all main verbs in the following sentences. Underline any verbals.

           HV   MV

1. Engineers will attempt <u>to complete</u> work on the dam by November.

2. The lost campers were waving at the helicopter circling above them.

3. Did you enjoy your recent trip to Utopia?

4. The Sphinx has a rather simple riddle to ask you.

5. Local students have been protesting the school's decision to replace hamburgers with broccoli burgers.

6. To please the audience, Woody has agreed to play his most popular folk song.

7. To tell the truth, the Trojans should never have accepted that strange gift.

8. Surprising everyone, the Academy did not nominate Forest Whitaker for an Oscar.

9. In the Middle Ages the fox was often used to symbolize the devil.

10. Does anyone recognize that man attacking that windmill with his lance?

Identifying Subjects and Verbs

Finding the Subject

Most sentences contain several nouns and pronouns used in a variety of ways. One of the most important ways is as the subject of a verb. To identify which of the nouns or pronouns in a sentence is the subject, you need to identify the complete verb first. After identifying the verb, it is easy to find the subject by asking yourself "Who or what __(verb)__?"

 EXAMPLE

          S   HV   MV

The **man** in the green hat **was following** a suspicious-looking stranger.

The complete verb in this sentence is *was following,* and when you ask yourself "Who or what was following?" the answer is "the man." Therefore, *man* is the subject.

Remember, most sentences contain several nouns and pronouns, but not all nouns and pronouns are subjects.

 EXAMPLE

          S   MV

The **people** from the **house** down the **street** often borrow our **tools**.

This sentence contains four nouns, but only *people* is the subject. The other nouns in this sentence are different types of **objects**. The noun *tools* is called a **direct object** because it receives the action of the verb *borrow*. The nouns *house* and *street* are called **objects of prepositions**. Direct objects will be discussed in Chapter Four. Objects of prepositions will be discussed later in this chapter. For now, just remember that not all nouns and pronouns are subjects.

 PRACTICE

In the following sentences, place an "HV" above any helping verbs, an "MV" above the main verbs, and an "S" above the subjects.

                                      S   HV MV

1. In Greek mythology, the Titans were called the Elder Gods.

2. Zeus was the son of the Titan Cronus.

3. Seizing the throne from his father, Zeus divided the universe with his

    brothers Poseidon and Hades.

4. Poseidon became ruler of the seas, creating storm and calm at his will.

5. To the god Hades, Zeus gave the underworld with its dead and all its

    precious metals.

Subject Modifiers

Words that modify or describe nouns or pronouns should not be included when you identify the subject.

 EXAMPLE

                S   MV
The red **wheelbarrow is** in the yard.

The subject is *wheelbarrow,* not *the red wheelbarrow.*
    Remember that the possessive forms of nouns and pronouns are also used to describe or modify nouns, so do not include them in the subject either.

 EXAMPLES

                   S   MV
My brother's **suitcase is** very worn.

        S   MV
His **textbook was** expensive.

The subjects are simply *suitcase* and *textbook,* not *my brother's suitcase* or *his textbook.*

Verb Modifiers

Just as words that describe or modify the subject are not considered part of the subject, words that describe or modify the verb are not considered part of the verb. Watch for such modifiers because they will often occur between helping verbs and main verbs and may be easily mistaken for helping verbs. Notice that in the following sentence the words *not* and *unfairly* are modifiers and, therefore, not part of the complete verb.

 EXAMPLE

      S   HV   MV
Parents should **not unfairly** criticize their children.

Some common verb modifiers are *not, never, almost, just, completely, sometimes, always, often,* and *certainly.*

 PRACTICE

Place "HV" over helping verbs, "MV" over main verbs, and "S" over the subjects of the following sentences.

              S   *HV*   *MV*
1. The fight for Little Round Top has not yet begun.

2. Biscotti were always offered at the neighborhood coffee shop.

3. Last night's championship football game did not attract a large crowd.

4. My favorite English teacher might very well enter the Spam sculpture contest.

5. Charging up the hill, Pickett's men bravely faced the rifles and cannons.

Multiple Subjects and Verbs

Sentences may contain more than one subject and more than one verb.

 EXAMPLES

  S   MV
Fred petted the dog.

  S   S   MV
Fred and **Mary petted** the dog.

  S   S   MV   MV
Fred and **Mary petted** the dog and **scratched** its ears.

  S   MV   S   MV
Fred petted the dog, and **Mary scratched** its ears.

  S   S   MV   S   MV
Fred and **Mary petted** the dog before **they fed** it.

 PRACTICE

Place "HV" over helping verbs, "MV" over main verbs, and "S" over subjects in the following sentences.

                               S   *MV*

1. For twenty years, Telemachus helped his mother.

2. The dish and the spoon ran away from the mad cow.

3. John Glenn and his assistants prepared for his historic flight and then ate

    a big dinner.

4. The Eighteenth Amendment was ratified in 1919, but it was repealed in 1933.

5. Mrs. Johnson expressed her opinion that assault rifles and other high-powered

    weapons should be banned.

Special Situations

SUBJECT UNDERSTOOD

When a sentence is a command (or a request worded as a polite command), the pronoun *you* is understood as the subject. *You* is the only understood subject.

 EXAMPLES

  MV
Shut the door. (Subject *you* is understood.)

        MV
Please **give** this book to your sister. (Subject *you* is understood.)

VERB BEFORE SUBJECT

In some sentences, such as in questions, the verb comes before the subject.

 EXAMPLE

MV   S
Is your **mother** home?

The verb also comes before the subject in sentences beginning with *there* or *here*, as well as in some other constructions.

 EXAMPLES

MV   S
There **is** a **bug** in my soup.

MV   S
Here **is** another **bowl** of soup.

MV   S
Over the hill **rode** the **cavalry**.

MV   S
On the front porch **was** a **basket** with a baby in it.

 PRACTICE

Place "HV" over helping verbs, "MV" over main verbs, and "S" over subjects in the following sentences. Verbals and verb modifiers should not be included in the complete verb.

   MV
1. Give the nose spray to Cyrano.

2. In the wheelchair was President Franklin D. Roosevelt.

3. Could John Philip Sousa have used fewer brass instruments in his marches?

4. There is an elephant in the middle of their living room.

5. Forget their predictions of failure.

 PRACTICE

Underline all subjects once and complete verbs twice in the following sentences. Remember that the complete verb contains the main verb and all helping verbs and that verbals and verb modifiers should not be included in the complete verb.

1. Her new <u>novel</u> <u>will</u> certainly <u>be</u> a success.

2. San Diego's wildfires must have been a terrifying experience.

3. Don Quixote will never forget the beautiful Dulcinea.

4. The pitcher's elbow had begun to ache more than ever.

5. Did *Life of Pi* win an Academy Award or a Golden Globe Award?

6. The young knight could not remove the sword from the stone.

7. Give the secret code to the man in the gray trench coat.

8. Bobby Zimmerman had always loved music, so he bought a harmonica.

9. There were two zebras and a chipmunk in my living room last night.

10. Charlie described the UFO and even drew a sketch of it for the police.

 PRACTICE   Write sentences of your own that follow the suggested patterns. Identify each subject (S), helping verb (HV), and main verb (MV).

1. A statement with two subjects and one main verb (S-S-MV):

   S   S   MV
   Sarah and Mireya met for lunch.

   _____

2. A statement with one subject and two main verbs (S-MV-MV):

   _____

   _____

3. A statement with one subject, one helping verb, and one main verb (S-HV-MV):

   _____

   _____

4. A question with one main verb and one subject (MV-S):

   _____

   _____

5. A command that begins with a main verb (MV):

   _____

   _____

6. A statement that starts with *there* and is followed by a main verb and a subject ("There"-MV-S):

7. A statement with two subjects and two main verbs (S-S-MV-MV):

8. A statement with one subject, one main verb, and *when* followed by another subject and another main verb (S-MV-"when"-S-MV):

9. A statement with a subject, a helping verb, and a main verb followed by *or* and another subject, helping verb, and main verb (S-HV-MV-"or"-S-HV-MV):

10. A statement with a subject, a helping verb, and a main verb followed by *because* and another subject and a main verb (S-HV-MV-"because"-S-MV):

Section One Review

1. A **noun** names a person, place, thing, or idea.

   a. **Proper nouns** name specific persons, places, things, or ideas. They begin with a capital letter. **Common nouns** name more general categories and are not capitalized.

   b. **A, an,** and **the** are noun markers. A noun always follows one of these words.

   c. If you are unsure whether or not a word is a noun, ask yourself if it could be introduced with **a, an,** or **the**.

   d. Words that end in -**ment**, -**ism**, -**ness**, -**ence**, -**ance**, and -**tion** are usually nouns.

2. A **pronoun** takes the place of a noun.

3. A **verb** either shows **action** or **links** the subject to another word.

4. Verbs appear in different **tenses** to show the time when the action or linking takes place.

5. The **complete verb** includes a **main verb** and any **helping verbs**.

6. **Verbals** are verb forms that do not function as verbs.

   a. The **infinitive** is a verbal that begins with the word *to*.

   b. **The "-ing" form of the verb without a helping verb is called a present participle** if it is used as an adjective.

   c. The "-ing" form of the verb without a helping verb is called a **gerund** if it is used as a noun.

7. To identify the **subject** of any sentence, first find the verb. Then ask, "Who or what <u>(verb)</u>?"

8. **Subject modifiers** describe or modify the subject. They should not be included when you identify the subject.

9. **Verb modifiers** describe or modify verbs. They are not considered part of the verb.

10. Sentences may contain **multiple subjects** and **multiple verbs**.

11. When a sentence is a command (or a request worded as a polite command), the pronoun *you* is understood as the subject. *You* is the only understood subject.

12. In some sentences the verb comes before the subject.

Exercise 1A

Listen to or watch the news, or read a magazine, newspaper, or book. Write down ten sentences that you find. Identify which news program, magazine, newspaper, or book you used. After writing down the sentences, underline the subject or subjects of each sentence once and the complete verbs twice.

1. _____

   _____

2. _____

   _____

3. _____

   _____

4. _____

   _____

5. _____

   _____

6. _____

   _____

7. _____

   _____

8. _____

   _____

9. _____

   _____

10. _____

    _____

Exercise 1B

In the spaces provided, indicate whether the underlined word is a subject (write "S"), a helping verb (write "HV"), or a main verb (write "MV"). If it is none of these, leave the space blank.

_MV_ 1. Sita <u>added</u> a lot of roasted cumin seed to her dal soup.

_____ 2. When *Breaking Bad* went off the <u>air</u>, many people were disappointed.

_____ 3. <u>Ulysses</u> knew that it would be ten more years before he saw his wife, Penelope.

_____ 4. After much soul searching, the big-game hunter <u>decided</u> to join PETA.

_____ 5. The New York <u>firefighters</u> gathered for a memorial at the church.

_____ 6. <u>Should</u> we be surprised that most house dust is made up of dead skin cells?

_____ 7. The film *The Hobbit* is based on a <u>novel</u> that J.R.R. Tolkien wrote in 1937.

_____ 8. Some of the olive trees in the Garden of Gethsemane <u>are</u> over two thousand years old.

_____ 9. In 1872 Susan B. Anthony <u>was</u> arrested for voting in the presidential election.

_____ 10. His trip on the raft with Jim <u>transformed</u> Huckleberry Finn.

_____ 11. Frustrated by the bad weather, <u>Icarus</u> canceled his flight.

_____ 12. Hillary Clinton <u>had</u> a challenging task as Secretary of State.

_____ 13. <u>Somebody</u> noticed that Santa had forgotten his suspenders.

_____ 14. The Chernobyl nuclear power plant <u>suffered</u> a major breakdown in 1986.

_____ 15. Anthropologists <u>have</u> always been fascinated by the Pre-Puebloan ruins in the Four Corners area.

Exercise 1C

A. Underline all subjects once and complete verbs twice in the following sentences. Remember that a sentence may have more than one subject and more than one verb.

1. A stranger in a gray suit was leaving the building.

2. Has Homer seen the Hillbilly Hall of Fame?

3. Someone must have found my wallet and car keys by now.

4. On the wall sat a gigantic egg in red shorts and a black sweater.

5. Mr. Capp and his wife liked the boy but did not want him as a son-in-law.

6. The symphony had not practiced for a month yet performed very well.

7. Arlo has been playing guitar in Alice's restaurant for many years.

8. Mount Rushmore impressed me, but my daughters were ready to go home.

9. Dan insisted that he would make a better MI6 agent than Sean or Pierce.

10. Tweedledum's brother has been thinking about changing his name.

B. Write sentences of your own that follow the suggested patterns. Identify each subject (S), helping verb (HV), and main verb (MV).

11. A statement with one subject and two main verbs (S-MV-MV).

   S   MV   MV
   Sharon took the case and won it.

   _____

12. A statement with two subjects, one helping verb, and one main verb (S-S-HV-MV).

   _____

   _____

13. A question that begins with a helping verb followed by the subject and a main verb (HV-S-MV).

   _____

   _____

Exercise 1C

continued

14. A statement with a subject, two helping verbs, and one main verb (S-HV-HV-MV).

_____

_____

15. A statement with a subject and main verb followed by a comma and *yet* and another subject and main verb (S-MV-"yet"-S-MV).

_____

_____

Exercise 1D

In the following paragraph, underline all subjects once and complete verbs twice.

1. An unfortunate <u>incident</u> in the fifth grade <u><u>was</u></u> one of the most traumatic experiences of my life. **2.** It started when both Raymond and I wanted to pitch the ball in a game of kickball. **3.** We started to argue about it, but recess ended in the middle of our argument. **4.** Ray was still angry, and he expressed his displeasure by striking me in the forehead. **5.** He had just hit me and turned to go back to our classroom when someone threw me the kickball. **6.** The large ball bounced twice before I caught it. **7.** In one motion, I gained control of the ball and lost control of myself. **8.** As if in slow motion, I drew back and then hurled the ball at Ray with the bitter words, "You can have the ball!" **9.** After leaving my hand and traveling through the air, the ball struck Ray in the back of the neck. **10.** He immediately collapsed, holding his neck with both hands. **11.** The teacher rushed to his side as Ray shouted, "I can't feel my legs!" **12.** I could not believe what I was seeing. **13.** As our teacher called for help, I found myself in line with my classmates watching as though a nightmare were unfolding before my eyes. **14.** I pressed my body against a pine tree and thought that I surely would go to jail. **15.** Then the sound of the sirens and the sight of the helicopter landing on the distant soccer field caused my stomach to twist, and a great feeling of sickness came over me.

Modifiers

Although subjects and verbs form the basis of any sentence, most sentences also contain many other words that serve a variety of purposes. One such group of words includes the modifiers, which limit, describe, intensify, or otherwise alter the meaning of other words. The word *modify* simply means "change." Notice how the modifiers change the meaning in each of the following sentences.

EXAMPLES

The dictator had **total** power.

The dictator had **great** power.

The dictator had **little** power.

The dictator had **no** power.

As you can see, the word *power* is significantly changed by the different modifiers in these sentences.

Although modifiers can change the meaning of words in many different ways, there are basically only two types of modifiers, **ADJECTIVES** and **ADVERBS**. You will be able to identify both types of modifiers more easily if you remember these three points:

1. Sentences often contain more than one modifier.

EXAMPLE

The **new** moon rose **slowly** over the desert.

In this example, the word *new* modifies *moon;* it describes the specific phase of the moon. The word *slowly* modifies *rose;* it describes the speed with which the moon rose.

2. Two or more modifiers can be used to modify the same word.

EXAMPLE

The moon rose **slowly** and **dramatically** over the desert.

In this example the words *slowly* and *dramatically* both modify *rose*. *Slowly* describes the speed, and *dramatically* describes the manner in which the moon rose.

3. All modifiers must modify *something*. You should be able to identify the specific word that is being modified as well as the modifier itself.

EXAMPLE

Slowly the **new** moon rose over the desert.

In this example, notice that the word *slowly* still modifies *rose*, though the two words are not close to each other. The arrows point from the modifiers to the words being modified.

PRACTICE   Draw an arrow from the underlined modifier to the word it modifies.

1. Stephanie wore <u>purple</u> hair to the party.

2. The fries were <u>hot</u> and <u>crispy</u>.

3. Craig <u>usually</u> eats a tuna sandwich for lunch.

4. The <u>tedious</u> movie was <u>mercifully</u> <u>short</u>.

5. <u>Tiny</u> animals ran <u>continually</u> down the path.

Adjectives

An adjective modifies a noun or a pronoun. In English most adjectives precede the noun they modify.

> **adjective**
> An adjective modifies a noun or a pronoun.

EXAMPLE

The **young** eagle perched on the **rocky** cliff.

In this example, the word *young* **modifies** *eagle,* and the word *rocky* **modifies** *cliff.*

    Although most adjectives precede the noun or pronoun they modify, they may also follow the noun or pronoun and be connected to it by a linking verb.

EXAMPLE

Poisonous plants are **dangerous.**

In this example, the word *poisonous* describes the noun *plants*. Notice that it **precedes** the noun. However, the word *dangerous* also describes the noun *plants*. It is **linked** to the noun by the linking verb *are*. Both *poisonous* and *dangerous* are adjectives that modify the noun *plants*.

    Many different types of words can be adjectives, as long as they **modify** a noun or pronoun. Most adjectives answer the questions **which?**, **what kind?**, or **how many?** Here are the most common types of adjectives.

1. Descriptive words

 EXAMPLES

I own a **blue** suit.

That is an **ugly** wound.

2. Possessive nouns and pronouns

 EXAMPLE

I parked **my** motorcycle next to **John's** car.

3. Limiting words and numbers

 EXAMPLES

Some people see **every** movie that comes out.

Two accidents have happened on **this** street.

4. Nouns that modify other nouns

 EXAMPLE

The **basketball** game was held in the **neighborhood** gym.

 PRACTICE

A. In the following sentences, circle all adjectives and draw an arrow to the noun or pronoun each adjective modifies.

1. A severe rash covered his left arm.

2. We attended an unusual concert last Saturday.

3. Five gray pelicans glided above the busy beach.

4. Those rickety old bleachers might collapse if our entire marching band

   tries to sit in them.

5. Next October Homer will spend his vacation time in

   his redecorated barn making a new Spam costume for the Halloween party.

B. Add two adjectives of your own to each of the following sentences.

6. The garage was filled with *dusty* boxes and *broken* tools.

7. An aardvark wandered into our yard and looked for ants.

8. The hermit lived in a cabin in the woods.

9. The dog in the street avoided the car and the truck.

10. Officials tried to blame the mess on the birds that lived near the pond.

Adverbs

An adverb modifies a verb, adjective, or another adverb. Adverbs are sometimes more difficult to recognize than adjectives because they can be used to modify three different types of words—verbs, adjectives, and other adverbs. They can either precede or follow the words they modify and are sometimes placed farther away from the words they modify than are adjectives.

> ### adverb
> An adverb modifies a verb, adjective, or another adverb.

 EXAMPLES

The president walked across the room **quickly**.
(adverb modifying a verb)

The president seemed **unusually** nervous.
(adverb modifying an adjective)

The president left **very** quickly after the press conference.
(adverb modifying an adverb)

Because adverbs are often formed by adding "-ly" to adjectives such as *quick* or *usual*, many adverbs end in "-ly" (*quickly* and *usually*). However, you cannot always use this ending as a way of identifying adverbs because some words that end in "-ly" are *not* adverbs and because some adverbs do not end in "-ly," as the following list of common adverbs illustrates:

already	now	still
also	often	then
always	quite	too
never	seldom	very
not	soon	well

Here are two ways to help you identify adverbs:

1. Find the word that is being modified. If it is a verb, adjective, or adverb, then the modifier is an adverb.

 EXAMPLES

Thelma **seriously** injured her finger during the tennis match.

My brother and I have **completely** different attitudes toward Spam.

Tuan **almost** always arrives on time for work.

2. Look for words that answer the questions **when?**, **where?**, **how?**, or **to what extent?**

 EXAMPLES

My grandparents **often** bring gifts when they visit. (**when?**)

The turnips were grown **locally**. (**where?**)

Rachel **carefully** removed the paint from the antique desk. (**how?**)

Homer is **widely** known as a trainer in a flea circus. (**to what extent?**)

NOTE: Adverbs are **not** considered part of the complete verb, even if they come between the helping verb and the main verb. (See page 29 for a list of common adverbs that come between the helping verb and the main verb.)

 EXAMPLE

HV Adv   MV
He has **not** failed to do his duty.

 PRACTICE

A. In the following sentences, circle all adverbs and draw an arrow to the word that each adverb modifies.

1. The (nearly) exhausted soldier ran (relentlessly) toward the fort.

2. The happy couple always said that they were extremely lucky.

3. The black widow sometimes gleefully destroys her mate.

4. As Ichabod Crane rode swiftly down the lane, he was already beginning to worry about the headless horseman.

5. Dido was excruciatingly sad as she stood on the rather sheer cliff.

B. Add one adverb of your own to each of the following sentences.

6. The full moon moved *slowly* across the sky.

7. The exuberant school children ran across the schoolyard.

8. Elmo opened the garbage can and looked for the puppet.

9. The dune buggy missed the cactus but smashed into the tree.

10. The ship escaped many perils and reached its destination.

Comparative and Superlative Forms

Adjectives and adverbs are often used to compare two or more people or things. **The comparative form is used to compare two people or things. The superlative form is used to compare three or more people or things.**

 EXAMPLES   (comparative)   He is **happier** than I am.
(superlative)   He is the **happiest** man in town.

Writing Comparatives

Use the following guidelines for most adjectives and adverbs.

- Add "-er" to adjectives and adverbs of one syllable.

  green   greener

  soon   sooner

- Use the word *more* before adjectives and adverbs of two or more syllables.

  tedious   more tedious

  swiftly   more swiftly

- If a two-syllable adjective ends in "-y," change the *y* to *i* and add "-er."

  crispy   crispier

  sunny   sunnier

Writing Superlatives

Use the following guidelines for most adjectives and adverbs.

- Add "-est" to adjectives and adverbs of one syllable.

  green   greenest

  soon   soonest

- Use the word *most* before adjectives and adverbs of two or more syllables.

  tedious   most tedious

  swiftly   most swiftly

- If a two-syllable adjective ends in "-y," change the *y* to *i* and add "-est."

  crispy   crispiest

  sunny   sunniest

PRACTICE   Write the comparative and superlative form of each of the following words.

1. loud   _louder_   _loudest_

2. clear   _____   _____

3. funny   _____   _____

4. joyful   _____   _____

5. suddenly   _____   _____

6. ugly   _____   _____

7. comfortable _____   _____

8. far   _____   _____

9. quickly   _____   _____

10. powerful   _____   _____

Using Adjectives and Adverbs Correctly

1. <u>Do not use an adjective when you need an adverb.</u>

EXAMPLES

(incorrect)   He does not speak very **clear**.

(correct)   He does not speak very **clearly**.

(incorrect)   He breathes **deep** whenever he is worried.

(correct)   He breathes **deeply** whenever he is worried.

2. <u>Distinguish between *good* and *well*, *bad* and *badly*, *real* and *really*.</u> The words *good*, *bad*, and *real* are always adjectives. The words *badly* and *really* are always adverbs. The word *well* is usually an adverb, although it is used as an adjective to describe someone's health.

EXAMPLES

(incorrect)   He sells a lot of novels because he writes **good**.

(correct)   He sells a lot of novels because he writes **well**. (The adverb **well** modifies the verb **writes**.)

(incorrect)   Joey says he feels fine, but he does not look **good** to me.

(correct)   Joey says he feels fine, but he does not look **well** to me. (The adjective *well* describes the health of *Joey*.)

(incorrect)	April felt **badly** when she accidentally insulted her friend.
(correct)	April felt **bad** when she accidentally insulted her friend. (The adjective *bad* modifies the noun *April*.)
(incorrect)	Slim says that it's **real** hot in Phoenix today.
(correct)	Slim says that it's **really** hot in Phoenix today. (The adverb *really* modifies the adjective *hot*.)

3. <u>Avoid doubling the comparative or superlative form.</u> Do not use *more* with an "-er" form or *most* with an "-est" form.

 EXAMPLES

(incorrect)	Michael is **more taller** than Oscar.
(correct)	Michael is **taller** than Oscar.
(incorrect)	Sabrina is the **most smartest** student in the class.
(correct)	Sabrina is the **smartest** student in the class.

4. <u>Avoid using the superlative when you are comparing only two persons or things.</u>

 EXAMPLES

(incorrect)	His Toyota seems to be the **fastest** of the two cars.
(correct)	His Toyota seems to be the **faster** of the two cars.

5. <u>Use *than*, not *then*, in comparisons.</u>

EXAMPLES

(incorrect)	Melissa is taller **then** her older sister.
(correct)	Melissa is taller **than** her older sister.

PRACTICE Correct any errors in the use of adjectives and adverbs (or in the use of *then* and *than*) in the following sentences.

1. My sister considers Will Smith a ~~more~~ better actor ~~then~~ *than* Sean Penn.

2. The worse mistake he made was deciding to buy the expensivest car on the lot.

3. Although Abraham Lincoln was one of our greatest presidents, some say he was the most ugly one.

4. Karl Marx was real intelligent though his theory of economics did not work very good.

5. Of the two, who was the most beautiful, Marie Antoinette or Anne Boleyn?

6. Russell Crowe, who is from Australia, is the most bestest actor on the screen today.

7. Robert de Niro felt badly when he forgot his lines during rehearsal.

8. The Trojans were more better prepared than the Greeks, but the Greeks were trickiest.

9. Halle Berry said that the interviews are worst then the filming.

10. Sofia always drives safe, even when she has to get somewhere as quick as possible.

Section Two Review

1. **Modifiers** limit, describe, intensify, or otherwise alter the meaning of other words.

   a. Sentences often contain more than one modifier.

   b. Two or more modifiers can be used to modify the same word.

   c. All modifiers must modify *something*.

2. An **adjective** modifies a noun or a pronoun.

3. Most adjectives answer the questions which?, what kind?, or how many?

4. Common types of adjectives are the following:

   a. Descriptive words

   b. Possessive nouns and pronouns

   c. Limiting words and numbers

   d. Nouns that modify other nouns

5. An **adverb** modifies a verb, adjective, or another adverb.

6. There are two ways to identify adverbs:

   a. Find the word that is being modified. If it is a verb, an adjective, or an adverb, then the modifier is an adverb.

   b. Look for words that answer the questions when?, where?, how?, or to what extent?

7. The **comparative form** is used to compare two people or things.

8. The **superlative form** is used to compare three or more people or things.

9. Use adjectives and adverbs correctly.

   a. Do not use an adjective when you need an adverb.

   b. Distinguish between *good* and *well*, *bad* and *badly*, *real* and *really*.

   c. Avoid doubling the comparative or superlative form.

   d. Avoid using the superlative when you are comparing only two persons or things.

   e. Use *than*, not *then*, in comparisons.

Exercise 2A

Take a magazine (such as *Time, U.S. News and World Report, National Geographic, Harper's,* etc.) and find five sentences that contain at least one adjective, five that contain at least one adverb, and five that have at least one adjective and at least one adverb.

Sentences with at least one adjective (underline the adjectives):

1.

2.

3.

4.

5.

Sentences with at least one adverb (underline the adverbs):

1.

2.

3.

4.

5.

Sentences with at least one adjective and one adverb (underline and label each one):

1.

2.

3.

4.

5.

Exercise 2B

A. In the following sentences, identify all adjectives by writing "Adj" above them, and identify all adverbs by writing "Adv" above them.

                 Adv   *Adj*

1. The curtain rose slowly, and the grateful actress accepted the roses.

2. In his dreams Nathaniel Hawthorne often chased the first letter of the alphabet.

3. Alice Walker, author of a famous novel, quietly lives in a California coastal town.

4. James Joyce knew without any doubt that he would always be misunderstood.

5. The Mad Hatter was angry because Alice stubbornly refused to share the mushrooms.

B. Add one adjective and one adverb to each of the following sentences. Do not use the same adjective or adverb more than once.

        carefully   *wooden*

6. Gepetto ^worked on the ^shoes all night.

7. The poet recited poems, answered questions, and joined people in the audience for coffee.

8. Our parents asked us to meet the stranger in the kitchen and talk to him.

9. On the stage the actors whispered to each other and glanced into the auditorium.

10. Many people volunteered to adopt the dogs that the football player had abused.

C. Correct any errors in the use of adjectives and adverbs (or in the use of *then* and *than*) in the following sentences.

         very   *well*

11. Christine was ~~real~~ happy when she did ~~good~~ on her test.

12. Mark Twain was more funnier then David Letterman.

13. The dog next door howls loud every night, more loud than the dogs across the street.

14. It was the worse dinner of my life because you treated the server so rude.

15. Sean, who tells jokes really good, is the most funniest person I know.

In the following sentences, write "Adj" above all adjectives and "Adv" above all adverbs. Underline all subjects once and all verbs twice.

1. Some people say that the most poignant story of all time is the myth of Pyramus and Thisbe. **2.** It has been used by many writers throughout the years. **3.** It is the source of the story of Romeo and Juliet, and Shakespeare also used it in *Midsummer Night's Dream.* **4.** *West Side Story*, a Broadway musical, was clearly based on this ancient tale. **5.** Pyramus and Thisbe were a young man and woman who were in love. **6.** However, their hostile families adamantly refused to allow them to be together. **7.** Their homes adjoined each other, so they were able to speak secretly through a hole in the common wall between their two houses. **8.** They became desperate and planned to sneak out to meet in the woods. **9.** They agreed to meet by a mulberry tree. **10.** Thisbe arrived first and waited eagerly for Pyramus, but she ran away when she saw a fierce lioness hunting in the woods. **11.** When Thisbe ran, she dropped her veil, which the lioness savagely tore to pieces with jaws that were stained by the blood of an ox. **12.** Pyramus soon arrived, and, seeing Thisbe's bloody veil, believed that she had been killed by a wild beast. **13.** In his grief, Pyramus stabbed himself. **14.** When Thisbe returned and saw her mortally wounded lover near the mulberry tree, she killed herself. **15.** According to legend, from that time on, the fruit of the mulberry, previously white, was always black. **16.** This sad story has always moved people and through time has been the basis of many other works.

In the following sentences, identify each of the underlined words as noun (N), pronoun (Pro), verb (V), adjective (Adj), or adverb (Adv).

1. The $\overset{N}{\underline{story}}$ of Oedipus, the $\overset{Adj}{\underline{Greek}}$ king, has caused audiences throughout the ages to reconsider their relationship with fate or "the gods." **2.** The source of <u>most</u> of the story <u>is</u> the play *Oedipus Rex* by Sophocles. **3.** Oedipus was a popular king of Thebes in <u>ancient</u> Greece, but he was <u>also</u> the victim of a curse placed on him when he was a baby. **4.** The curse said that he would kill <u>his</u> father, Laius, and <u>marry</u> his mother, Jocasta. **5.** His father tried to avoid the curse by abandoning the baby Oedipus on a mountain with his <u>ankles</u> connected by wires, hoping he would die; however, the baby Oedipus was <u>quickly</u> rescued by shepherds. **6.** The king and queen of Corinth adopted the baby, and Oedipus <u>naturally</u> thought that they were his <u>birth</u> parents. **7.** When he <u>eventually</u> <u>learned</u> about the curse, he left Corinth to protect them. **8.** On the road, Oedipus met Laius and his <u>company</u>, <u>who</u> did not let him pass. **9.** Unaware that Laius was <u>really</u> his <u>true</u> father, the aggressive Oedipus killed him. **10.** When he approached <u>Thebes</u> and met the Sphinx, she asked him a now <u>famous</u> riddle: "What creature walks on four legs in the morning, two legs at noon, and three legs in the evening?" **11.** Because Oedipus answered the riddle <u>correctly</u>, "a man," the Sphinx <u>allowed</u> him to enter Thebes, where he met Queen Jocasta, not knowing she was his real mother. **12.** Oedipus married <u>her</u> and <u>had</u> children by her. **13.** When he <u>eventually</u> learned that he had married his mother, Oedipus gouged out his eyes with a <u>sharp</u> pin from Jocasta's robe. **14.** Because she was <u>so</u> ashamed, Jocasta hanged <u>herself</u>. **15.** Oedipus, having <u>innocently</u> become the victim of the curse, <u>went</u> into exile. **16.** In the end, Oedipus's <u>fate</u> became a <u>cautionary</u> tale about not trying to avoid the will of the gods.

Connectors

The final group of words consists of the connectors. These are signals that indicate the relationship of one part of a sentence to another. The two types of connectors are **conjunctions** and **prepositions**.

Conjunctions

A conjunction joins two parts of a sentence. The word *conjunction* is derived from two Latin words meaning "to join with." The definition is easy to remember if you know that the word *junction* in English refers to the place where two roads come together.

> **conjunction**
>
> A conjunction joins two parts of a sentence.

The two types of conjunctions are **coordinating** and **subordinating**. In Chapter Two we will discuss the subordinating conjunctions. You will find it much easier to distinguish between the two types if you memorize the coordinating conjunctions now.

The **coordinating conjunctions** are *and, but, or, nor, for, yet,* and *so*.

NOTE: An easy way to learn the coordinating conjunctions is to remember that their first letters can spell **BOYSFAN:** (<u>B</u>ut <u>O</u>r <u>Y</u>et <u>S</u>o <u>F</u>or <u>A</u>nd <u>N</u>or).

Coordinating conjunctions join elements of the sentence that are <u>equal</u> or <u>parallel</u>. For instance, they may join two subjects, two verbs, two adjectives, or two parallel groups of words.

EXAMPLE

   S   Conj S   MV Conj   MV
Ernie **and** Bert often disagree **but** never fight.

In this example the first conjunction joins two subjects and the second joins two verbs.

EXAMPLE

   S   MV   Adj Conj   Adj   Conj   MV
Susan often felt awkward **or** uncomfortable **yet** never showed it.

In this example the first conjunction joins two adjectives, and the second joins two verbs.

Coordinating conjunctions may even be used to join two entire sentences, each with its own subject and verb.

EXAMPLES

       S   HV   MV   S   MV

The rain had fallen steadily all week long. The river was close to overflowing.

       S   HV   MV   Conj   S   MV

The rain had fallen steadily all week long, **so** the river was close to overflowing.

  Notice that the coordinating conjunctions have different meanings and that changing the conjunction can significantly change the meaning of a sentence. *A person should never drink **and** drive* communicates a very different idea from *A person should never drink **or** drive.*

- The conjunction *and* indicates **addition.**

 EXAMPLE

  Jules **and** Jim loved the same woman.

- The conjunctions *but* and *yet* indicate **contrast.**

 EXAMPLES

  She wanted to go **but** didn't have the money.

  I liked Brian, **yet** I didn't really trust him.

- The conjunctions *or* and *nor* indicate **alternatives.**

EXAMPLES

  You can borrow the record **or** the tape.

  He felt that he could neither go **nor** stay.

- The conjunction *for* indicates **cause.**

EXAMPLE

  The plants died, **for** they had not been watered.

- The conjunction *so* indicates **result.**

EXAMPLE

  Her brother lost his job, **so** he had to find another.

PRACTICE

A. In the following sentences, circle all coordinating conjunctions. Underline all subjects once and all complete verbs twice.

 1. My mother (or) my father will give you a ride home.

 2. Do you know when Meryl Streep won both an Oscar and a Golden Globe Award for best actress?

 3. Miriam experienced painful boredom, yet the musical would last another hour.

 4. Sam did not like Gollum, nor did he care much for Shelob.

 5. The sink in the kitchen was not draining, so we called the plumber.

B. In the following sentences, add coordinating conjunctions that show the relationship indicated in parentheses.

6. We can go to the baseball game, ____*or*____ we can see a movie, but we can't do both. (alternatives)

7. Columbus was convinced he could reach Asia, _____ very few people agreed with him. (contrast)

8. President Franklin Delano Roosevelt had to face war _____ harsh financial conditions. (addition)

9. President Obama faced similar circumstances in his first term, _____ he had to deal with wars in Iraq and Afghanistan and serious economic issues. (cause)

10. Cesar Chavez was concerned about the conditions of Mexican American farm workers, _____ he organized the National Farm Workers Association. (result)

Prepositions

> **preposition**
> A preposition relates a noun or pronoun to some other word in the sentence.

A preposition relates a noun or a pronoun to some other word in the sentence. Prepositions usually indicate a relationship of **place** (in, near), **direction** (toward, from), **time** (after, until), or **condition** (of, without).

 EXAMPLE

                Prep
The boy ran **to** the store.

Notice how the preposition *to* shows the relationship (direction) between *ran* and *store*. If you change prepositions, you change the relationship.

 EXAMPLES

                Prep
The boy ran **from** the store.

                Prep
The boy ran **into** the store.

                Prep
The boy ran **by** the store.

Here are some of the most common prepositions:

about	because of	during	near	to
above	before	except	of	toward
across	behind	for	on	under
after	below	from	onto	until
among	beneath	in	over	up
around	beside	in spite of	past	upon
as	between	into	through	with
at	by	like	till	without

NOTE: *For* can be used as a coordinating conjunction, but it is most commonly used as a preposition. *To* can also be used as part of an infinitive, in which case it is not a preposition.

 PRACTICE

Write "Prep" above the prepositions in the following sentences.

1. Mr. Duong sat *Prep* in the waiting room and thought *Prep* about his wife.

2. Without hesitation, he lifted his new laptop from the box.

3. During the hotly contested election, the nominees remained friendly on the campaign trail.

4. When they were near La Mancha, Dulcinea and Sancho Panza called for Don Quixote.

5. The prophet Muhammad fled from Mecca to Medina.

Prepositional Phrases

The word *preposition* is derived from two Latin words meaning "to put in front." The two parts of the word (pre + position) indicate how prepositions usually function. They are almost always used as the first words in **prepositional phrases**.

> **prepositional phrase**
> Preposition + Object (noun or pronoun) = Prepositional Phrase

A prepositional phrase consists of a preposition plus a noun or a pronoun, called the object of the preposition. This object is almost always the last word of the prepositional phrase. Between the preposition and its object, the prepositional phrase may also contain adjectives, adverbs, or conjunctions. A preposition may have more than one object.

EXAMPLES

Prep   Obj
after a short **lunch**

Prep   Obj   Obj
with his very good **friend** and his **brother**

Prep Obj   Obj
to you and **her**

   Prep   Obj
through the long and dismal **night**

Although prepositions themselves are considered connectors, prepositional phrases actually act as modifiers. They may function as adjectives, modifying a noun or pronoun, or they may function as adverbs, modifying a verb.

 EXAMPLES

The cat (**from next door**) caught a gopher.

The burglar jumped (**from the window**).

In the first example, the prepositional phrase functions as an adjective, modifying the noun *cat,* and in the second example, the prepositional phrase functions as an adverb, modifying the verb *jumped.*

NOTE: If you can recognize prepositional phrases, you will be able to identify subjects and verbs more easily **because neither the subject nor the verb of a sentence can be part of a prepositional phrase.**

In the following sentence it is difficult at first glance to determine which of the many nouns is the subject.

In a cave near the village, a member of the archaeological team found a stone ax from an ancient civilization.

If you first eliminate the prepositional phrases, however, the true subject becomes apparent.

                                    S
 EXAMPLES

(In a cave) (near the village), a member (of the archaeological team)

   MV
found a stone ax (from an ancient civilization).

 PRACTICE

Place parentheses around the prepositional phrases and write "Prep" above all prepositions and "Obj" above the objects of the prepositions.

       Prep   *Obj*   *Prep*   *Obj*
1. (From the earliest years) (of our country), overeager reporters have

pursued our presidents. **2.** Anne Royall, who was one of the first female journalists in the United States, was determined to interview John Quincy Adams, our sixth president. **3.** She had been trying for weeks to get an interview with him. **4.** President Adams would often bathe naked in the Potomac River, and Anne Royall learned of this habit. **5.** One morning she followed him to the riverbank, where he undressed and stepped into the cold water. **6.** She crept near the shore and positioned herself on his clothes. **7.** When President Adams began to move toward the bank, she introduced herself and asked for an interview. **8.** In spite of his pleas, she refused to give him his clothes unless he agreed to talk to her. **9.** Remaining decently submerged in the water, Adams answered the questions posed by the determined reporter. **10.** After this incident, John Quincy Adams became one of Anne Royall's close friends.

Section Three Review

1. A **conjunction** joins two parts of a sentence.

2. The **coordinating conjunctions** are *and, but, or, nor, for, yet,* and *so.*

3. A **preposition** relates a noun or pronoun to some other word in the sentence.

4. A **prepositional phrase** consists of a **preposition** plus a noun or a pronoun, called the **object of the preposition**.

5. Neither the subject nor the verb of a sentence can be part of a prepositional phrase.

Exercise 3A

Prepositional phrases are all around us, and we use them constantly. Since they are so important (and so helpful in determining what cannot be a subject), it is useful to be able to recognize them easily. Pay attention to your everyday conversation with people and write down ten sentences that you used or heard somebody use that contain at least one prepositional phrase. Find prepositional phrases using different prepositions. There should be at least six different prepositions in the ten sentences you write down below.

1. _____

_____

2. _____

_____

3. _____

_____

4. _____

_____

5. _____

_____

6. _____

_____

7. _____

_____

8. _____

_____

9. _____

_____

10. _____

_____

Exercise 3B

A. Combine each pair of sentences into one sentence. Use the coordinating conjunction indicated in parentheses.

1. (contrast)
   Freddie Mercury was born in Zanzibar and lived there and in India until he was 17.
   He tends to be known as a British rock star and lead singer of the group Queen.

   Freddie Mercury was born in Zanzibar and lived there and in India until he was 17, yet he tends to be known as a British rock star and lead singer of the group Queen.

2. (addition)
   Carla liked *Alchemy*, her new computer game.
   She could get one level higher than everyone else in her house.

3. (cause)
   Donald Trump missed the Trivial Pursuit question.
   He could not recall why Abraham Lincoln was called "Honest Abe."

4. (alternative)
   The Steelers could fumble.
   They could throw an interception.

5. (alternative)
   Mrs. Peacock had not committed the murder.
   She was not a very good actress.

continued

6. (result)

It was the seventh year of the drought.
We were ordered to use less water.

_____

_____

B. In each of the following sentences, change the underlined *and* to a coordinating conjunction that expresses the relationship between the ideas in the sentence. If the *and* does not need to be changed, do nothing to it.

7. Jenna loves her cockatiels, <u>and</u> she buys only the best birdseed for them.

Jenna loves her cockatiels, so she buys only the best birdseed for them.

_____

8. "Betty Crocker" is the name on many cookbooks, <u>and</u> no one who writes those books is really named Betty Crocker.

_____

_____

9. Tonight you can go with me to the jazz club, <u>and</u> you can stay home and watch *Harry Potter* reruns.

_____

_____

10. Enrique could not remember how to get to Albuquerque, <u>and</u> he looked up the directions on *MapQuest*.

_____

_____

11. Victoria refused to ride the new horse, <u>and</u> it was dangerous and mean.

_____

_____

continued

12. Marilyn Monroe's original name was Norma Jean Baker, <u>and</u> Judy Garland's name was Frances Gumm.

_____

_____

13. Claudia agreed to play miniature golf, <u>and</u> she was not excited about riding go-carts.

_____

_____

14. Hinh's new Mustang is a fast car, <u>and</u> Steve's Prius gets much better gas mileage.

_____

_____

15. Signs along the freeway in New Mexico warn drivers not to pick up hitchhikers, <u>and</u> a federal penitentiary is in the area.

_____

_____

Exercise 3C

Place all prepositional phrases in parentheses and circle all conjunctions. For additional practice, underline all subjects once and all complete verbs twice.

A.

1. The <u>soldiers</u> (and) the <u>captain</u> <u><u>stood</u></u> (at attention).

2. Sully had been trying to hit a homerun for three seasons.

3. Michelangelo stared at the ceiling and started to paint.

4. In his nose, ears, and tongue were gold and silver rings.

5. Snow White and one of her favorite dwarfs have eloped to Magic Mountain.

6. The symbol of the caduceus is often associated with the medical profession.

7. The caduceus is a staff with two entwined serpents, and it was carried by Mercury.

8. A total of thirty thousand people saw the play, but not one of them liked it.

B.

9. Michelle's great-grandfather served as an officer during World War I. 10. He saw battle at the Somme Offensive, one of the bloodiest battles of the war. 11. In World War II, her grandfather was stationed at a remote airfield in Burma. 12. His living conditions were rather crude, for there was no indoor plumbing. 13. He shared a thatched hut with another pilot, and he flew fuel and other supplies over the Himalayas. 14. The Himalayas are the world's highest mountain range and dangerous to fly over. 15. The pilots called the Himalayan range "The Hump," so the pilots were called "Hump pilots." 16. Today the Himalayas are a destination for mountain climbers who want to ascend their challenging peaks.

Exercise 3D

In the following sentences, identify each of the underlined words as noun (N), pronoun (Pro), verb (V), adjective (Adj), adverb (Adv), conjunction (Conj), or preposition (Prep).

1. On March 25, 1944, Nicholas Alkemade reserved a place for himself[Pro] in aviation[Adj] history.

2. He was in the tail of a plane flying at 18,000 feet when the plane was hit by antiaircraft fire. 3. Alkemade looked for his parachute only to find that he could not reach it because the plane was on fire. 4. He knew that he had two choices: burn alive in the tail of the plane or jump out without his parachute. 5. Believing he would be unconscious before he hit the ground, he decided to jump out. 6. As he plummeted toward the ground, he had no sensation of falling. 7. In fact, he later said that he felt as if he were floating on a soft cloud up to the point when he passed out. 8. Moments after he had jumped from the plane, Alkemade's unconscious body was falling to the earth at a speed of 120 mh. 9. However, before he hit the ground, Alkemade crashed into a forest of fir trees where thick branches broke his fall. 10. Then, below the trees, he came to rest in eighteen inches of soft snow, which acted as a cushion. 11. When he finally regained consciousness several hours later, Alkemade was being cared for by a German patrol. 12. He told them his incredible story, but they did not believe that he had fallen from a plane without a parachute. 13. After all, Alkemade had very little to show as a result of his 18,000-foot fall. 14. He had a burned hand, a strained back, a scalp wound, and a twisted knee. 15. Nicholas Alkemade's story was later verified, and his fall became part of the folklore of aviation history.

Sentence Practice: Embedding Adjectives, Adverbs, and Prepositional Phrases

You have now learned to identify the basic parts of a sentence, but this skill itself is not very useful unless you can use it to compose clear and effective sentences. Obviously, you have some flexibility when you compose sentences, but that flexibility is far from unlimited. The following sentence has a subject, a verb, five modifiers, one conjunction, and two prepositional phrases, but it makes no sense at all.

> Architect the quickly president for the drew up building new and plans the them to showed company.

With the parts arranged in a more effective order, the sentence, of course, makes sense.

> The architect quickly drew up plans for the new building and showed them to the company president.

There is no single correct pattern for the English sentence. The patterns you choose will be determined by the facts and ideas you wish to convey. For any given set of facts and ideas, there will be a relatively limited number of effective sentence patterns and an enormous number of ineffective ones. Knowing the parts of the sentence and how they function will help you choose the most effective patterns to communicate your thoughts.

Assume, for example, that you have four facts to communicate:

1. *Moby Dick* was written by Herman Melville.

2. *Moby Dick* is a famous novel.

3. *Moby Dick* is about a whale.

4. The whale is white.

You could combine all these facts into a single sentence:

> *Moby Dick* was written by Herman Melville, and *Moby Dick* is a famous novel, and *Moby Dick* is about a whale, and the whale is white.

Although this sentence is grammatically correct, it is repetitious and sounds foolish.

If you choose the key fact from each sentence and combine the facts in the order in which they are presented, the result is not much better:

> *Moby Dick* was written by Herman Melville, a famous novel about a whale white.

A much more effective approach is to choose the sentence that expresses the fact or idea you think is most important and to use that as your **base sentence.** Of course, the sentence you choose as the base sentence may vary depending on the fact or idea you think is most important, but, whichever sentence you choose, it should contain the essential fact or idea that the other sentences somehow modify or explain. Once you have found the base sentence, you can **embed** the other facts or ideas into it as **adjectives, adverbs,** and **prepositional phrases.**

For example, let's use "*Moby Dick* is a famous novel" as the base sentence since it states an essential fact about *Moby Dick*—that it is a famous novel. The idea in sentence number one can be embedded into the base sentence as a **prepositional phrase:**

> by Herman Melville
> *Moby Dick* ∧is a famous novel.

The idea in sentence three can now be embedded into the expanded base sentence as another **prepositional phrase:**

> about a whale
> *Moby Dick* by Herman Melville is a famous novel∧.

Sentence number four contains an **adjective** that modifies the noun *whale,* so it can be embedded into the sentence by placing it before *whale:*

> *Moby Dick* by Herman Melville is a famous novel
>
> white
> about a ∧whale.

Thus, your final sentence will read:

> *Moby Dick* by Herman Melville is a famous novel about a white whale.

The same facts could be embedded in a number of other ways. Two of them are:

> *Moby Dick,* a famous novel by Herman Melville, is about a white whale.

> Herman Melville's *Moby Dick* is a famous novel about a white whale.

This process of embedding is called **sentence combining.** The purpose of practicing sentence combining is to give you an opportunity to apply the grammatical concepts you have learned in the chapter. For instance, in the above example the base sentence was expanded into a more interesting sentence by means of prepositional phrases and an adjective. Practicing this process will also help you develop greater flexibility in your sentence structure and will show you how to enrich your sentences through the addition of significant details. After all, the use of specific details is one of the most important ways of making writing interesting and effective.

PRACTICE

a. The farmer was old.
b. The farmer waited in front of the bank.
c. The farmer was in overalls.
d. The overalls were faded.
e. The farmer was patient.

1. In the space below, write the base sentence, the one with the main idea.

_____

2. Embed the **adjective** from sentence a into the base sentence by placing it before the noun that it modifies.

_____

3. Embed the **prepositional phrase** from sentence c into the sentence by placing it after the word that it modifies.

_____

4. Embed the **adjective** from sentence d into the sentence by placing it before the noun that it modifies.

_____

_____

5. Change the **adjective** in sentence e into an adverb (add "-ly") and embed it into the sentence by placing it after the verb that it modifies.

_____

_____

Sentence Combining: Exercise A

In each of the following sets of sentences, use the first sentence as the base sentence. Embed into the base sentence the adjectives, adverbs, and prepositional phrases underlined in the sentences below it.

 EXAMPLE
    a. The tiger paced in its cage.
    b. The tiger was <u>rare</u>.
    c. The tiger was <u>black and white</u>.
    d. The tiger paced <u>impatiently.</u>
    e. The tiger paced <u>during the entire night</u>.

The rare black and white tiger impatiently

paced in its cage during the entire night.

1. a. The editor fired the reporter.
    b. The editor was <u>enraged</u>.
    c. The reporter was <u>incompetent</u>.

_____

_____

2. a. The cab driver honked his horn.
    b. The cab driver was <u>angry</u>.
    c. He honked <u>at the pedestrian</u>.
    d. The pedestrian was <u>confused</u>.

_____

_____

3. a. A duck was watching a movie.
    b. The duck was <u>strange</u>.
    c. It was <u>in a sailor suit</u>.
    d. The movie was <u>about two chipmunks</u>.
    e. The chipmunks were <u>fat</u>.

_____

_____

Sentence Combining: Exercise A

continued

4. a. The bullfighter waved his cape.
   b. The bullfighter was waving <u>at the bull</u>.
   c. The bullfighter was <u>young</u>.
   d. The bullfighter was <u>in the arena</u>.
   e. The bull was <u>angry</u>.

_____

_____

5. a. The guard handed the list.
   b. The guard was <u>nervous</u>.
   c. The guard handed the list <u>quietly</u>.
   d. The list was of <u>missing items</u>.
   e. The guard handed the list <u>to the detective</u>.
   f. The detective was <u>frowning</u>.

_____

_____

Sentence Combining: Exercise B

First, choose a base sentence and circle the letter next to it. Then, using adjectives, adverbs, and prepositional phrases, embed the other facts and ideas into the base sentence.

 EXAMPLE
   a. The mountains were tall.
   b. The mountains were snow-covered.
   ⓒ The mountains towered over the hikers.
   d. There were three hikers.
   e. The hikers were from France.
   f. The hikers were lost.
   g. The mountains towered menacingly.

The tall, snow-covered mountains towered menacingly over the three lost hikers from France.

1. a. The poet was frustrated.
   b. The poet threw the letter.
   c. The letter was a rejection.
   d. He threw it into the trashcan.
   e. The trashcan was next to his desk.

_____

_____

2. a. The dancer was lonely.
   b. The dancer walked.
   c. She walked silently.
   d. She walked across the stage.
   e. The stage was empty.

_____

_____

3. a. The girl was frightened.
   b. The dog was tiny.
   c. The scarecrow was in the field.
   d. The girl and her dog stared.
   e. They stared at the scarecrow.

_____

_____

Sentence Combining: Exercise B

continued

4. a. The flames were red.
  b. The flames were fierce.
  c. They were the flames of a forest fire.
  d. The flames destroyed the village.
  e. The village was ancient.

_____

_____

5. a. The children were excited.
  b. The children placed their hands on the fur.
  c. They placed their hands carefully.
  d. The tiger was sleeping.
  e. Its fur was rough.

_____

_____

6. a. The Wright brothers are usually given credit.
  b. They are given credit for building the first successful flying machine.
  c. It was built at Kitty Hawk.
  d. Kitty Hawk is in North Carolina.
  e. It was built in 1903.

_____

_____

7. a. Samuel Langley built a flying machine.
  b. It was unmanned.
  c. He built it at the Potomac River.
  d. It was 1889.

_____

_____

continued

8. a. It was on December 8, 1903.
   b. It was just nine days before the Wright brothers' flight.
   c. Langley tried a manned flight, but it failed.
   d. It failed due to a catapult problem.

   _____

   _____

9. a. The Wright brothers' famous flight is considered the first manned flight.
   b. It is considered the first powered flight.
   c. It is also considered the first controlled flight.
   d. It is also considered the first sustained flight in a heavier-than-air craft.

   _____

   _____

10. a. Langley was discouraged about his failed flight.
    b. He was discouraged about the Wright brothers' successful flight.
    c. Langley gave up aviation.
    d. He gave it up forever.

    _____

    _____

Paragraph Practice: Narrating an Event

If you have ever sat for hours before a blank sheet of paper or stared for what seemed like forever at a blank computer screen, you know how difficult and frustrating it can be to write a paper. In fact, some people have such trouble simply <u>starting</u> their papers that for them writing becomes a truly agonizing experience.

Fortunately, writing does not have to be so difficult. If you learn how to use the steps involved in the process of writing, you can avoid much of the frustration and enjoy more of the satisfaction that comes from writing a successful paper. In this section, you will practice using the three general activities that make up the writing process—**prewriting, writing,** and **rewriting**—to produce a paragraph based on the following assignment.

Writing Assignment

Exercises 1D (page 25), 2C (page 38), 2D (page 39), and 3D (page 52) of this chapter are about four memorable events: a traumatic experience in fifth grade, Pyramus and Thisbe's tragic love story, the fate of Oedipus, and Nicholas Alkemade's 18,000-foot fall from an airplane. Although few of us have had experiences as dramatic as these, we all have had things happen to us that we remember either with warm, positive feelings or with uncomfortable, negative ones.

For this writing assignment, use the writing process explained below to describe an event that has happened to you. Ask yourself, "What events—either from the distant past or from more recent times—have happened to me that I remember well?" Perhaps you remember your first date, your first traffic ticket, or even the birth of your first child. Or perhaps you remember the day you won a race in a track meet, performed alone on a stage, or attended your first college class. Often the <u>best</u> event to write about will not be the first one you think of.

Reading Assignment

The reading selections in the "Narrating an Event" section of Chapter Six can help you see how professional writers tell their stories. Read one or more of the selections, as assigned by your instructor, and use the questions that follow them to develop ideas for your own paper.

Prewriting to Generate Ideas

Prewriting is the part of the writing process that will help you get past "writer's block" and into writing. It consists of <u>anything</u> you do to generate ideas and get started, but three of the most successful prewriting techniques are **freewriting**, **brainstorming**, and **clustering**.

Freewriting

Freewriting is based on one simple but essential idea: When you sit down to write, you write. You don't stare at your paper or look out the window, wondering what in the world you could write about. Instead, you <u>write down</u> your thoughts and questions even if you have no idea what topic you should focus on. In addition, as you freewrite, you do not stop to correct spelling, grammar, or punctuation errors. After all, the purpose of freewriting is to generate ideas, not to write the final draft of your paper.

Here is how some freewriting might look for the assignment described above.

> To describe an event? What could I write about that? I don't have a lot of "events" that I can think of—but I suppose I must have some. What do I remember? How about recently? Have I gone anywhere or has anything happened to me? I went skiing last month and took a bad fall—but so what? That wouldn't be very interesting. How about something I remember that I didn't like—like what? Death? Too depressing. Besides, I have never been closely involved in death. I was in a car accident once, but that was too long ago, and it doesn't really interest me. How about—what? I'm stuck. How about events I have good memories about—wait—I remember almost drowning when I was practicing for water polo in high school. <u>That</u> was a wild event. I could do it. Any other possibilities? How about good memories—like the time I made that lucky catch in Little League. That would be good. Or the fish I caught with my dad when I was a kid. Lots of good memories there. Any others? Yeah—I joined a softball league recently—that was a real experience, especially because it'd been so long since I'd played baseball. But I can't think of any particular thing I'd write about it.—Of all these, I think I like the drowning one best. I <u>really</u> remember that one and all the feelings that went with it.

You can tell that the above writer was not trying to produce a clean, well-written copy of his paper. Instead, he wrote down his thoughts as they occurred to him, and the result was a very informal rush of ideas that eventually led him to a topic, a near-drowning that occurred when he was in high school. Now that he has his topic, he can continue to freewrite to generate details about the event that he can use in his paper.

Prewriting Application: Freewriting

1. Freewrite for ten minutes about any memories you have of events that were important to you. Don't stop to correct any errors. Just write about as many events as you can remember. If you skip from one event to another, that's fine. If you get stuck, just write "I'm stuck" or something like that over and over—but keep writing for ten minutes.

2. Now reread your initial freewriting. Is there some event in there that interests you more than the others? Choose one event and freewrite only on it. Describe everything you can remember about the event, but don't stop to correct errors—just write.

Brainstorming

Brainstorming is another prewriting technique that you can use to generate ideas. Brainstorming is similar to freewriting in that you write down your thoughts without censoring or editing them, but it differs in that the thoughts usually appear as a list of ideas rather than as separate sentences. Here is an example of how the above freewriting might have looked as brainstorming.

An event I remember well—what could I use?
    recently?
        fall while skiing—no
    things I didn't like
        death? too depressing
        car accident I was in? too long ago
        almost drowned at practice—<u>good one</u>
    good memories?
        lucky catch in Little League
        fishing with Dad
<u>Use the one about almost drowning</u>.

Prewriting Application: Brainstorming

1. Make a brainstorming list of events from your life that were important to you. Include events from as far back as your early childhood to as recently as yesterday.

2. Choose the event that interests you the most. Make a brainstorming list of everything you can remember about it.

Clustering is a third prewriting technique that many people find helpful. It differs from brainstorming and freewriting in that it is written almost like an informal map. To "cluster" your ideas, start out with an idea or question and draw a circle around it. Then connect related ideas to the circle and continue in that way. Here is how you might use clustering to find a memorable event to write about.

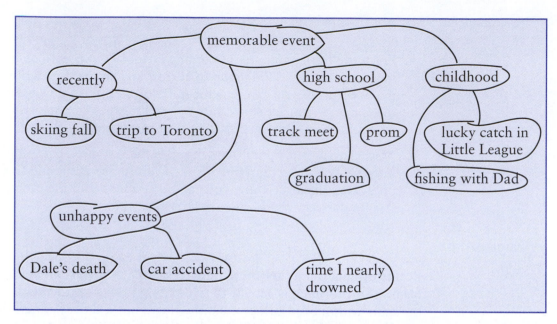

As you can see, clustering provides a mental picture of the ideas you generate. As such, it can help you organize your material <u>as</u> you think of it.

Prewriting Application: Clustering

1. Develop a "memorable events" cluster of your own. Include as many associations as you can to find the one event that interests you the most.

2. Now choose the event that interests you the most and use it as the center of a new cluster. Write in as many memories of the event as you can.

Freewriting, brainstorming, and clustering are only three of many techniques to help you get started writing. When you use them, you should feel free to move from one to the other at any time. And, of course, your instructor may suggest other ways to help you get started. Whatever technique you use, the point is to <u>start writing</u>. Do your thinking on paper (or at a computer), not while you are staring out a window. Here's a good motto that you should try to follow whenever you have a writing assignment due: **Think in ink.**

Choosing and Narrowing the Topic

Choosing the Topic

Perhaps you have already found the event that most interests you. If you have, continue to prewrite to develop as many details as you can. If you are still undecided about a topic, use the following suggestions to think of possibilities.

1. What experiences of yours have been particularly exciting, happy, or pleasant?

2. What experiences are you most proud of?

3. What events bring you disappointing, unpleasant, or fearful memories?

4. What are your most embarrassing memories?

5. What strange or unusual things have happened to you?

6. What dangerous or frightening experiences have you had?

7. What are the "firsts" in your life? Consider your first day in high school, your first day on a team or as part of a group, your first performance, your first date, your first camping trip, your first traffic ticket.

8. What experiences have inspired you, changed the way you think about life, or made you into a different person?

9. What events do you remember from your early childhood?

10. What events do you remember from elementary school or high school, from vacations or trips?

Narrowing the Topic

Many topics that interest you might be too broad—that is, explaining them might require a much longer paper than has been assigned. And sometimes instructors provide only broad topic ideas when they assign a paper, expecting you to narrow the topic to something appropriate for the length of the assignment. In such cases you need to *narrow* your topic, discussing, perhaps, only part of the event rather than the entire thing. Learning to narrow a topic is an important step in the writing process because broad topics usually lead to general, unconvincing papers.

For example, let's say you have chosen a high school football game as your topic, the championship game in which you scored the winning touchdown. It would be natural to want to cover the entire game because all of it was important to you, but the topic is much too large to be covered in one paragraph. So you must narrow the topic. A successful single paragraph might describe only one play, the one in which you made the winning play. It would describe everything about the play, from the noise in the stands to the looks on your teammates' faces in the huddle, to the smell of the grass, to the sound of the quarterback's voice—everything you can think of to provide detail and excitement to the event.

Prewriting Application: Narrowing the Topic

Consider the following events as possible topics for a paragraph. Write "OK" next to any that you think would work. If any seem too broad, explain why and discuss how you might narrow them.

_____ 1. Giving birth to my first child

_____ 2. My vacation to Atlanta

_____ 3. The car accident that changed my life

_____ 4. The last time I saw my father

——————— **5.** A day at Disneyland

——————— **6.** Prom night dinner

——————— **7.** Skiing in Aspen

——————— **8.** My first date

——————— **9.** Getting lost in Tijuana

———————**10.** Moving to Texas

Prewriting Application: Talking to Others

Once you have your topic, form groups of two, three, or four and tell your experiences to each other. Telling others about an event is a good way to decide what details to include and how much to say. And listening to someone else's story will help you learn what will keep an audience interested in your own story.

As you describe your event to others, make it as interesting as you can by describing what happened, how you felt, and what you thought. As you listen to the stories of others and as you describe your own experience, consider these questions:

1. What are the time and place of the event? How old were you? What time of day did it occur? What time of year? What was the weather like?

2. Can you visualize the scene? What is the name of the place where the event occurred? What physical features are in the area—trees? buildings? furniture? cars? other people?

3. How did you feel as the event progressed? What were you thinking each step of the way?

4. Did your thoughts and feelings change as the event occurred?

5. What parts of the event would be clearer if they were explained more?

Writing a Topic Sentence

The topic sentence is the one sentence in your paragraph that states both your **narrowed topic** and the **central point** you intend to make about the topic. To find your central point, reread your prewriting. Look for related details that seem to focus on *one particular reaction* to the event. That reaction is your central point.

College texts and your own college papers describe events in order to make a point. In a psychology text, for example, an airplane crash might be described in detail to help the reader understand how such an event can affect the relatives of those involved. And a history text might describe what happened at the Battle of Gettysburg to help the reader understand why it was a major turning point in the Civil War. Certainly in your own college papers, you will be expected to describe events to illustrate the points you are trying to make.

Although the topic sentence can appear in a variety of places, in college paragraphs you should usually write it as the first sentence so that your central point is clear from the very start. Here are some examples of topic sentences drawn from the exercises in this chapter. Note that each topic sentence contains a topic and a central point and that each one is the first sentence of its paragraph.

 EXAMPLES

      topic   central point

An **unfortunate incident in the fifth grade** was one of <u>the most traumatic</u>

<u>experiences of my life</u>.

    central point   topic

<u>One of the most poignant stories of all time</u> **is the myth of Pyramus**

and Thisbe.

      topic   central point

The story of Oedipus, the Greek king, has caused audiences throughout

the ages to reconsider their relationship with fate or "the gods."

     topic

On March 25, 1944, Nicholas Alkemade <u>reserved a place</u>

    central point

<u>for himself in aviation history.</u>

The **central point** of your topic sentence needs to be *limited* and *precise* so that it is not too broad, general, or vague. For example, in the topic sentence *My first date was an interesting experience,* the central idea that the date was *interesting* is much too vague. It could mean the date was the best experience of your life or that it was absolutely horrible. As a general rule, the more precise the topic sentence, the more effective your paragraph will be. Consider the following characteristics of a well-written topic sentence.

1. A topic sentence must include a central point.

 EXAMPLE

(weak)   My paragraph is about my youngest sister's wedding.

In this sentence the topic (my youngest sister's wedding) is clear, but no central point about that wedding is expressed. An improved topic sentence might be:

 EXAMPLE

(improved)   My youngest sister's wedding last year was one of the most hilarious events I have ever experienced.

In this sentence, a central point—that the wedding was hilarious—has been clearly expressed.

2. A topic sentence does not merely state a fact.

EXAMPLE

    (weak)   A few months ago I saw a car accident.

This sentence simply states a fact. There is no central point to be explained after the fact is stated. An improved topic sentence might be:

EXAMPLE

    (improved)   I will never forget how horrified I was a few months ago when I was an unwilling witness to a major car accident.

This sentence now makes a statement about the accident that causes the reader to want more explanation.

3. A topic sentence must include a narrowed topic and central point.

EXAMPLE

    (weak)   My spring break this year was really something.

Both the topic (spring break) and the central point (it was "something") are far too general to describe in detail in one paragraph. Here is a more focused topic sentence:

EXAMPLE

    (improved)   On the last day of spring break this year, my vacation in Palm Springs, California, turned from wonderful to absolutely miserable in just one hour.

This sentence now focuses on a specific event—the last day of spring break in Palm Springs—and on a precise central point—that it changed from wonderful to miserable.

Prewriting Application: Working with Topic Sentences

In each sentence below, underline the topic once and the central point twice.

1. When walking my dog around the lake last evening, I had a life-changing insight.

2. Reducing possible distractions is a key strategy in successfully preparing for an exam.

3. When I received my first chemistry kit for my eleventh birthday, I did not know that the doors to my future career had opened.

4. My first flight on an airplane turned out to be much more of an adventure than I had anticipated.

5. There was feeling of accomplishment and of a tangible connection with the earth when I harvested the vegetables from my first attempt at gardening.

Prewriting Application: Evaluating Topic Sentences

Write "No" before each sentence that would not make a good topic sentence and "Yes" before each sentence that would make a good one. Using ideas of your own, rewrite the unacceptable topic sentences into topic sentences that might work.

_____   **1.** Last year I went skiing.

_____

_____

_____   **2.** Giving birth to my first child made me wonder if I would ever want to have children again.

_____

_____

_____   **3.** My heart nearly broke the day I decided it was time to take my dog, Jasper, on his last ride to the veterinarian's office.

_____

_____

_____   **4.** My first night camping was interesting.

_____

_____

_____   **5.** One of my earliest memories of my father and me spending time together is also one of my most disappointing ones.

_____

_____

_____   **6.** It all went downhill when I started to make breakfast after our first night together.

_____

_____

_____   **7.** My paragraph will be about my favorite computer game.

_____

_____

_____   **8.** I was amazed at everything that happened to us while driving from Amarillo, Texas, to Atlanta, Georgia.

_____

_____

_____   **9.** When I stepped into the sunlight the next morning, I wondered if the party the night before had been a bad dream.

_____

_____

_____   **10.** When I opened my email inbox, I could not have known that I was in for a big surprise.

_____

_____

Organizing Details

When describing an event, you will usually present the details in **chronological order.** That is, you will organize them according to how they occurred in time. However, other assignments might require different organizations to present your supporting details effectively. (Other organizational patterns are discussed in later chapters.)

Prewriting Application: Organizing Supporting Details

Number the details in the following brainstorming list so that they appear in their probable chronological order.

_____   joined water polo

_____   volunteered to try the challenge set

_____ two laps underwater

_____ felt okay at first

_____ woke up in coach's arms

_____ choking underwater

_____ second lap seemed okay at first

_____ determined to make it

_____ everyone around me when I woke up

_____ everything went black

_____ lungs gave out

_____ saw lane markers just before passed out

What Is a Paragraph?

Since you are going to write a paragraph about an experience of your own, it is time to explain what a paragraph is. First and foremost, a paragraph is a kind of visual aid. Just imagine how a text would look if there were no paragraphs; one would end up with one long uninterrupted block of sentences, possibly going on for pages. Such a block would look intimidating and discourage the reader. Paragraphs visually indicate where one idea—or a portion of an idea—starts and ends. When you start a new paragraph, you signal to a reader that you shift the topic slightly, or that you turn to another portion of the larger idea that your essay as a whole is pursuing, or that you are moving to another section of your story. Therefore, the general rule is that one paragraph should explore and develop one idea, or one event, or a portion of a more complicated event or idea. Since that is the case, an event or an idea you want to write about in one paragraph cannot be too complicated. An appropriate paragraph topic has to be specific.

Writing the Paragraph

Writing a full draft of your paragraph is the next step in the writing process. The trick to writing your first draft without getting stuck is to remember that what you write now is not your final copy, so you can allow yourself to make mistakes and to write awkward sentences. Don't worry about how "correct" your writing is. Instead, just describe your experience as thoroughly as you can.

Here is a sample first draft of the paragraph on drowning. As you read it, notice that the writer has not yet corrected any errors it may contain.

The Challenge Set (First Draft)

I almost drowned when I was sixteen. It all happened one day at practice for water polo. I was a sophomore on the Kearney High School water polo team. One day I volunteered for the dreaded "Challenge Set." I had just finished the first lap underwater. I still felt good. As I come to the wall, I make the decision to go for another lap, I keep swimming, but my lungs collapse. I took a few more strokes, and then it happened. I blacked out. All I remember was seeing black. I felt completely relaxed. Then I remember hearing voices. Suddenly, starting to cough violently. When I opened my eyes, the first person I saw was my coach. He told me what had happened, I was a little shaken. I couldn't believe that I almost died. This was really a frightening experience that I remember whenever I go for a swim.

The above first draft is far from perfect. It contains writing errors and could use more descriptive details. However, it has accomplished its purpose: *It has given the writer a draft to work with and to improve with revision.*

Writing Application: Producing Your First Draft

Now write the first draft of your paragraph. Remember that your goal is <u>not</u> to write an error-free draft. Rather, it is to write a <u>first</u> draft that opens with a preliminary topic sentence, a draft that you can then continue to work on and improve.

Rewriting and Improving the Paragraph

Rewriting consists of two stages: **revising** and **editing**. In the **revising** stage of the writing process, you work on the "larger" areas of your paper—its content, organization, and sentence structure. Here are some suggestions.

■ <u>Improve your preliminary topic sentence.</u>

You can often improve your topic sentence <u>after</u> you have written your first draft because now you really have something to introduce. In fact, if you look at the <u>concluding</u> sentences of your first draft, you may find a clearer statement of the central point of your paragraph than the one you have in your opening sentence. If that is the case, rewrite your opening sentence to include that statement.

■ Add more details.

After you have written the first draft, add any further details that might improve your paper. Look especially for those that will emphasize the central point of your topic sentence.

■ Reorganize the details in the first draft.

There are many ways to organize a paper, but one of the most common ones is to save the most important details for last. Another way to organize details, especially if you are describing an event, is to list the details in chronologic order. Whichever way you choose, now is the time to make any changes in the order of your material.

■ Combine related sentences and ideas.

Combine sentences that are obviously related. Where possible, use sentence combining techniques to embed material from one sentence into another. (Sentence combining techniques are discussed in Section Four of each chapter.)

Improving Supporting Details

The supporting details in many first drafts tend to be vague, colorless, and mediocre. But with just a little work they can be transformed into strong, dramatic sentences. Consider adding details that emphasize specific sights and sounds. Wherever you can, use the precise names of people, places, and things. Look especially for new details and words that will emphasize the central point of your paragraph. Note how the colorless example below is transformed with precise, descriptive details.

 EXAMPLE   (weak)   My father went in one direction while I went in another. I saw a fence covered with all sorts of decorations from local Indians. Inside the fence on the ground was the medicine wheel. I stared at it silently.

 EXAMPLE   (improved)   My father veered off to the west as I continued straight ahead, toward what I perceived to be the main attraction. On this fist of land was a protective, circular chain link fence sixty feet in diameter, decorated with ribbons, scraps of paper, little totem bags made by the local Indian women and girls, eagle feathers, and strings of beads. All of these decorations were meant as offerings and prayers. Inside the fence was the medicine wheel, a fifty-foot spoked wheel etched into the dust. I stopped and felt the wind and the still sacredness of the view.

Rewriting Application: Improving Supporting Details

Read the following brief paragraphs and identify places where the support could be more descriptive and precise. Then rewrite the paragraphs, adding stronger, more dramatic details.

A. My trip to the grocery store turned into a complete nightmare. When I walked down one of the aisles, I saw a person shoplifting, so I told the manager. She stopped the shoplifter, and they argued. Then the manager said I had to stay to talk to the police. I had some important things to do, so I said I had to leave. As I walked to my car, the manager became really mad at me too.

B. One of the highlights of my short career playing Little League baseball happened when my best friend was at bat. He and I played on opposing teams. I was in the outfield when he hit the ball toward me. It was going to go over my head, so I backed up. When I reached the fence, I stuck up my glove and caught the ball. I looked at the stands and saw people standing and cheering for me. It was a great experience.

Proofreading

Proofreading is the final step in the writing process. It consists of correcting spelling, grammar, and punctuation errors. **Do not skip this step.** A paper focused on an excellent topic and developed with striking details will almost always still receive a poor grade if it is full of distracting writing errors. Here are some suggestions to help you proofread successfully.

- If you use a computer, run the spelling-checker program. (But don't rely only on that program. Read each word carefully yourself.)

- Use a dictionary to check the spelling of any words you are unsure of.

- Watch for incomplete sentences and run-on sentences. (These errors will be discussed in Chapter Two.)

- Look closely at your verbs and pronouns. If you are describing an event from the past, use past tense verbs. (Verb and pronoun errors will be discussed in Chapter Four.)

- Ask someone you trust to read your paper. If your school has tutors available, use them. They can help you find many writing errors that you might have overlooked. **However, please note:** If a friend reads your paper, do not allow him or her to rewrite sentences for you. Most instructors consider that kind of help to be plagiarism.

- When you are satisfied with your paper, print a final copy (if you are using a computer), and then *read that copy one more time*. You will be surprised how often more errors seem to appear out of nowhere. If you find more errors, fix them and print another copy.

Rewriting Application: Responding to Writing

Reread the first draft of "The Challenge Set" on page 72. Then respond to the following questions:

1. What is the writer's central feeling about his experience? Where is it stated? How would you reword the opening sentence to express that central feeling?

2. Where should the writer add more details? What kind of details would make his paragraph more colorful and descriptive?

3. Should any of the details be reorganized or presented in a different order?

4. What sentences would you combine because they contain related ideas?

5. What changes should the writer make in spelling, grammar, or punctuation?

Here is how the student who nearly drowned revised his first draft. Compare it to his first draft.

The Challenge Set

Revised opening sentence includes reaction to the event.

When I was sixteen, I had a frightening experience that I still remember whenever I go for a swim. This took place when I was a sophomore on the Kearney High School water polo team. One day at practice, I volunteered to try the dreaded "Challenge Set." **It consisted of three to four players attempting to swim fifty yards, two laps of the pool, on a single breath.**

Added details

I dove into the cool, clear water full of confidence, but I had no idea what was about to happen. When I came to the wall at the end of the first lap, I was well ahead of my teammate, Bryan, who was in the lane to my right. I felt great, as if I could hold my breath forever, so I decided to go for the second lap. I made the flip turn and pushed off the blue tiles. I still felt okay, but without my knowing it, my lungs had started to collapse. I

Added details

remember beginning to feel pressure in my chest when I saw the blue hash marks, the halfway markers. I had just a little way to go, but my head was whirling, and my chest felt like it was about to explode. Suddenly everything slowed down. I knew I should stop and take a breath, but I refused to do it. I took a few more strokes, and then it happened. I started to black

Combined sentences

out. **All I remember is seeing black and feeling completely relaxed. The next thing I knew, it seemed like someone was shaking me. As I began to hear voices, I started to cough violently. Every time I tried to take a breath, a searing pain shot through me. I was terrified.** When I opened my eyes, the

Added details

first person I saw was Coach Leonard, a state beach lifeguard. I was lying in his arms, not knowing where I was or what had happened to me. When he told me that I had passed out in the pool and that Bryan had pulled me

Added details

out, I was really shaken. I couldn't believe I had almost drowned. **I got out of the pool, got dressed, and sat in the stands waiting for practice to end.** I don't think I'll ever forget that day.

Rewriting Application: Revising and Editing Your Own Draft

Now revise and edit your first draft. As you do so, remember to <u>revise</u> first.

1. Improve your topic sentence.

2. Add more details, especially those that emphasize the central point.

3. Reorganize the details.

4. Combine related sentences and ideas.

Once you have revised, then <u>edit</u> for spelling, grammar, and punctuation errors. As you can tell, thorough revising and editing will involve several new drafts, not just one. Once you have a draft with which you are satisfied, prepare a clean final draft, following the format your instructor has requested.

Chapter 1 Practice Test

A. Identify the underlined words by writing "S" over subjects, "HV" over helping verbs, and "MV" over main verbs. If the underlined word is none of these, leave it blank.

1. The quartz <u>crystal</u> in my watch <u>will</u> vibrate 32,768 times per second.

2. The vampire <u>staring</u> into my window <u>looked</u> very thirsty.

3. Here <u>are</u> three <u>people</u>, so here must be a crowd.

4. <u>Siddartha</u> taught his followers to <u>live</u> what he called "The Middle Way."

5. <u>Ask</u> Zeus if he <u>has</u> ever heard of Jupiter.

B. Underline all subjects once and all complete verbs twice in the following sentences.

6. Jackie Chan and Chris Tucker cause many people to laugh.

7. There is an elephant's footprint on the floor of my living room.

8. Some of the people in the audience did not enjoy Taylor Swift's singing.

9. Don Quixote just ignored all of the insults and smiles.

10. The tarantula crawled onto her arm, but Abbie did not seem to mind.

11. A Greek won the Nobel Prize for literature, and an American was awarded the Pulitzer Prize for editorial writing.

12. No falling raindrop can exceed the speed of eighteen miles per hour.

13. What image is on the front of a fifty-dollar bill, or are you more familiar with twenty-dollar bills?

14. Dorian Gray had not changed in decades, but the picture of him had changed radically.

15. Although some Brits will deny it, England has always been smaller than the state of Georgia.

C. Write sentences of your own that follow the suggested patterns.

16. A statement with one subject and two main verbs joined by "and" (S-MV-"and"-MV):

_____

_____

17. A question with one helping verb, one subject, and one main verb (HV-S-MV):

_____

_____

continued

18. A statement with two subjects joined by "and," one helping verb, and one main verb. (S-"and"-S-HV-MV):

_____

_____

19. A statement with one subject, two helping verbs, and a main verb (S-HV-HV-MV):

_____

_____

20. A statement with a subject and a main verb followed by "after" and another subject and main verb (S-MV-"after"-S-MV):

_____

_____

D. In the following sentences, identify all adjectives by writing "Adj" above them, and identify all adverbs by writing "Adv" above them.

21. During the walk with an angry Elmo, Ernie suddenly started to sing.

22. Merle did not know the name of the third planet from the sun.

23. Peter Parker was suddenly bitten by a radioactive spider.

24. Tommy, the main character in *Rescue Me,* usually broods about the past.

25. Eddie Murphy once played an African prince in *Coming to America.*

E. In the following sentences, correct any errors in the use of adjectives and adverbs (or in the use of *then* and *than*) by crossing out any incorrect words and writing the correct words above them.

26. It was real hot at the beach yesterday, but it was even more hotter today.

27. I would rather visit Monterey then Los Angeles because it has the cleanest air of the two.

28. Gregory finished the test quick because he had prepared so good.

29. The people in *Under the Dome* felt badly because their worse fear had come true.

30. Would you say Herbert Hoover had more wiser economic policies then

Franklin Delano Roosevelt?

continued

F. In the following sentences, place all prepositional phrases in parentheses.

31. Could a better thing have happened to a better person at a better time?

32. Charon refused to ferry us across the river Styx because of our healthy glow.

33. Brad got into his Chevy and Angelina followed with her Harley.

34. Igor opened the door and stared at the package of spiders that had just arrived from Transylvania.

35. Between the two, Keisha has a more sophisticated sense of style than Katie.

G. In the following sentences, add coordinating conjunctions that show the relationship indicated in parentheses.

36. Bill is taking care of the dog, _____ Hillary is traveling around the world. (addition)

37. Willie could not face the truth, _____ he asked Biff to lie to him. (result)

38. Ernesto did his best to arrive on time, _____ traffic conditions conspired against him. (contrast)

39. Cole could be playing with his Elmo doll, _____ he could spend time with one of his grandfathers. (alternative)

40. Ulysses was feeling lonesome, _____ he had not been home for almost twenty years. (cause)

H. In the following sentences, identify the underlined words by writing one of the following abbreviations above each word: noun (N), pronoun (Pro), verb (V), adjective (Adj), adverb (Adv), conjunction (Conj), preposition (Prep).

41. After the <u>angry</u> chimpanzee had collected the stones, he threw <u>them</u> at the people in the zoo.

42. The school <u>changed</u> its <u>name</u> to Howard Zinn Memorial High School.

43. An ancient mariner watched the <u>albatross</u> drift lazily <u>toward</u> his ship.

44. Katie <u>quietly</u> arose, went into the nursery, and picked up the <u>hungry</u> baby.

continued

45. Closely watching the gas consumption of the car, Henrik <u>was</u> delighted <u>at</u> its

energy efficiency.

46. Stevie Wonder performed at the awards show, <u>but</u> he did <u>not</u> understand how some

of the performers could have been given the praise they received.

47. Last night, <u>someone</u> broke into Jessica's house and stole her <u>collection</u> of Guns N'

Roses records.

48. Does anyone still remember Gangnam Style, <u>or</u> is there a <u>new</u> YouTube sensation?

49. The poet smiled to <u>himself</u> as he stood on the stage in New York and recited his poem

"Where There Was No Pattern" <u>before</u> a crowded auditorium.

50. Stanley stumbled <u>drunkenly</u> into the street, where he <u>screamed</u> "Stella!"

Understanding Sentence Patterns

In Chapter One you learned the terms that describe how words function in a sentence. These terms will help you understand how the various word groups operate in a sentence. Understanding these word groups will help you see not only how sentences are put together but also how to revise your writing effectively and systematically. Without some knowledge of these word groups, you really can't even define what a sentence is.

Consider, for example, two common definitions of a sentence:

1. A sentence is a group of words that expresses a complete thought.

2. A sentence is a group of words that contains a subject and a verb.

These definitions may seem adequate, but, if you consider them carefully, you will see that neither of them is really accurate. For example, some sentences do not seem to express "a complete thought." Consider the sentence *It fell.* Do these two words really convey a complete thought? In one sense they do: A specific action is communicated, and a subject, though an indefinite one, is identified. However, the sentence raises more questions than it answers. What fell? Why did it fall? Where did it fall to? The sentence could refer to an apple, a star, the sky, or the Roman empire. If someone walked up to you in the street and said, *It fell,* you certainly would not feel that a complete thought had been communicated to you, and yet the two words do form a sentence.

The second definition is no more satisfactory. The words *Because his father was sleeping* do <u>not</u> make up a sentence even though they contain both a subject (*father*) and a verb (*was sleeping*). Although it is true that all sentences must contain a subject and a verb, it does not necessarily follow that every group of words with a subject and a verb is a sentence.

The only definition of a sentence that is <u>always</u> correct is the following one: A sentence is a group of words that contains at least one main clause.

---

sentence

A sentence is a group of words that contains at least one main clause.

You will understand this definition easily if you know what a **main clause** is, but it will be incomprehensible if you do not. Thus, it is critical that you be able to identify this word group, for, if you cannot identify a main clause, you cannot be certain that you are using complete sentences in your writing.

Clauses

Main Clauses and Subordinate Clauses

A clause is a group of words that contains at least one subject and at least one verb.

> **clause**
>
> A clause is a group of words that contains at least one subject and at least one verb.

The two types of clauses are **main clause** and **subordinate clause**.

1. A **main clause** is a group of words that contains at least one subject and one verb and that <u>expresses a complete idea</u>.

2. A **subordinate clause** is a group of words that contains at least one subject and one verb but that <u>does not express a complete idea</u>. All subordinate clauses begin with **subordinators.**

 EXAMPLE

            sub. clause   main clause
[Although he seldom plays,] [Raymond is an excellent golfer.]

This example contains two clauses, each with a subject and a verb. As you can see, the clause *Raymond is an excellent golfer* could stand by itself as a sentence. But the clause *Although he seldom plays* cannot stand by itself (even though it has a subject and a verb) because it needs the main clause to complete its thought and because it begins with the subordinator *although*.

Subordinators

Subordinators indicate the relationship between the subordinate clause and the main clause. Learning to recognize the two types of subordinators—subordinating conjunctions and relative pronouns—will help you identify subordinate clauses.

Subordinating Conjunctions		*Relative Pronouns*	
<u>after</u>	so that	that	who(ever)
although	than	which	whom(ever)
<u>as</u>	though		whose
as if	unless		
as long as	<u>until</u>		
because	when		
<u>before</u>	whenever		
even though	where		
if	wherever		
<u>since</u>	while		

NOTE: Some of the words in the above list of subordinators are underlined (*after, as, before, since, until*). These words are used as prepositions when they do not introduce a subordinate clause.

 EXAMPLES

prepositional phrase: after dinner

subordinate clause: after I eat dinner

The following are examples of sentences containing subordinate clauses. (Note that each subordinate clause begins with a subordinator.)

 EXAMPLES

                      sub. clause   main clause
[**Before** his horse had crossed the finish line,] [the jockey suddenly stood up in his saddle.]

        main clause   sub. clause
[Fried Spam is a dish] [that few people love.]

            main clause   sub. clause
[Antonio won the spelling bee] [**because** he spelled *penicillin* correctly.]

 PRACTICE

Identify the following word groups as main clauses (MC), subordinate clauses (SC), or neither (N).

_*SC*___ **1.** When Susan thought of running the marathon.

_____ **2.** She was anxious.

_____ **3.** Then she became eager.

_____ **4.** To begin the race.

_____ **5.** As she approached the starting line.

———— **6.** On September 16, 2014.

———— **7.** The runners stretched their legs.

———— **8.** Because she had prepared for the long run.

———— **9.** She knew she would reach her destination.

————**10.** Many arduous miles later.

◎ **PRACTICE**   Identify the following word groups as subordinate clauses (SC) or prepositional phrases (PP).

——*SC*—— **1.** Until you begin to diet.

———— **2.** Until the beginning.

———— **3.** Until next October.

———— **4.** As the main character in *Mad Men*.

———— **5.** As I was watching *Mad Men*.

———— **6.** Before she sang her first song.

———— **7.** Before dawn.

———— **8.** After the first inning.

———— **9.** After we eat breakfast.

————**10.** After the class with Professor Gomez.

◎ **PRACTICE**   Underline the subordinate clauses in the following sentences and circle the subordinators. Not all sentences contain subordinate clauses.

1. People clapped (as) the president approached the microphone.

2. After their fight, Ali shook Joe's hand.

3. Shamu splashed the people who were sitting by the tank.

4. If the creek does not rise, Mr. Murdoch will buy the newspaper.

5. The government cannot operate effectively until both political parties

agree to compromise.

6. The dinner was delicious although some people became sick from the shrimp.

7. The student loved Emily Dickinson, whose poem she was reading.

8. The DJ played hip-hop music while the crowd danced.

9. Stonewall stared at the mountain where the Yankees were loading their cannons.

10. Maria and Jackson listened to the wind that blew through the trees.

Adverb and Adjective Subordinate Clauses

Subordinate clauses may function as adverbs, adjectives, or nouns in their sentences. Therefore, they are called **adverb clauses, adjective clauses,** or **noun clauses.** We will be discussing adverb and adjective clauses, but not noun clauses. Although we frequently use noun clauses in our writing, they seldom present problems in punctuation or clarity.

Adverb Clauses

Like single-word adverbs, adverb subordinate clauses can modify verbs. For example, in the sentence *Clare ate a big breakfast because she had a busy day ahead of her,* the adverb clause *because she had a busy day ahead of her* modifies the verb *ate.* It explains <u>why</u> Clare ate a big breakfast.

Another characteristic of adverb clauses is that they begin with a **subordinating conjunction,** not a relative pronoun. In addition, in most cases an adverb clause can be moved around in its sentence, and the sentence will still make sense.

 EXAMPLES

[**When** she ate the mushroom,] Alice grew taller.

Alice grew taller [**when** she ate the mushroom.]

Alice, [**when** she ate the mushroom,] grew taller.

NOTE: When the adverb clause begins the sentence, it is followed by a comma, as in the first example. When the adverb clause ends a sentence, no comma is needed. When the adverb clause interrupts the main clause, it is enclosed by commas.

PRACTICE   Underline the adverb clauses in the following sentences. Circle the subordinating conjunctions.

1. (Until) you are given permission, do not board the airplane.

2. When General Lee left his tent, Traveller was waiting for him.

3. Miley was hurt because Elton John called her a "meltdown waiting to happen."

4. Before Admiral Nelson could make a choice, he consulted his wife.

5. Someone threw a water balloon as the senator started to speak.

 PRACTICE   Add adverb clauses of your own to the following main clauses in the spaces indicated. Use commas where they are needed. (Answers will vary.)

1. The train could not make it across the mountain _because snow was blocking the tracks._

2. _____

   _____ Howard forgot to leave a tip.

3. Vincent moved to France _____

   _____

4. _____

   _____ Delilah cut Samson's hair.

5. The children threw their Brussels sprouts under the table_____

   _____

Adjective Clauses

Adjective subordinate clauses modify nouns or pronouns just as single-word adjectives do. Adjective clauses follow the nouns or pronouns they modify, and they usually begin with a **relative pronoun**—*who, whom, whose, which, that* (and sometimes *when* or *where*). As you can see in the examples below, relative pronouns sometimes serve as subjects of their clauses. We will discuss the rules for punctuating adjective clauses in Chapter Three.

 EXAMPLES   The horse [that Mr. Lee liked best] was named Traveller. (The adjective clause modifies *horse.*)

On the top shelf was the trophy [**that** Irma had won for her model of the Battle of Shiloh]. (The adjective clause modifies *trophy.*)

Hampton, [**which** is Michelle's hooded rat,] resides at the foot of her bed. (The adjective clause modifies *Hampton,* and the relative pronoun *which* is the subject of the clause.)

NOTE: As you can see in the example above, the adjective clause often appears between the subject and the verb of the main clause. In addition, as you can see in the following example, sometimes the relative pronoun is left out.

 EXAMPLE   The man [I met yesterday] works for the CIA. (Here the adjective clause modifies the noun *man,* but the relative pronoun *whom* is left out.)

A note about relative pronouns:

1. Use *who* or *whom* to refer to people only.

2. Use *which* to refer to nonhuman things only, such as animals or objects.

3. Use *that* to refer to either people or nonhuman things.

 PRACTICE   Underline the adjective clauses in the following sentences and circle the relative pronouns.

1. Holesome Gatherings is the new bagel and jazz place (that) opened this week.

2. A saxophone player whom we all like was the first act. 3. A drummer who lives next door to us played with her. 4. The Billie Holiday Special, which is my favorite, is a bagel in the shape of a gardenia. 5. A Dalmatian that everyone calls Thelonious greets people at the door.

PRACTICE   Add adjective clauses of your own to the following main clauses.

1. Jason noticed a light go on in an upper floor of the building.

   Jason noticed a light go on in an upper floor

   of the building that he was passing.

2. Joshua looked up at the walls of Jericho.

   _____

   _____

3. Nathaniel showed his new house to Herman.

   _____

   _____

4. The princes were kept in the tower.

   _____

   _____

5. One of the fiercest battles of the Civil War was the Battle of Antietam.

   _____

   _____

 PRACTICE   In the following sentences, underline the subordinate clauses and identify them as adverb clauses (Adv) or Adjective clauses (Adj).

Adv   1. After Rojelio gets home, we can start dinner.

_____   2. Ophelia asked Hamlet if he still loved her.

_____   3. Stephanie likes to play the Bob Dylan songs that are on her iPhone.

_____   4. My mother plays croquet whenever she can.

_____   5. Darby likes to run in Brady Park, which is near my home.

PRACTICE   Add subordinate clauses of your own to the following main clauses and indicate whether you have added an adverb clause (Adv) or an adjective clause (Adj).

1. Waldo played his new computer game.

    Waldo played his new computer game, which he had purchased at Best Buy. (Adj)

2. Sheila loaded her skis onto her car.

    Sheila loaded her skis onto her car, after she got packed for her trip. (Adv)

3. The snake crawled under the house.

    The snake crawled under the house, when the kids scared it. (Adv)

4. Meredith refused to go to classes.

    Meredith refused to go to classes, when she wanted to go to Olive Garden. (Adj)

5. The candle at the edge of the table flickered.

    The candle at the edge of the table flickered, when Dan opens the window. Adv

Section One Review

1. A **clause** is a group of words <u>that contains at least one subject and at least one verb</u>.

2. A **main clause** is a group of words that contains at least one subject and one verb and that <u>expresses a complete idea</u>.

3. A **subordinate clause** is a group of words that contains at least one subject and one verb but that <u>does not express a complete idea</u>.

4. **Subordinate clauses** begin with <u>subordinators</u>.

5. **Adverb subordinate clauses** usually modify verbs and begin with <u>subordinating conjunctions</u>.

6. **Adjective subordinate clauses** modify nouns or pronouns and begin with <u>relative pronouns</u>.

Exercise 1A

Listen to or watch the news, or read a magazine, newspaper, or book. Identify which news program, magazine, newspaper, or book you used. Write down five sentences that contain adjective subordinate clauses and five that contain adverb subordinate clauses. Underline and identify each subordinate clause.

1. _____

   _____

2. _____

   _____

3. _____

   _____

4. _____

   _____

5. _____

   _____

6. _____

   _____

7. _____

   _____

8. _____

   _____

9. _____

   _____

10. _____

   _____

Exercise 1B

Underline all subordinate clauses and circle the subordinators. In the spaces provided, indicate whether the subordinator is an adverb clause (Adv) or an adjective clause (Adj). If a sentence contains no subordinate clause, do nothing to it.

Adj   **1.** Alec Baldwin was proud of the advertisement (that) he had developed for the credit card company.

_____   **2.** Caesar was quite surprised when he saw all the daggers.

_____   **3.** Because of the phase of the moon, the general decided to attack.

_____   **4.** Everyone was laughing at Homer's new Volkswagen, which had been painted like a can of Spam.

_____   **5.** If the rain continues for much longer, the mud on the hillside might slide into our backyard.

_____   **6.** Because he had researched it so thoroughly, Allan Gurganus took seven years to write his first novel.

_____   **7.** The woman who sang the National Anthem was cheered by the fans.

_____   **8.** Beethoven took questions from the audience after he had premiered his Ninth Symphony.

_____   **9.** Whenever Achilles griped, his friends laughed at him.

_____   **10.** Before the services, the minister put a black veil over his face.

_____   **11.** Monk asked the officer to arrest the man who had been sneezing in public.

_____   **12.** The political decision that had closed all of the national parks angered 85 percent of the population.

_____   **13.** Although Michael Vick was a masterful quarterback, few people would forgive him.

_____   **14.** Prometheus would be a very happy Titan if the eagle ever lost its appetite.

_____   **15.** Even though the woman had been severely wounded at the Boston Marathon, she was determined to run again.

Exercise 1C

A. Join the pairs of sentences below by making one of them either an adverb or an adjective subordinate clause. You may need to delete or change some words.

1. The farmer stared at the barn.
   The barn had been destroyed by the tornado.

   The farmer stared at the barn that

   had been destroyed by the tornado.

2. Nathaniel Hawthorne wanted to write a great novel.
   He needed to support his family.

   _____

   _____

3. Naomi Watts starred in the film *Impossible*.
   The film was about a family that survived a tsunami in Thailand.

   _____

   _____

4. The bombings occurred during the 2013 Boston Marathon.
   The bombings were in the news for weeks afterward.

   _____

   _____

5. Lang Lang began his piano solo.
   The orchestra played the introduction to the concerto.

   _____

   _____

B. Write subordinate clauses (adjective or adverb) in the blanks as indicated in parentheses at the beginning of the sentence. Make sure your clauses have subjects and verbs.

6. (Adv) *After the ants carried away the okra,* _____

   Hortense decided to call an exterminator.

7. (Adv) The coach was worried about getting uniforms for his team _____

   _____

continued

8. (Adj) Sister Agatha drove a motorcycle _____

_____

9. (Adj) Charlie Parker, _____

_____ became addicted to several drugs.

10. (Adv) _____

Dierdre enjoyed the party.

C. To the main clauses below, add the types of subordinate clauses indicated in parentheses. Add your clause at any place in the sentence that you feel is appropriate. For instance, you may add an adjective clause to any noun in a sentence.

11. (Adv) Mr. Barth resumed reading his newspaper.

After he had eaten his dinner, Mr. Barth resumed

reading his newspaper.

12. (Adj) In the last Harry Potter novel, Harry Potter makes some strange decisions.

_____

_____

13. (Adv) Lindsay Lohan stared at the judge.

_____

_____

14. (Adj) My iPhone made some insulting statements last Friday.

_____

_____

15. (Adv) Joy is looking forward to seeing the latest version of *The Great Gatsby*.

_____

_____

Underline all subordinate clauses and identify the type of clause (adjective or adverb) in the spaces provided.

1. A number of "London bridges" span the Thames River at London, England, but the bridge that is the source of the famous nursery rhyme has an especially interesting history. _Adj_

2. The song "London Bridge Is Falling Down" probably refers to an early wooden version of the bridge that was destroyed by King Olaf of Norway in the eleventh century. _____

3. On the other hand, because the tolls to pay for the bridge's repair were rarely collected, the song might also refer to the general shabbiness of the bridge. _____ **4.** Between 1176 and 1209, the wooden bridge was rebuilt by Peter of Colechurch, who constructed nineteen stone arches to support the new bridge. _____ **5.** Because of an ancient superstition that the river gods had to be appeased, its cornerstones were spattered with the blood of little children. _____ **6.** In the middle of the river on the largest pier stood a chapel. _____ **7.** All across the surface of the bridge were buildings that were used as residences and businesses. _____ **8.** Three years after it was completed, the bridge was severely damaged by a fire. _____ **9.** Despite such setbacks, for centuries the bridge remained a choice residential and business site for the people who owned the houses and shops on it. _____ **10.** During Shakespeare's time, people would cross the bridge to Southwark, where the theaters and other places of entertainment were. _____ **11.** Until the 1740s, it was the only bridge that crossed the Thames. _____ **12.** Although it was extensively rebuilt in the 1750s, it was demolished in the 1820s and replaced by New London Bridge. _____ **13.** New London Bridge, which was itself replaced in the 1960s, was dismantled and shipped across the Atlantic. _____ **14.** It was re-erected at Lake Havasu, Arizona, where it is now a tourist attraction. _____ **15.** The old bridge built by Peter of Colechurch stood for more than six hundred years, five hundred years more than the one that was built to replace it. _____

Simple, Compound, Complex, and Compound-Complex Sentences

Sentences are categorized according to the number and types of clauses they contain. The names of the four types of sentences are **simple, compound, complex,** and **compound-complex.** You need to be familiar with these sentence patterns for a number of reasons:

1. **Variety.** Varying your sentence patterns creates interest and avoids monotony. Repeating a sentence pattern endlessly will bore even your most interested reader.

2. **Emphasis.** You can use these sentence patterns to emphasize the ideas that you think are more important than others.

3. **Grammar.** A knowledge of the basic sentence patterns of English will help you avoid the major sentence structure errors discussed in Section Three.

Being able to recognize and use these sentence patterns will help you control your writing and thus express your ideas more effectively.

The Simple Sentence

The introduction to this chapter points out that a sentence must contain at least one main clause. A sentence that contains only one main clause and no other clauses is called a **simple sentence.** However, a simple sentence is not necessarily an uncomplicated or short sentence because, in addition to its one main clause, it may also contain a variety of phrases and modifiers.

The basic pattern for the simple sentence is subject–verb (SV). This pattern may vary in several ways:

 EXAMPLES

subject–verb (SV): The plane flew over the stadium.

verb–subject (VS): Over the stadium flew the plane.

subject–subject–verb (SSV): The plane and the helicopter flew over the stadium.

subject–verb–verb (SVV): The plane flew over the stadium and turned north.

                                          S   S   V
subject–subject–verb–verb (SSVV): The plane and the helicopter flew

                        V
over the stadium and turned north.

                                  S   V
A simple sentence can be brief: It rained.

                                                                    S
Or it can be rather long: Enraged by the taunting of the boys, the huge gorilla

     V   V
leaped from his enclosure and chased them up a hill and down a pathway to
the exit gates.

   The important thing to remember about the simple sentence is that it has
only one main clause and no other clauses.

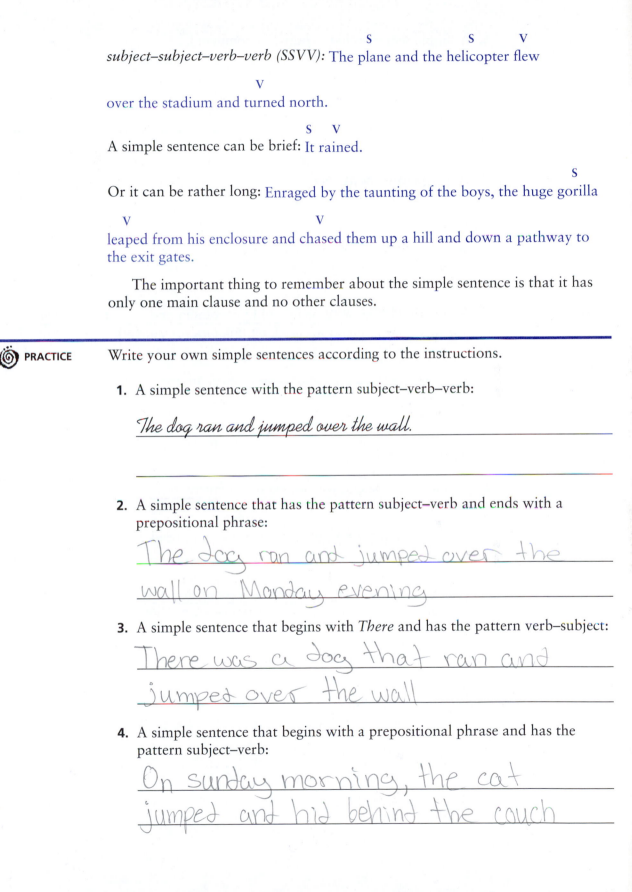

PRACTICE   Write your own simple sentences according to the instructions.

1. A simple sentence with the pattern subject–verb–verb:

The dog ran and jumped over the wall.

2. A simple sentence that has the pattern subject–verb and ends with a
   prepositional phrase:

The dog ran and jumped over the
wall on Monday evening

3. A simple sentence that begins with *There* and has the pattern verb–subject:

There was a dog that ran and
jumped over the wall

4. A simple sentence that begins with a prepositional phrase and has the
   pattern subject–verb:

On sunday morning, the cat
jumped and hid behind the couch

5. A simple sentence that expresses a command.

_____

_____

The Compound Sentence

Simply put, a **compound sentence** contains two or more main clauses but no subordinate clauses. The basic pattern of the clauses may be expressed subject–verb/subject–verb (SV/SV). The main clauses are always joined in one of three ways:

1. Two main clauses may be joined by a comma and one of the seven coordinating conjunctions (*and, or, nor, but, for, so, yet*).

EXAMPLE

    S   V   S   V

Maria registered for all of her classes by mail, but Brad was not able to do so.

Remember, the two main clauses must be joined by **both a comma and a coordinating conjunction**, and the comma always comes before the coordinating conjunction.

2. Two main clauses may be joined by a semicolon (;).

EXAMPLE

    S   V   S   V

Maria registered for all of her classes by mail; Brad was not able to do so.

3. Two main clauses may be joined by a semicolon and a transitional word or phrase. Such transitional words or phrases are followed by a comma.

EXAMPLE

    S   V   S

Maria registered for all of her classes by mail; **however,** Brad

    V

was not able to do so.

Below is a list of the most commonly used transitional words and phrases. Do not confuse these words or phrases with coordinating conjunctions or subordinating conjunctions.

accordingly	for instance	moreover	similarly
also	further	namely	still
as a result	furthermore	nevertheless	that is
besides	hence	next	then
consequently	however	nonetheless	therefore
finally	instead	on the other hand	thus
for example	meanwhile	otherwise	undoubtedly

 PRACTICE Write compound sentences of your own according to the instructions.

1. A compound sentence that uses a comma and *and* to join two main clauses:

   Myrtle likes to grow okra, and she likes to

   serve it to Vergil.

2. A compound sentence that joins two main clauses with a semicolon, followed by *however* and a comma:

   Jan likes to eat cheesecake; however she is lactose intolerant, but is okay

3. A compound sentence that joins two main clauses with a semicolon and an appropriate transitional word or phrase followed by a comma:

4. A compound sentence that joins two main clauses with a comma and *yet*:

   Dan wants to play videogames, yet he has homework

5. A compound sentence that joins two main clauses with a semicolon, followed by *therefore* and a comma:

PRACTICE   In the following paragraph, write "S" above each subject and "V" above each verb. Then, in the spaces provided, identify each sentence as either **simple** or **compound**.

S   **V**

1. Captain Bush flew airplanes during WWII. _Simple_   2. He was stationed

in Burma and flew planes over the mountains into China. _____

3. The mountains were very high, so the flights were dangerous. _____

4. The mountains were called the Himalayas; the pilots were known as "hump"

pilots. _____   5. Because of primitive navigational devices on these Dakota

aircraft, the pilots sometimes lost their way. _____   6. Captain Bush lived

in a grass hut in Burma; one day he found a mongoose in the thatch of the

ceiling. _____   7. The mongoose had made a nest, so he allowed her to

stay there. _____   8. Captain Bush's mother would send him food in

packages, and he would share it with the mongoose. _____   9. After a

while, he noticed babies in her nest. _____   10. A mongoose can kill a

cobra; as a result, the hut was safe from those deadly snakes. _____

The Complex Sentence

The **complex sentence** has the same subject–verb pattern (SV/SV) as the compound sentence. However, the complex sentence features only one main clause and always contains at least one subordinate clause and sometimes more than one. The subordinate clauses in a complex sentence may occur at any place in the sentence.

 EXAMPLES

                                         S   V   S   V

Before a main clause: <u>After he retired from the army,</u> Eisenhower ran for president.

                             S   V   S   V

After a main clause: Rugby is a sport <u>that I have played only once</u>.

                                    S   S   V

Interrupting a main clause: Emilio's grandfather, <u>who fought in World</u>

V
<u>War II,</u> told him about his experiences during the war.

S   V
Before and after a main clause: <u>When the pianist sat down at the piano,</u>

S   V   S   V
she played a melody <u>that she had written recently.</u>

PRACTICE   Write complex sentences of your own according to the instructions.

1. A complex sentence with a main clause followed by an adverb clause beginning with *because:*

   Vergil burned the cornbread because he was

   talking on the telephone.

2. A complex sentence with an adverb clause beginning with *When* followed by a main clause:

   When he finally retired, my grandpa had a lot more freetime.

3. A complex sentence that contains a noun modified by an adjective clause beginning with *that:*

   _____

   _____

4. A complex sentence that contains a main clause and an adverb clause beginning with *even though:*

   Even though he had a lot of money, he wasn't happy.

5. A complex sentence that contains one main clause and one adjective clause:

   After he earned a lot of fans, he has gained a lot of haters on YouTube

The Compound-Complex Sentence

The **compound-complex sentence** is a combination of the compound and the complex sentence patterns. It is made up of two or more main clauses and one or more subordinate clauses. Therefore, it must contain a minimum of three sets of subjects and verbs (<u>at least</u> two main clauses and <u>at least</u> one subordinate clause).

 EXAMPLES

main clause   sub. clause
[On the day-long bicycle trip, Ophelia ate the food] [that she had packed,]

main clause
[but Henry had forgotten to bring anything to eat.]

sub. clause   main clause
[Although he was exhausted,] [Ernesto cooked dinner for his mother,]

main clause
[and after dinner he cleaned the kitchen.]

main clause   sub. clause
[The travelers were excited] [when they arrived in Paris;]

main clause
[they wanted to go sightseeing immediately.]

 PRACTICE

Write compound-complex sentences of your own according to the instructions.

1. A sentence that contains two main clauses joined by *but* and one adjective clause beginning with *where*:

   Cassandra went to the drugstore, where she found the memory

   medicine, but then she forgot to buy the toothpaste.

2. A compound-complex sentence that contains a main clause and an adjective clause followed by a semicolon and another main clause:

   _____

   _____

3. A compound-complex sentence that contains two main clauses joined by a semicolon and a transitional word or phrase. Modify one of the nouns in either main clause with an adjective clause beginning with *who* or *which*.

   _____

   _____

4. A compound-complex sentence that contains two main clauses joined by *or* and one adverb subordinate clause beginning with *since, after,* or *though:*

_____

_____

5. A compound-complex sentence with a pattern of your own choice:

_____

_____

PRACTICE

In the following paragraph, write S above each subject and V above each verb. Then, in the spaces provided, identify the sentences as simple, compound, complex, or compound-complex.

1. According to Greek mythology, the Minotaur, which was part bull and part man, lived deep within the labyrinth on Crete. *Complex* **2.** The story about the Minotaur concerns Theseus and Ariadne. _____ **3.** Each year King Minos of Crete ordered Athens to send seven boys and seven girls, who were to be devoured by the Minotaur. _____ **4.** One year, however, Theseus, the hero, accompanied the children. _____ **5.** Ariadne was the daughter of Minos, and she fell in love with Theseus. _____ **6.** Ariadne gave Theseus a ball of string to take with him into the labyrinth of the Minotaur. _____ **7.** Theseus took the string with him, and he unraveled it as he went into the maze. _____ **8.** He planned to unravel the string until he wanted to leave the labyrinth; then he would follow it out to the opening. _____ **9.** Theseus listened for the sound of the bellowing of the Minotaur, and at last he found the beast. _____ **10.** When he reached the Minotaur, he killed it and led the children to safety. _____

Section Two Review

1. A **simple sentence** contains only one main clause and no other clauses.

2. A **compound sentence** contains two or more main clauses that are joined by a comma and a coordinating conjunction **or** a semicolon **or** a semicolon and a transitional word or phrase.

3. A **complex sentence** contains only one main clause and one or more subordinate clauses.

4. A **compound-complex sentence** contains two or more main clauses and one or more subordinate clauses.

Exercise 2A

Examine one of your textbooks, a newspaper, a magazine, or a book from your home and find two simple sentences, three compound sentences, three complex sentences, and two compound-complex sentences. Label the types of sentences you have found as simple, compound, complex, or compound-complex.

1. _____

_____

2. _____

_____

3. _____

_____

4. _____

_____

5. _____

_____

6. _____

_____

7. _____

_____

8. _____

_____

9. _____

_____

10. _____

_____

Exercise 2B

In the spaces provided, identify the sentences in the following paragraph as simple, compound, complex, or compound-complex.

1. Writers come and go, but Shakespeare remains the favorite of many. *Compound*

2. As the twenty-first century progresses, several movies of Shakespeare's plays are being filmed. _____ **3.** Even a new *Hamlet* is in production. _____ **4.** In fact, *Hamlet* is an industry of its own; at any hour of any day, somewhere *Hamlet* is being performed. _____

5. Hamlet is one of the top five most written about people in history even though he is only a character in a play. _____ **6.** Many writers have tried to explain the popularity of Shakespeare's plays, but there is not just one explanation. _____ **7.** Among the reasons given are the vivid stories, the compelling characters, and the beautiful use of the language. _____

8. Although there have been many great writers, not one has combined these elements so well. _____ **9.** Even though Shakespeare borrowed almost all of his stories, he transformed them, and they came to life in his hands. _____ **10.** *Hamlet,* for instance, contains as much killing and double-crossing as a Mafia movie. _____ **11.** *Macbeth* has an ambitious husband-and-wife team; it could be the story of a modern business executive clawing his way to the top. _____ **12.** The sad tale of the star-crossed lovers Romeo and Juliet is one that has been told over and over. _____ **13.** Characters like Othello, Brutus, and King Lear have enthralled people over the centuries. _____ **14.** Even less major characters like Iago, Falstaff, and Lady Macbeth have captivated audiences, and actors still compete to play them. _____

15. Because Shakespeare's use of language is so eloquent, authors use phrases from his works for their titles; we come across expressions like "Something is rotten in the State of Denmark" every day. _____

Exercise 2C

A. Combine each pair of sentences according to the instructions. You may need to delete or change some words.

1. A simple sentence with the pattern verb–subject:
   a. The men stood at the entrance of the bank.
   b. The men were wearing clown masks and carrying assault rifles.

   At the entrance of the bank stood men wearing clown masks and

   carrying assault rifles.

2. A compound sentence that uses a semicolon as the connector:
   a. At first, Roosevelt was despondent over his disease.
   b. Then he turned it to his advantage.

   _____

   _____

3. A complex sentence that uses the subordinator *although*:
   a. Six months was a long time to spend in Hades.
   b. Persephone persevered and soon saw her mother.

   _____

   _____

4. A simple sentence in the form of a question:
   a. Can you bring some M&M's for the movie?
   b. Can you also pay for the tickets?

   _____

   _____

5. A compound sentence that uses *for* as a connector:
   a. Carmel was in a state of anxiety and despair.
   b. She thought she had been rejected by her favorite college.

   _____

   _____

Exercise 2C

continued

6. A complex sentence:
   a. Both houses of the United States Congress were trying to cooperate.
   b. The country was facing an economic crisis.

   _____

   _____

7. A simple sentence:
   a. Around midnight, the cow jumped over the moon.
   b. The spoon jumped over the moon as well.

   _____

   _____

8. A compound-complex sentence:
   a. The two men represented a religious organization.
   b. They were going door to door seeking converts.
   c. They were not having much success.

   _____

   _____

9. A compound-complex sentence:
   a. Homer was determined to discover Elvis's covert hideout.
   b. He bought the secret map.
   c. It had been offered on the *Elvis Lives!* website for $5,000.

   _____

   _____

B. Following the instructions, construct sentences of your own.

   10. A complex sentence that uses the subordinator *if:*

   _____

   _____

continued

11. A compound sentence that uses *yet* as the connector:

_____

_____

12. A simple sentence that begins with a prepositional phrase:

_____

_____

13. A complex sentence that uses *where* to begin the subordinate clause:

_____

_____

14. A compound sentence that uses a semicolon as the connector, followed by the transitional words *therefore* or *in fact*:

_____

_____

15. A compound-complex sentence that uses *than, though,* or *unless* to begin a subordinate clause:

_____

_____

Identify the sentences in the following paragraph as simple, compound, complex, or compound-complex.

1. Most of the theaters where Shakespeare put on his plays were circular. _Complex_ **2.** Some were made from bear-baiting pits. _____ **3.** In a bear-baiting pit, a bear was chained in the center, and dogs were sent to attack it. _____ **4.** Some people bet on the bear; some people bet on the dogs. _____ **5.** Because these theaters were renovated bear-baiting pits, they were open to the sky, and the floors were bare dirt. _____ **6.** Around the inside of the theater and extending to the roof were boxes for spectators. _____ **7.** These were the higher-priced seats; the lower-priced ones were on the floor around the stage, where the "groundlings" sat. _____ **8.** The stage was a platform that was about forty feet wide and twenty-five feet deep. _____ **9.** Most of the stage was covered by a projecting roof known as the "shadow" or the "heavens." _____ **10.** It was called the "heavens" because the underside was decorated with pictures of the sun, the moon, the planets, and the constellations. _____ **11.** Near the middle of the stage was a door in the floor, which led below the stage; this space below the stage was called "hell," for obvious reasons. _____ **12.** Ghosts could appear from this door. _____ **13.** In the back of the stage was the tiring-house, which, as the name (attiring-house) implies, contained the actors' dressing rooms. _____ **14.** Here also were the two doors where the actors entered and exited. _____ **15.** These doors were important because there was no opening or closing of curtains in these theaters. _____ **16.** The stage represented the world, with the heavens above and hell below. _____

Fragments, Fused Sentences, and Comma Splices

Now that you are combining main and subordinate clauses to write different types of sentences, we need to talk about a few of the writing problems you might encounter. Fortunately, the most serious of these problems—the **fragment**, the **fused sentence**, and the **comma splice**—are also the easiest to identify and correct.

Fragments

The easiest way to identify a **sentence fragment** is to remember that <u>every sentence must contain a main clause</u>. If you do not have a main clause, you do <u>not</u> have a sentence. You can define a fragment, then, like this: A sentence fragment occurs when a group of words that lacks a main clause is punctuated as a sentence.

> **sentence fragment**
>
> A sentence fragment occurs when a group of words that lacks a main clause is punctuated as a sentence.

Using this definition, you can identify almost any sentence fragment. However, you will find it easier to locate fragments in your own writing if you know that fragments can be divided into three basic types.

Three Types of Sentence Fragments

1. Some fragments contain <u>no clause at all</u>. This type of fragment is simple to spot. It usually does not even sound like a sentence because it lacks a subject or verb or both.

 EXAMPLE   The snow in the street.

2. Some fragments contain <u>a verbal but still no clause</u>. This fragment is a bit less obvious because a verbal can be mistaken for a verb. But remember, neither a participle nor an infinitive is a verb. (See Chapter One, page 12, if you need to review this point.)

 EXAMPLES   (participle)   The snow **falling** on the street.

(infinitive)   To slip on the snow in the street.

3. Some fragments contain a **subordinate clause** but no **main clause**. This type of fragment is perhaps the most common because it does contain a subject and a verb. But remember, <u>a group of words without a main clause is not a sentence</u>.

 EXAMPLES

After the snow had fallen on the street.

Because I had slipped on the snow in the street.

Repairing Sentence Fragments

Once you have identified a fragment, you can correct it in one of two ways.

1. Add words to give it a main clause.

 EXAMPLES

(fragment)	The snow in the street.
(sentence)	**I gazed** at the snow in the street.
(sentence)	The snow **was** in the street.
(fragment)	The snow falling in the street.
(sentence)	The snow falling in the street **covered my car.**
(sentence)	The snow **was** falling in the street.
(fragment)	After the snow had fallen in the street.
(sentence)	**I looked for a shovel** after the snow had fallen in the street.

2. Join the fragment to a main clause written before or after it.

 EXAMPLES

(incorrect)	I love to see the ice on the lake. And the snow in the street.
(correct)	I love to see the ice on the lake and the snow in the street.
(incorrect)	My back was so sore that I could not stand straight. Because I had slipped on the snow in the street.
(correct)	My back was so sore that I could not stand straight because I had slipped on the snow in the street.

One final point might help you identify and correct sentence fragments. Remember that we all speak in fragments every day. (If a friend asks you how you are, you might respond with the fragment "Fine.") Because we speak in fragments, you may find that your writing seems acceptable even though it contains fragments. When you work on the exercises in this unit, do not rely on your "ear" alone. Look at the sentences. **If they do not contain main clauses, they are fragments, no matter how correct they may sound.**

PRACTICE   Underline any fragment you find. Then correct it either by adding new words to give it a main clause or by joining it to a main clause next to it.

1. The rain dripped slowly from the trees. <u>Falling quietly from the dark green leaves.</u>

   The rain dripped slowly from the trees as it fell quietly from the dark green leaves.

2. <u>The man who helped rescue the kidnapped woman.</u>

   The man who helped rescue the kidnapped woman brought her home to kept her company for the night.

3. <u>While Persephone was in Hades.</u> Her mother was worried. <u>That she might never see her again.</u>

   Her mother was worried that she might never see her again becauses she's been gone for three days.

4. <u>Arrive early at the theater.</u> <u>To ensure that you get a good seat.</u>

   Arrive early at the theater to ensure that you get a good seat and fresh popcorn.

5. <u>When John F. Kennedy was assassinated in Dallas.</u>

   When John F. Kennedy was assassinated, riots were caused in Dallas.

6. If he wanted to live on his own. <u>Arnie needed to find a job.</u>

   If he wanted to live on his own Arnie needed
   to find a job to pay for the house.

7. The Chocolate Shoppe owner was locking the door. Even as Craig was

   dashing across the street. Begging for him to let him in.

   _____

   _____

8. Odysseus continued to love his daughters. <u>Although he would always be

   ashamed of his actions.</u>

   Odysseus continued to love his daughters but no matter
   what he would always be ashamed of his actions.

9. <u>To join his parents at the theater to see *Les Miserables*.</u>

   Andre left work early to join his parents at the
   theater to see Les Miserables

10. Deborah and Carlton headed for Arrowhead Pond. <u>Even though U2 had

    canceled the Saturday concert.</u>

    Deborah and Carlton headed for Arrowhead Pond. Even
    though U2 had canceled the Saturday concert due to snow.

Fused Sentences and Comma Splices

The **fused sentence** and **comma splice** are serious writing errors that you can correct with little effort. Either error can occur when you write a compound or compound-complex sentence. The fused sentence occurs when two or more main clauses are joined without a coordinating conjunction and without punctuation.

> ### fused sentence
>
> The fused sentence occurs when two or more main clauses are joined without a coordinating conjunction and without punctuation.

 EXAMPLE   (fused)   Raoul drove by his uncle's house he waved at his cousins.

As you can see, the two main clauses in the above example (*Raoul drove by his uncle's house* and *he waved at his cousins*) have been joined without a coordinating conjunction and without punctuation of any kind.

The comma splice is a similar error: The comma splice occurs when two or more main clauses are joined with a comma but without a coordinating conjunction.

> ### comma splice
>
> The comma splice occurs when two or more main clauses are joined with a comma but without a coordinating conjunction.

 EXAMPLE   (comma splice)   The hot sun beat down on the construction workers, they looked forward to the end of the day.

In this example, the two main clauses (*The hot sun beat down on the construction workers* and *they looked forward to the end of the day*) are joined by a comma, but a comma alone is not enough to join main clauses.

NOTE: One of the most frequent comma splices occurs when a writer joins two main clauses with a comma and a transitional word rather than with a semicolon and a transitional word.

EXAMPLE   (comma splice)   I wanted a dog for Christmas, however, my parents gave me a cat.

Repairing Fused Sentences and Comma Splices

Because both fused sentences and comma splices occur when two main clauses are joined, you can correct either error using one of five methods. Consider these two errors:

⊙ **EXAMPLES**   (fused)   Jack left for work early he arrived late.

(comma splice)   Jack left for work early, he arrived late.

Both of these errors can be corrected in one of five ways:

1. <u>Use a comma and a coordinating conjunction.</u>
   Jack left for work early, **but** he arrived late.

2. <u>Use a semicolon.</u>
   Jack left for work early; he arrived late.

3. <u>Use a semicolon and a transitional word or phrase.</u>
   Jack left for work early; **however,** he arrived late.

NOTE: Do <u>not</u> use a semicolon before a transitional word that does <u>not</u> begin a main clause. For example, in the following sentence, *however* does not need a semicolon.

⊙ **EXAMPLE**   I have not seen my father, **however,** for ten years.

4. <u>Change one of the clauses to a subordinate clause by beginning it with a subordinator.</u>
   Although Jack left for work early, he arrived late.

5. <u>Punctuate the clauses as two separate sentences.</u>
   Jack left for work early. He arrived late.

NOTE: Sometimes the two main clauses in a fused sentence or comma splice are interrupted by a subordinate clause. When this sentence pattern occurs, the two main clauses must still be connected in one of the five ways.

⊙ **EXAMPLES**   (fused)   Alma bought a new Mercedes even though she could not afford one she fell behind in her monthly payments.

(comma splice)   Alma bought a new Mercedes even though she could not afford one, she fell behind in her monthly payments.

These errors can be corrected in any of the five ways mentioned above.

⊙ **EXAMPLE**   Alma bought a new Mercedes even though she could not afford one; consequently, she fell behind in her monthly payments.

🌀 **PRACTICE**   Identify the following sentences as fused (F), comma splice (CS), or correct (C). Then correct the incorrect sentences. Use a different method of correction each time.

_CS_   **1.** Pierre walked down the hall and insulted Erica, Erica forgave him later.

Pierre walked down the hall and insulted Erica;

however, Erica forgave him later.

_F_   **2.** Bottom went peacefully to sleep he awoke with the head of an ass.

Bottom went peacefully to sleep. He awoke with the

head of an ass.

_C_   **3.** The rescuers had been searching the collapsed building for sixteen days. Then they found a nineteen-year-old woman.

_CS_   **4.** The series *Bones* is about police forensics, therefore, viewers are exposed to many gory scenes involving dead bodies.

The series Bones is about police forensics, therefore

viewers are exposed to many gory scenes involving

dead bodies

_C_   **5.** Doc Ford opened the door to his laboratory, all of his crabs were on the floor.

CS 6. Siddhartha was raised in a royal household, eventually, he left home and sought enlightenment.

Siddhartha was raised in a royal household, eventually he left home and sought enlightenment

F 7. You can cut off your cat's tail it will not grow back again.

You can cut off your cat's tail, but it will not grow back again

C 8. Adrian was happy, *Justified* still had five segments to go.

_____

_____

C 9. Dr. Frankenstein searched all night until he finally found the body that he needed.

_____

_____

F 10. All of the Dracula-themed films and series are becoming boring I am not going to watch them anymore.

All of the Dracula-themed films and series are becoming boring. I am not going to watch them anymore.

Section Three Review

1. A **sentence fragment** occurs when a group of words that lacks a main clause is punctuated as a sentence.

2. There are three types of sentence fragments.

   a. Some contain no clause at all.

   b. Some contain a verbal but still no clause.

   c. Some contain a subordinate clause but no main clause.

3. You can correct a sentence fragment in one of two ways.

   a. Add words to give it a main clause.

   b. Join it to an already existing main clause.

4. The **fused sentence** occurs when two or more main clauses are joined without a coordinating conjunction and without punctuation.

5. The **comma splice** occurs when two or more main clauses are joined with a comma but without a coordinating conjunction.

6. You can correct fused sentences and comma splices in one of five ways.

   a. Use a comma and a coordinating conjunction.

   b. Use a semicolon.

   c. Use a semicolon and a transitional word or phrase.

   d. Change one of the clauses to a subordinate clause by adding a subordinator at the beginning of it.

   e. Punctuate the clauses as two separate sentences.

Exercise 3A

Identify each of the following as correct (C), fused (F), comma splice (CS), or sentence fragment (Frag). Then correct each error using any of the methods discussed in this unit.

Frag **1.** Although Aaron called as many people as he could think of to find where the computer had gone.

Although Aaron called as many people as he could think of to find where the computer had gone, he did not think to call his business partner.

2. The coach wanted to forfeit the game, however, the team begged him to wait at least another half-hour.

3. Order a pizza with mushrooms, sausage, and pepperoni.

4. At first Harker liked the man in the black cape then he realized there was something strange about his teeth.

5. All of the brothers and sisters of the lottery winner.

Exercise 3A

continued

_____ **6.** *Hamlet* is a great play, *Death of a Salesman* is also.

_____

_____

_____ **7.** The sinking ship almost cost Ishmael his life, but luckily a floating coffin saved him.

_____

_____

_____ **8.** Many claimed that the Ironman was weakening however he insisted that he was in perfect health.

_____

_____

_____ **9.** Job was hoping things would get better soon, nothing he did seemed to make a difference.

_____

_____

_____ **10.** Baz Luhrman, while directing *The Great Gatsby*.

_____

_____

_____ **11.** Justin Bieber was unable to control his temper, therefore the police officers took him into custody.

_____

_____

continued

_____ **12.** Macbeth's wife was ambitious for her husband, she persuaded him to kill the king.

_____

_____

_____ **13.** Most of my friends do not like Vegemite on the other hand my relatives in Australia think it is delicious.

_____

_____

_____ **14.** Many Sioux lay dead and dying at Wounded Knee after the American soldiers returned to the fort.

_____

_____

_____ **15.** The Labrador retriever saw the duck fall into the water, even though the water was freezing, she jumped into it.

_____

_____

Exercise 3B

A. Correct the following sentence fragments by adding words to them to make them complete sentences.

1. Trinh, who had been studying for three hours.

   Trinh, who had been studying for three hours, finally

   decided it was time for bed.

2. Bob Dylan singing "Forever Young."

   _____

   _____

3. As President Obama walked the dog that Michelle had given him.

   _____

   _____

4. Who participated in the rescue efforts on September 11, 2001.

   _____

   _____

5. Addressing the audience after the performance.

   _____

   _____

B. Join the following main clauses by using a comma and a coordinating conjunction, a semicolon, a semicolon and a transitional word or phrase, or by making one of the clauses a subordinate clause. Use each of these four methods at least once.

6. Harry loved to skateboard. His wife said he had outgrown the activity and handed him his cane.

   Harry loved to skateboard; however, his wife said he had

   outgrown the activity and handed him his cane.

continued

7. Hemingway wanted to fish. Fitzgerald wanted to go to Paris.

_____

_____

8. Seamus Heaney was searching for an idea for a poem. He remembered his father.

_____

_____

9. Little Red Riding Hood was confident walking through the woods. She had a large
   container of pepper spray under her cloak.

_____

_____

10. Chicken Little tried desperately to warn people. No one would listen.

_____

_____

C. Expand each of the following sentences by adding a **clause** to it. Identify the subject and verb
of each clause you use and vary the placement of the clauses. (Don't place every clause at the
end of its sentence.) When you add the clauses, use each of the following methods at least
once: (a) use a comma and a coordinating conjunction; (b) use a semicolon; (c) use a semicolon
and a transitional word or phrase; (d) make one clause a subordinate clause.

11. Near the corner of the yard, a toy poodle cowered in fear before a Siamese cat.

    Near the corner of the yard, a toy poodle cowered in fear before

    a Siamese cat; however, the cat only wanted to make a new friend.

12. Wynton Marsalis was polishing his new trumpet.

_____

_____

Exercise 3B

continued

13. The prime minister of Afghanistan was becoming impatient with the length of the war.

_____

_____

14. One tower is being built at the site of the former Twin Towers.

_____

_____

15. Katrina was angry that the hurricane was named after her.

_____

_____

Exercise 3C

In the following paragraph, correct any fragments, fused sentences, or comma splices.

1. After dark, the shore near my cabin is a mysterious place ~~2. Where~~ *, where* the absence of light creates a new reality. 3. As I was walking along the beach one night recently. 4. I surprised a snow crab in the beam of my flashlight. 5. Hiding in a pit just above the surface. 6. As if he were watching the sea and waiting. 7. When I turned off the flashlight, I could feel the darkness around me, I felt alone with the snow crab. 8. I could hear nothing but the elemental sounds of wind blowing over sand and water and waves crashing on the beach. 9. Time seems suspended when I am on that beach at night I feel alone with the creatures of the shore. 10. Those creatures, like the sea anemones and the shore birds, have been there since the dawn of time. 11. As my eyes accustom themselves to the dark. 12. The gulls and sanderlings become shadows. 13. When I am surrounded by those sights, sounds, and smells, I feel transported. 14. Into another, older world before humankind. 15. The rhythm of the sea becomes the rhythm of the whole world, the smell becomes a fundamental smell. 16. On that recent night, I sat near that snow crab. 17. And watched the sea with it. 18. Hidden beneath the water before me were patches of bright coral they were the home for blood-red starfish and green sea cucumbers. 19. All seemed peaceful then, but on the shore the battle for survival rages incessantly. 20. The largest shark and the smallest plankton must search constantly. 21. For the food that sustains them. 22. In the dim light I saw several hermit crabs scurrying across the sand, I turned from the dark shore toward the lights of my home.

Sentence Practice:
Combining Main and Subordinate Clauses

In this chapter you have learned the basic sentence patterns of English, and you have seen that you can combine the major word groups of a sentence—the clauses—in various ways. Of course, how you present your ideas in your sentences can affect the way a reader perceives your ideas. Take, for instance, the following sentences.

1. Subcompact cars are economical.

2. Subcompact cars are easy to handle.

3. Subcompact cars are simple to park.

4. Full-size sedans are roomier.

5. Full-size sedans are safer.

6. Full-size sedans are quieter.

You can present these ideas in six simple sentences like those above, but doing so makes the writing choppy and simplistic. On the other hand, you can use the sentence patterns discussed in this chapter to combine these six ideas in several ways.

1. You can present these ideas as two simple sentences.

 EXAMPLE

Subcompact cars are economical, easy to handle, and simple to park. Full-size sedans are roomier, safer, and quieter.

2. Or you can group the ideas into one compound sentence by using a comma and a coordinating conjunction.

 EXAMPLE

Subcompact cars are economical, easy to handle, and simple to park, but full-size sedans are roomier, safer, and quieter.

Note that the coordinating conjunction *but* allows you to emphasize the contrast between the ideas in the two main clauses.

3. You can also group these ideas into a compound sentence by using a semicolon as a connector.

 EXAMPLE

Subcompact cars are economical, easy to handle, and simple to park; full-size sedans are roomier, safer, and quieter.

In this sentence the contrast in the ideas is implied rather than directly stated.

4. Of course, you can add a transitional word after the semicolon.

 EXAMPLE   Subcompact cars are economical, easy to handle, and simple to park; however, full-size sedans are roomier, safer, and quieter.

Note that *however* now signals the contrast between the ideas in the two clauses.

5. Finally, you can group the ideas into a main clause and a subordinate clause by adding a subordinator. Now you have a complex sentence.

 EXAMPLE   Although subcompact cars are economical, easy to handle, and simple to park, full-size sedans are roomier, safer, and quieter.

Like the other sentences, this sentence shows the reader the contrast between the ideas in the two clauses. However, it also shows the ideas the writer thinks are most important—the ones in the main clause.

Sentence Combining Exercises

Using the knowledge of sentence patterns that you have gained from this chapter, combine the following lists of sentences into longer sentences according to the directions. Be sure to punctuate carefully to avoid comma splices or fused sentences. Remember to look for a base sentence or a main idea to build on. The most important idea should be in a main clause.

 EXAMPLE   First, combine these ideas into a compound sentence, using one of the three methods presented in Section Two of this chapter. Then form a complex sentence, using a subordinator to make one clause subordinate.

1. Cooking can be enjoyable.
2. Cooking can be creative.
3. Cooking can be satisfying.
4. Someone has to shop for ingredients.
5. Someone has to chop onions.
6. Someone has to put everything away.
7. Someone has to wash the dishes.

A. Compound sentence:

> *Cooking can be enjoyable, creative, and satisfying, but someone has to shop for ingredients, chop onions, put everything away, and wash the dishes.*

B. Complex sentence:

> *Although cooking can be enjoyable, creative, and satisfying, someone has to shop for ingredients, chop onions, put everything away, and wash the dishes.*

Sentence Combining Exercises

continued

1. Combine these sentences into a complex sentence. Use sentence a to create an adverb clause starting with *although*.

   a. Dennis Leary's character in *Rescue Me* is a heroic firefighter.
   b. He has trouble with his love life.
   c. He has trouble with his parenting skills.
   d. He has trouble with his drinking.

   _____

   _____

   _____

2. First combine these ideas into a compound sentence. Then combine them into a complex sentence. Begin each sentence with a prepositional phrase.

   a. It was morning.
   b. Luisa was jogging.
   c. She was at the Oakland waterfront.
   d. The waterfront was beautiful.
   e. Suddenly she slipped on a wet spot.
   f. She sprained her arm.
   g. The sprain was severe.

   _____

   _____

   _____

   _____

Sentence Combining Exercises

continued

3. Combine these sentences into a complex sentence. Form sentences a through c into a main clause. Use sentence d as a subordinate clause beginning with *because*.

   a. Jackie Robinson was a great baseball player.
   b. Jackie Robinson was courageous pioneer.
   c. He was a pioneer in race relations.
   d. Jackie Robinson was the first African American to break the color barrier in Major League Baseball in the United States.

   _____

   _____

   _____

   _____

4. Combine these sentences into one compound sentence. Use sentences a and b as a main clause. Use sentence c as a main clause starting with *and*. Use sentences d and e as a subordinate clause starting with *when*.

   a. Steve Martin was a popular comedian.
   b. He was on *Saturday Night Live*.
   c. He became an international celebrity.
   d. He starred in films.
   e. He wrote novels.

   _____

   _____

   _____

   _____

Sentence Combining Exercises

continued

5. Combine these sentences into one compound sentence. Use the most effective pattern you can find. At the end of your new sentence, indicate which type of sentence you have written.

    a. Wolves are among the most misunderstood of animals.
    b. They have a bad reputation.
    c. Their reputation is partly the result of stories.
    d. There is the story of *Little Red Riding Hood*.
    e. There is the story of *The Three Little Pigs*.
    f. There is the story of *The Werewolf*.

    _____

    _____

    _____

    _____

6. Combine these sentences into one sentence. Use the most effective pattern you can find. At the end of your new sentence, indicate which type of sentence you have written.

    a. Enrique wanted to go to McDonald's.
    b. His daughter preferred Chili's.
    c. His son preferred Baskin-Robbins.
    d. His wife preferred Red Lobster.

    _____

    _____

    _____

    _____

Sentence Combining Exercises

continued

7. Combine these sentences into one sentence. Indicate which type of sentence you have written.

    a. Paul Desmond played alto saxophone.
    b. He played it with the Dave Brubeck Band.
    c. He wrote "Take Five."
    d. "Take Five" is one of the most popular jazz tunes.

_____

_____

_____

_____

8. Combine these sentences into one sentence. Indicate which type of sentence you have written.

    a. At first no singer wanted to record "Rudolf the Red-Nosed Reindeer."
    b. Gene Autry agreed to record the song.
    c. "Rudolph, the Red-Nosed Reindeer" became the second-best-selling record of all time.

_____

_____

_____

_____

Sentence Combining Exercises

continued

9. Combine these sentences into one sentence. Indicate which type of sentence you have written.

   a. It is an interesting fact.
   b. The fact is about "Rudolph, the Red-Nosed Reindeer."
   c. Sociologists have studied the song.
   d. Sociologists have called it the only new addition to the folklore of Santa Claus in the twentieth and twenty-first centuries.

   _____

   _____

   _____

   _____

10. Combine these sentences into one sentence. Indicate which type of sentence you have written.

    a. Reindeer may look like deer.
    b. Reindeer may have a deerlike name.
    c. Reindeer are actually the same as caribou.
    d. Caribou are found in the Western Hemisphere.
    e. They are referred to as reindeer in northern Europe and Asia.

    _____

    _____

    _____

    _____

Paragraph Practice: Describing a Place

Writing Assignment

In Chapter Two you have read paragraphs that describe a variety of places. Exercise 1D (page 95) presents a history of London Bridge, Exercise 2D (page 110) describes a Shakespearean theater, and Exercise 3C (page 126) describes the shore of the sea at night. Your assignment in this writing section is to describe a place that you remember for one particular reason. As you do so, you will practice limiting your paragraph to one idea that is expressed in a topic sentence and developing your paragraph with details that are both specific and concrete.

Reading Assignment

The reading selections in the "Describing a Place" section of Chapter Six can help you see how professional writers describe memorable places. Read one or more of the selections, as assigned by your instructor, and use the questions that follow them to develop ideas for your own paper.

Prewriting to Generate Ideas

To find a topic, use freewriting, brainstorming, or clustering (or all three) to generate ideas about places that you remember well. Try to develop a list of as many places as you can. Sometimes the most interesting place to describe will be buried deep in your memory, so give prewriting a chance to uncover that memory before you decide on a topic.

Choosing and Narrowing the Topic

As you prewrite, avoid topics that are too broad to cover in one paragraph. For example, a city or an amusement park would be too large of a topic to cover in detail in a brief piece of writing. However, one particular part of a small town or one particular section of an amusement park might work very well.

Prewriting Application: Finding Your Topic

Consider the following questions as you prewrite:

1. What places have you visited in the past several years? Think about vacations you have taken or places you have traveled to.

2. Where have you been in the past two weeks? Make a list of everywhere you have gone.

3. What places from your childhood give you the most pleasant memories?

4. Where do you go to relax, to meditate, or to find peace of mind?

5. Have you ever been somewhere when you felt frightened or concerned for your safety?

6. What are the most beautiful places you have ever seen?

7. What are the most unpleasant ones? What are the strangest ones?

8. Have any places ever made you feel confused or lost?

9. Do you know any places that are particularly chaotic and noisy?

10. Where have you been today? Can you describe an ordinary, everyday place so that a reader sees it in a new way?

Once you have chosen the one place that is most interesting to you, keep prewriting about it. Try to remember as many details as you can about the place. Don't worry about writing well at this point—just brainstorm (make lists) or freewrite to get down as many of the details as you can remember.

Writing a Topic Sentence

After you have written for a while, read over what you have. Look for related details that focus on *one particular impression* of the place. These details and others that give the same impression are the ones you should emphasize in your paragraph. Once you have identified that particular impression, you are ready to write a preliminary **topic sentence.**

Remember, a topic sentence contains both a **topic** and a **central point.** In this writing assignment, your topic will be the place you are describing, and your central point will be the particular impression about the place that your details emphasize and illustrate.

Prewriting Application: Working with Topic Sentences

In each sentence below, underline the topic once and the central point twice.

1. Mammoth Cave, in southwestern Kentucky, is full of eerie, unearthly sights.

2. One of the most confusing places I have ever visited was the Los Angeles International Airport.

3. Snow Summit, in Big Bear, California, is a popular ski resort because it has such a variety of ski runs to choose from.

4. My grandmother's kitchen was one of the few places where I always felt safe and welcome.

5. The artificial decorations and dreary atmosphere were not at all what I had expected when I decided to visit the Excalibur casino in Las Vegas.

Prewriting Application: Evaluating Topic Sentences

Write "No" before each sentence that would not make a good topic sentence and "Yes" before each sentence that would make a good one. Using ideas of your own, rewrite the unacceptable topic sentences into topic sentences that might work.

_____ 1. Last year I spent three days hiking through Yellowstone National Park.

_____

_____

_____ 2. Balboa Island, near Newport Beach, California, is clearly a place designed for the rich and famous.

_____

_____

_____ 3. Whenever I look around my bedroom, I become thoroughly depressed.

_____

_____

_____ 4. One of my favorite places to visit is the beach.

_____

_____

_____ **5.** The waiting area in Dr. Larson's dentist's office is one of the most welcoming, relaxing places that I have ever seen.

_____

_____

_____ **6.** Last December 30, we had the opportunity to visit Stone Mountain in Atlanta, Georgia.

_____

_____

_____ **7.** My paragraph will describe the Hearst Castle in San Simeon, California.

_____

_____

_____ **8.** The undeveloped canyon behind my house is one place where I can feel free and unrestricted.

_____

_____

_____ **9.** The most unusual restroom that I have ever seen was the one at the Bahia de Los Angeles Research Station in Baja California, Mexico.

_____

_____

_____ **10.** The Deep South is one of the most memorable places that I have ever seen.

_____

_____

Prewriting Application: Talking to Others

Before you write your first draft, form groups of two, three, or four people and describe the place that you have decided to write about. Tell the members of your group what central point you are trying to emphasize, and then describe as many details as you can to make that point. As you tell others about the place you have chosen, describe all of the sights, sounds, and smells that contributed to your overall impression of the place. As you listen to the places described by others and as you describe your own place, consider these questions:

1. Where exactly is this place? Has its location been clearly identified? What time of year is it? What time of day? What is the weather like?

2. Can you visualize the place? What physical features are in the area—trees? buildings? furniture? cars? other people? What colors should be included?

3. How did you feel about this place? Is the central point or impression of the place clear?

4. Were there sounds, smells, or physical sensations that should be included in the description of the place?

5. What parts of the scene should be described in more detail?

Organizing Descriptive Details

Writers of descriptive papers use **spatial order** to organize supporting details. Unlike **chronological order,** which describes events as they occur in time, **spatial order** presents details according to their physical placement or characteristics. For example, you might describe the larger, more obvious details of a scene first and then move to the smaller, less obvious details. Or you might mention the details closer to you first and then move to those farther away. Other spatial organizations might involve describing details from left to right or top to bottom or describing the most dominant sense impression first, such as a strong smell, and then moving to other sense impressions.

Descriptions of places often combine spatial and chronological order, especially if you are moving as you describe the place. In such a situation, you might describe what you encounter first in time, then what you encounter second, and so on. If you take such an approach, remember that the purpose of this assignment is to describe the place itself, not to describe what you are doing there.

Prewriting Application: Organizing Supporting Details

Read Exercise 2D on page 110. Examine the details and explain why they are organized as they are.

Writing the Paragraph

Once you have a preliminary topic sentence and a list of related details, it is time to write the first draft of your paragraph. Open your paragraph with your topic sentence and then write out the details that illustrate the central point of your topic sentence. Do not worry about writing a "perfect" first draft. You will have the chance to improve the draft when you revise it.

Rewriting and Improving the Paragraph

1. When you have completed the first draft, read it over to see if your preliminary topic sentence accurately states the central point of your paper. If you can improve the topic sentence, do so now.

2. As you read over your draft, see if you can add still more descriptive details that relate to your central point. Add those that come to mind.

3. Finally, check the words and phrases you have used in your first draft. You will find that many of them can be more descriptive if you make them more **specific** and **concrete**.

Adding Specific and Concrete Details

A **specific** detail is limited in the number of things to which it can refer. For example, the word *poodle* is more specific than the word *dog,* and the word *elm* is more specific than *tree*. A **concrete** detail appeals to one of the five senses. It helps a reader **see, hear, smell, taste,** or **feel** what you describe. For instance, rather than writing that your grandmother's kitchen smelled "wonderful," you might write that it was always "filled with the aromas of freshly baked bread and my grandfather's cigar smoke."

Unfortunately, most writers—even most professional writers—do not write specific and concrete details naturally. You need to *add* these details to your draft. You do so by reading back through what you have written and changing words from general to specific and from abstract to concrete. As you read, consider these areas.

- Specificity: Which words could be made more specific? Use precise names of people, places, things, emotions, and actions wherever you can.

- Sight: What sights can be included? Consider colors, shapes, and sizes.

- Sound: What sounds should be added? Were there loud noises; subtle background sounds; peaceful, relaxing sounds; piercing, metallic, or unpleasant sounds?

- Smell: Were any smells present? Were you in a kitchen, near the ocean, passing by a newly oiled street? Were you at a produce stand or in a gymnasium? Many places have distinctive smells that you should include.

- Taste: Taste might be involved even if you did not eat or drink anything. A strong smell often evokes a taste sensation too. A dusty field as well as a dry desert might also elicit a taste reaction.

- Touch: Consider the less obvious touch sensations as well as obvious ones involving pain or pleasure. Were you standing in sand or on hot pavement? Did you touch anything with your hands? Was there a breeze? Was it raining? Did your collar blow up against your face? All of these might involve touch sensations.

Not all senses need to be included, especially if they don't emphasize your central point, but most first drafts have too few specific and concrete details rather than too many.

Rewriting Application: Adding Specific and Concrete Details

In each of the following sentences, identify which words could be made more specific or concrete. Then rewrite the sentence to replace and improve the general, abstract words.

 EXAMPLE   The house was run down.

The three-bedroom tract house on the corner of Elm and Vine

had deteriorated into a ruin of broken windows, peeling

paint, and splintered, termite-infested walls.

1. The woman walked through the entrance.

   _____

   _____

   _____

2. The food tasted terrible.

   _____

   _____

   _____

3. The man looked angry.

_____

_____

_____

4. Her bedroom walls were colorful.

_____

_____

_____

5. The trees along the driveway smelled wonderful.

_____

_____

_____

Rewriting Application: Responding to Writing

Read the following description of Breaks Interstate Park. Then respond to the questions following it.

> ### Breaks Interstate Park
>
> There is no more beautiful place in the spring than the Breaks Interstate Park. Last year I spent part of the spring with my father and my grandmother in the Smokey Mountains of Virginia. Because the Smokey Mountains are a very remote area, there was not much to do during my vacation until some of my cousins wanted to go to a place called "The Breaks." We drove into the mountains for about an hour. When we got to the entrance, the first thing I noticed was the incredible number of flowers. There were flowers on the ground, flowers in the trees and on the rocks, and there were some on the log cabins and picnic tables. We pulled off the road to one of the campsites and got out of the car. The smell of spring was everywhere. We could smell honeysuckle, strawberry, and the heady scent of wild flowers. All we could hear were bees working the blossoms and birds bathing in the springs trickling out of the mountainside. My cousin Charon came up to me and told me to follow her. We went across the road and down a winding dirt path, past a sign that said "Twin Towers Overlook." I then beheld one of the most striking and magnificent views I have ever seen in my life. I was on an overlook, looking down at a gorge where the river flowing through it makes a horseshoe-shaped bend and the mountains on

the other side look like twin towers. I ran back to the car to get my camera. While on my way back, I slipped on a moss-covered rock and skinned my knee. When I got back to the overlook, I sat down on some strawberry vines, ate wild strawberries, and took pictures. I finally ran out of film and deliciously sweet strawberries, not to mention daylight. We packed it up and went back home; however, I will never forget about the Breaks Interstate Park in the springtime.

1. Identify the topic sentence. State its topic and central idea. Is it an effective topic sentence? Why or why not?

2. Identify specific and concrete details. What words do you find particularly effective?

3. Which of the five senses does the writer employ in the description? Identify each of them in the paragraph.

4. What details would you make still more specific or concrete? Would you omit any details because they do not support the central point of the paragraph?

5. What sentences would you combine because they contain related ideas?

Adding Subordinate Clauses

In this chapter you have studied main and subordinate clauses and the four sentence types: simple, compound, complex, and compound-complex. As you rewrite papers, look for opportunities to change main clauses to subordinate clauses.

Rewriting Application: Adding Subordinate Clauses

A. Combine the following sentences by changing some of them to subordinate clauses.

1. a. We pulled off the road to one of the campsites and got out of the car.
   b. The smell of spring was everywhere.

   _____

   _____

2. a. My cousin Charon came up to me and told me to follow her.
   b. We went across the road and down a winding dirt path, past a sign that said "Twin Towers Overlook."
   c. I then beheld one of the most striking and magnificent views I have ever seen in my life.

   _____

   _____

   _____

3. a. Bright, warm sunlight filters through eucalyptus trees and presses against my shoulders.
 b. An old man greets me with a warm smile.
 c. The old man is raking leaves in the middle of the yard.

_____

_____

4. a. My grandfather sits on an old rust-covered metal stool.
 b. The stool used to be painted yellow.
 c. He tells me stories about my father's boyhood.

_____

_____

5. a. I have visited my grandparents' house many times during my childhood.
 b. I have not fully appreciated it until recently.

_____

_____

B. Revise each of the following sentences by changing one of the main clauses to a subordinate clause.

6. I looked to the right, and I could see an astonishingly high water slide.

_____

_____

7. I visited the cemetery in Escondido, California, to attend the funeral of my friend Jake McDonnell, for he had died in a head-on motorcycle accident.

_____

_____

8. The brevity of life was impressed on me, and I read the short accounts of unknown people's lives on the hundreds of tombstones.

_____

_____

9. Each weekend our family visited the Waimanalo Beach Park, and it is surrounded by the evergreen mountain range that towers over the valley below.

_____

_____

10. We took off our jackets and sweaters, but we still felt uncomfortably warm.

_____

_____

C. Now examine your own draft. Identify any main clauses that would work better as subordinate clauses. Consider changing some of your compound sentences to complex sentences. If you have a series of short sentences, combine them by changing some of the short main clauses to subordinate clauses.

Proofreading

When you are finished, proofread your paper. Check the spelling of words you are uncertain about. Examine each sentence closely to be sure it is not a **fragment, comma splice,** or **fused sentence.** If it is, repair the error using the techniques you have studied in this chapter. Once you have a draft you are satisfied with, prepare a clean final draft, following the format your instructor has asked for.

Chapter 2 Practice Test

I. Review of Chapter One

A. In the following sentences, identify the underlined words by writing one of the following abbreviations above the words: noun (N), pronoun (Pro), verb (V), adjective (Adj), adverb (Adv), conjunction (Conj), or preposition (Prep).

1. The football <u>team</u> in blue <u>beat</u> the football team in white in the last two seconds.

2. The citizens of Boston are <u>extremely</u> proud <u>of</u> their city.

3. After the war, Admiral Nelson <u>hoped</u> Lady Hamilton and <u>her</u> child would be safe.

4. Teddy Roosevelt <u>and</u> the Rough Riders <u>cheerfully</u> began the charge up San Juan Hill.

5. Sisyphus <u>patiently</u> placed his hands upon the <u>large</u> stone and started pushing.

6. When Little Miss Muffet sat down, it seemed like a safe <u>place</u>, <u>but</u> it wasn't.

7. After sewing the letter <u>onto</u> her dress, Hester thought <u>it</u> was rather attractive.

8. Portia skillfully <u>saved</u> a pound of <u>precious</u> flesh.

9. <u>During</u> the storm, Gatsby looked at the <u>green</u> light.

10. <u>Anyone</u> who left <u>before</u> the last episode of *Justified* missed some interesting violence.

B. For the following sentences, underline all subjects once and all complete verbs twice. Place parentheses around all prepositional phrases.

11. Has everyone received the new mysterious application in her or his email?

12. The dog with three heads stood before the castle and howled.

13. Will the tsunami reach us tonight, or will it miss us altogether?

14. While Icarus and Daedalus lived in the labyrinth, they tried to develop a plan of escape.

15. Chelsea has not told her father about her plan to visit Afghanistan.

continued

C. In the following sentences, correct any errors in the use of adjectives and adverbs (or in the use of *then* or *than*) by crossing out any incorrect words and writing the correct words above them.

16. I was real happy to see the news this morning; both the Padres and the Cubs were playing more better.

17. At last night's party, Sven's older daughter behaved more rude then his younger one.

18. As Elena heard the worse news of her life, she wore the most saddest look I have ever seen.

19. Irene clapped loud because the *Cirque du Soleil* artists performed so good.

20. Amy said *The Golden Compass* was the best of the two movies, but Ed said it was received poor in his town.

Chapter 2 Practice Test

II. Chapter Two

A. Underline the subordinate clauses and identify the type of clause (adjective or adverb) in the space provided.

_____ 1. The hummingbirds that visit my backyard are quite tame.

_____ 2. Some of them will even sit on my shoulder if I am very still.

_____ 3. There is a special one that has a bright, iridescent red throat and extra long

tail feathers.

_____ 4. When several of the birds are at the feeder at the same time, it is a colorful sight.

_____ 5. Unless I keep the feeder filled, they will stop coming.

B. To the main clauses below, add the types of subordinate clauses indicated in parentheses. Add your clause at any place in the sentence that is appropriate.

6. (adverb clause) The ten-year-old boy safely crossed the intersection.

_____

_____

7. (adjective clause) The marathon will be delayed by one day.

_____

_____

8. (adjective clause) The firefighters hurried up the ladder toward the window.

_____

_____

9. (adverb clause) My mother introduced me to the joys of reading.

_____

_____

10. (adverb clause) Bruce is always an easy grader.

_____

_____

Chapter 2 Practice Test

continued

C. In the spaces provided, identify the following sentences as simple, compound, complex, or compound-complex.

_____ **11.** After raining for nearly two weeks, the weather finally began to clear up.

_____ **12.** An Australian shepherd chased our car down the driveway; even though it was barking loudly, it seemed happy to see us.

_____ **13.** Rob refused to come home until he had caught at least one yellowtail.

_____ **14.** My son's soccer team practiced every afternoon for two months, but it still lost every game of the season.

_____ **15.** In early spring, Mark began to practice his golf swing, take afternoon walks, and enjoy the warmer weather.

D. Compose sentences of your own according to the instructions.

16. Write a simple sentence. End it with a prepositional phrase.

_____

_____

17. Write a compound sentence. Use the coordinating conjunction *yet* and appropriate punctuation.

_____

_____

18. Write a complex sentence. Use *while* as the subordinator.

_____

_____

19. Write a compound sentence. Use a semicolon and *however* to join the two main clauses.

_____

_____

continued

20. Write a compound–complex sentence. Use the coordinating conjunction *and* and the subordinator *as* or *before*.

_____

_____

E. Identify each of the following sentences as correct (C), fused (F), comma splice (CS), or fragment (Frag). Then correct any errors by using the methods discussed in Chapter Two.

_____ **21.** Although he preferred *The Great Gatsby* with Robert Redford in the leading role.

_____

_____

_____ **22.** Billie Holiday walked onto the stage, then she noticed Ella was already there.

_____

_____

_____ **23.** Bring your sister and her boyfriend to the picnic.

_____

_____

_____ **24.** The high school student texting during class.

_____

_____

_____ **25.** Lindbergh stared at his plane it was named after a famous city.

_____

_____

continued

_____ **26.** His haircut was finished, he had a narrow line of bright red hair in the middle of his head.

_____

_____

_____ **27.** Because a skull and crossbones had suddenly appeared on the screen of his iPad.

_____

_____

_____ **28.** Tiger looked irritated he stared at the person talking on the cell phone.

_____

_____

_____ **29.** After returning from his journey, Odysseus killed several men and kissed his wife Penelope.

_____

_____

_____ **30.** Romeo fell in love with Juliet at first sight, therefore, he pestered her day and night.

_____

_____

Improving Sentence Patterns

Now you have a fundamental knowledge of the sentence patterns of English. Although sentences may fall into four broad categories according to the number and types of clauses, the ways to express any thought in a sentence are almost infinitely variable.

You may make a sentence short and to the point:

> Eniko sold her netsuke collection.

Or, through the addition of modifying words, phrases, and additional clauses, you can expand it:

> After much soul searching and after seeking the advice of her mother, her brother, and her best friend, Eniko, a person who always carefully considered important decisions, sold her netsuke collection, which was worth several thousand dollars, but she kept one special carving of a frog and a sacred bird.

The essential idea—*Eniko sold her netsuke collection*—is the same for both sentences. Sometimes you will want to be short and to the point, and a five-word sentence will serve your purpose best. Other times you will want to be more explanatory, and then you may need to use more words.

The difference between the five words of the first sentence and the fifty words of the second one is the addition of modifying words, phrases, and clauses. These modifiers can help you write more clearly and vividly. The second sentence, though admittedly a bit overdone, tells a story, paints a picture. Modifying words, phrases, and clauses can be overused and should never be substituted for strong verbs and nouns, but most writers err in the opposite direction, leaving their writing limp and colorless.

You need to follow certain guidelines when you use the various modifying phrases and clauses. First we will discuss the most effective ways to use phrases and clauses in your sentences, and then we will discuss how to avoid the typical errors that writers make in using these devices. We hope that by the end you will have gained an appreciation of the wonderful flexibility of the English sentence and that you will have acquired more tools for making your own writing more interesting and effective.

Modifying with Participial and Infinitive Phrases

You can use **participial** and **infinitive phrases** as modifiers in your sentences. These phrases can help you streamline your sentences and achieve sentence variety. In most cases, participial and infinitive phrases take the place of subordinate clauses.

 EXAMPLES

(subordinate clause) **As he drove to work,** Harry saw a black cat run in front of his car.

(participial phrase) **Driving to work,** Harry saw a black cat run in front of his car.

As you already know, **a clause is a word group that contains a subject and a verb. A phrase,** on the other hand, **is a word group that does not contain a subject and a verb.** You are already aware of prepositional phrases. Other phrases, generally called verbal phrases, include **present participial phrases, past participial phrases,** and **infinitive phrases.**

Present Participial Phrases

As we mentioned in Chapter One, the present participle is a verbal. It is the form of the verb that ends in "ing" (*running, typing, looking*). Without a helping verb it cannot be used as the verb of a sentence. Instead, it is used as an adjective. For example, you can use it as a one-word adjective.

 EXAMPLE

The **running** woman stumbled as she rounded the corner.

In this sentence, the present participle *running* modifies the noun *woman*.

You can also use the present participle as part of a phrase that functions as an adjective. Such a phrase is called a **participial phrase,** and it is often used to begin sentences.

 EXAMPLE

Rounding the corner, the running woman stumbled.

In this sentence, the present participial phrase *Rounding the corner* is an adjective phrase modifying the noun *woman*. The present participle is *Rounding*.

The present participial phrase, then, is an adjective phrase consisting of the present participle plus any other words attached to it. When a present participial phrase introduces a sentence, it is always followed by a comma.

Past Participial Phrases

The past participle is the form of the verb that you use with the helping verbs *have, has,* or *had* (*have eaten, has defeated, had bought*). Like the present participle, the past participle is a verbal when used without a helping verb. And, like the present participle, it is used as an adjective.

You can use a past participle as a single-word adjective.

 EXAMPLE   The **defeated** army retreated into the mountains.

In this sentence, the past participle *defeated* modifies the noun *army.*

Or you can use the past participle as part of a past participial phrase.

 EXAMPLE   **Pursued by the enemy,** the army retreated into the mountains.

In this sentence, the past participial phrase *Pursued by the enemy* modifies the noun *army.* Notice that it is followed by a comma. As with the present participial phrase, when the past participial phrase introduces a sentence, you should place a comma after it.

Participial phrases make good introductions to sentences, but you can use them anywhere. To avoid confusion, though, you should place them as closely as possible to the words they modify.

 EXAMPLES   All of the students **submitting essays for the contest** used word processors.

The man **bitten by the rattlesnake** walked ten miles to the hospital.

The present participial phrase *submitting essays for the contest* modifies the noun *students.* The past participial phrase *bitten by the rattlesnake* modifies the noun *man.*

 PRACTICE   Underline the participial phrases in the following sentences and circle the words they modify.

1. Shocked by his own indiscretion, (Kevin) immediately apologized.

2. (The server) apologized to the customers sitting by the front door.

3. Leaping gracefully, (the gazelle) crossed the valley.

4. Dancing across the stage, (Bill) gave his best performance ever.

5. Because she is a responsible citizen of the world, (Amina) does not buy any

jewelry produced by child labor.

6. The mockingbird perching on the telephone pole imitated the blue jay in the pine tree.

7. Blaise wanted to meet the woman giving the lecture on South Africa.

8. Hurt by her remark, Chris slowly turned red.

9. Wondering about the trustworthiness of Napoleon, Toussaint walked out of his house in Port-au-Prince.

10. Antonia, threatened by the pitbull for the fifth time, called the police.

Infinitive Phrases

The infinitive is a verbal that you can use as a noun, an adjective, or an adverb. You form the infinitive by adding *to* to the present tense form of the verb (*to write, to run, to listen*).

You can use the infinitive by itself.

 EXAMPLE   **To fly,** you must first take lessons and get a license.

Or you can use the infinitive to form an infinitive phrase.

 EXAMPLE   **To play the saxophone well,** you must practice often.

Notice that the infinitive phrase consists of the infinitive plus any words attached to it. Like the two participial phrases, it is followed by a comma when it introduces a sentence. However, when you use the infinitive as a noun, it can act as the subject of a sentence. In this case, you do not use a comma.

 EXAMPLE   **To be a good husband** was Clint's ambition.

The infinitive phrase *To be a good husband* is the subject of the verb *was*.

Generally, like the two participial phrases, the infinitive phrase can appear in a variety of places in a sentence.

 EXAMPLE   Carla's motives were hard **to understand at first.**

Here the infinitive phrase *to understand at first* acts as an adverb to modify the adjective *hard.*

 EXAMPLE   Eduardo liked having a sister **to talk to** even though she teased him constantly.

Here, the infinitive phrase *to talk to* acts as an adjective to modify the noun *sister.*

PRACTICE   Underline the modifying participial and infinitive phrases in the following sentences and circle the words they modify.

1. Mrs. Tran bought a (thesaurus) to give to her son.

2. Staring at their (history book), they realized they could not celebrate Columbus Day any longer.

3. Most of the shoppers were glad to buy the (Girl Scout Cookies) from Tomasita.

4. Overwhelmed by its beauty, (Narcissus) stared at the image in the pond.

5. Peter's (determination) to find customers for his herbal supplement business irritated many of his friends.

6. Pandora could not resist her (desire) to open the box.

7. Reading her travel guide, Alicia eagerly (researched) Tokyo's jazz scene.

8. Frustrated by the recipe, (Sarah) simply added ten more cloves of garlic.

9. (Wallace) stood and stared at the man playing the blue guitar.

10. Reading *Heart of Darkness,* (Chinua Achebe) became more and more enraged.

Section One Review

1. The **present participle** is a verbal that ends in "ing" and that is used as an adjective. (When the "ing" form is used as a noun, it is called a **gerund**.)

2. A **present participial phrase** consists of the present participle plus any words attached to it.

3. A comma follows a **present participial phrase** that introduces a sentence.

4. The **past participle** is the form of the verb used with the helping verbs *have, has,* and *had.*

5. The **past participle** is a verbal used as an adjective.

6. A **past participial phrase** consists of the past participle plus any words attached to it.

7. A comma follows a **past participial phrase** that introduces a sentence.

8. An **infinitive** is formed by adding *to* to the present tense of a verb.

9. The **infinitive** is a verbal that can be used as a noun, an adjective, or an adverb.

10. An **infinitive phrase** consists of the infinitive plus any words attached to it.

11. A comma follows an **infinitive phrase** that introduces a sentence and acts as a modifier.

Exercise 1A

From a magazine, newspaper, book, or online source (such as *Wikipedia*), copy three sentences that contain an infinitive phrase, three that contain a present participial phrase, and three more that contain a past participial phrase. Underline the phrase in each sentence.

A. Sentences with infinitive phrases:

1. _____

_____

2. _____

_____

3. _____

_____

B. Sentences with present participial phrases:

4. _____

_____

5. _____

_____

6. _____

_____

C. Sentences with past participial phrases:

7. _____

_____

8. _____

_____

9. _____

_____

Exercise 1B

Underline all participial and infinitive phrases. Circle the words that they modify. In the spaces, identify the phrase as present participle (Pres P), past participle (Past P), or infinitive (Inf).

Past P **1.** Born on February 27, 1897, (Marian Anderson) became one of the most famous singers of classical music in the twentieth century. _____ **2.** Performing with the best orchestras and conductors throughout the United States and Europe, she was admired by music lovers everywhere. _____ **3.** Her many records, ranging from opera arias to concert songs to African American spirituals, show her incredible range and vocal ability. _____ **4.** Marian Anderson also played a role in the struggle to overcome racial prejudice in the United States. _____ **5.** In 1939, the Daughters of the American Revolution did not allow Anderson to sing at Constitution Hall in Washington, DC. _____ **6.** Providing her with a much larger stage, First Lady Eleanor Roosevelt and President Franklin D. Roosevelt arranged a concert on the steps of the Lincoln Memorial instead. _____ **7.** As a result, more than 75,000 people at the Lincoln Memorial and millions listening to radio heard her remarkable voice. _____ **8.** In 1955, Marian Anderson became the first African American singer to perform at the world-famous Metropolitan Opera in New York City. _____ **9.** Later on, serving as "goodwill ambassador" for the United States Department of State, Anderson became a delegate to the United Nations Human Rights Committee. _____ **10.** She was also an active member of the civil rights movement, performing at the 1963 March on Washington, DC, where Martin Luther King gave his "I Have a Dream" speech. _____ **11.** Awarded the Presidential Medal of Freedom in 1963, the Kennedy Center Honors in 1978, the National Medal of Arts in 1986, and a Grammy Lifetime Achievement Award in 1991, Anderson became one of the most decorated classical music performers of her time. _____ **12.** Admired by fans of classical music all over the world, she died in Portland, Oregon, on April 8, 1993.

Exercise 1C

In the places indicated by ^, add your own participial or infinitive phrases to the following sentences. Use the verbs in parentheses. Be sure to place a comma after any phrase that introduces a sentence.

1. ^ Francis turned on the lights, closed the draperies, and locked the doors. (leave)

    Leaving the house, Francis turned on the lights, closed the draperies, and locked the doors.

2. Whenever Randy visits the orphanage, he takes extra clothing ^ . (give)

    _____

    _____

3. The dog ^ barked one more time at the cat. (stand)

    _____

    _____

4. ^ Sofia started laughing. (surprise)

    _____

    _____

5. Bao-yu had not expected that Hao would like the pizza ^ . (cover)

    _____

    _____

6. ^ He found it necessary to set three alarm clocks. (wake up)

    _____

    _____

7. The riverboat gambler ^ decided it was time to bet it all. (stare)

    _____

    _____

Exercise 1C

continued

8. ^ Arthur said goodbye to Queen Guinevere. (hope)

_____

_____

9. The treasure ^ was discovered two hundred years later by a local surfer. (hide)

_____

_____

10. ^ Trenton created beats on his laptop. (nod)

_____

_____

11. The congressperson ^ vowed that he would never cooperate with the opposing party. (elect)

_____

_____

12. ^ Usain Bolt crossed the finish line. (run)

_____

_____

13. Tommy's little brother searched for a rock ^ . (throw)

_____

_____

14. ^ Do not eat too many refined carbohydrates. (lose)

_____

_____

15. ^ The ship reached the Andromeda galaxy in two days. (fly)

_____

_____

Exercise 1D

Underline all infinitive and participial phrases and circle the words that they modify.

1. Many of the historical (stories) told to us as children are really not at all accurate. **2.** For example, many stories say that Christopher Columbus had trouble financing his voyage because people of his time thought that the world is flat. **3.** In reality, thinkers of Columbus's day knew that the world is round. **4.** That knowledge, developed by the Greeks nearly fifteen hundred years earlier, was not at all unfamiliar to the people of Columbus's world. **5.** However, there was another reason that people did not offer money to pay for Columbus's voyage. **6.** They correctly believed that the ocean separating Europe from the Orient could not be crossed successfully because it is too vast. **7.** Running out of food and water, Columbus and his men survived their journey only because an entire continent blocked their way to the Orient. **8.** Another example of inaccurate history is the story of the Liberty Bell cracking on July 4, 1776. **9.** Commissioned in the 1750s for the state house in Pennsylvania, the Liberty Bell cracked when it was first tested, so it was then recast. **10.** Although it was rung on July 8 (not July 4) in celebration of the Declaration of Independence, there is no record to indicate any damage to the bell at that time. **11.** Ringing for the death of Chief Justice John Marshall in 1835, the Liberty Bell suffered its now famous crack. **12.** Finally, many people believe that Thomas Edison invented the first electric light, but he did not. **13.** Passing electricity through a wire, Sir Humphrey Davy invented the first electric light in 1802, some fifty years before Edison's work. **14.** Between 1840 and 1870, electric lights developed by inventive people included arc lamps, lightbulbs with filaments, and even fluorescent lights. **15.** Edison began his work to design a long-lasting filament lightbulb in 1877, and his famous breakthrough occurred in 1879, long after the invention of the electric light itself. **16.** As one can see, not every story taught to us as history when we were young is necessarily the way it really was.

SECTION 2

Modifying with Adjective Clauses and Appositives

Adjective Clauses

We discussed adjective clauses earlier in a section on subordinate clauses. An adjective clause is an important option when you want to modify a noun or pronoun in a sentence. Using an adjective clause instead of single-word adjectives or modifying phrases tends to place more emphasis on what you are saying about the noun or pronoun you are modifying. Consider the following sentences, for instance.

 EXAMPLES

(adjective)   My **insensitive** neighbor plays her trombone all night long.

(adjective clause)   My neighbor, **who is insensitive,** plays her trombone all night long.

Using the adjective clause *who is insensitive* places more importance on the neighbor's insensitivity. Sometimes you need only single-word modifiers, but it is good to be aware of all of your choices for modifying words.

Here is a brief review of adjective clauses.

1. Adjective clauses follow the noun or pronoun they modify.

2. Adjective clauses begin with the relative pronouns *who, whom, whose, which, that* (and sometimes *when* or *where*).

 EXAMPLES

We returned the money to the *person* **who had lost it.** (*Who* introduces an adjective clause that modifies the noun *person.*)

I remember the *time* **when Homer and Hortense were married at the Spam factory.** (*When* introduces an adjective clause that modifies the noun *time.*)

Sidney decided to move to *Colorado,* **where his family used to spend summer vacations.** (*Where* introduces an adjective clause that modifies the noun *Colorado.*)

3. If the adjective clause provides information that is necessary to identify the noun or pronoun, do not set it off with commas.

 EXAMPLE

The woman **who was sitting next to my uncle at the banquet** is a famous sportswriter.

The information in this adjective clause is necessary to identify which woman at the banquet is the famous sportswriter.

4. If the adjective clause provides information that is merely descriptive and is not necessary to identify the noun or pronoun, then set off the clause with commas.

 EXAMPLE

Merlin Olsen, **who was an all-pro football player,** became a famous sportscaster.

Merlin Olsen's name already identifies him, so the adjective clause contains added but unnecessary information. Therefore, you need the commas.

We will discuss the rules for the use of commas with adjective clauses again in Chapter Five.

 PRACTICE

Underline all adjective clauses and circle the words they modify. For further practice, try to determine which clauses need commas and add them where necessary.

1. The (man) who was chosen to succeed the governor was a political cartoonist.

2. *Walden* which was written by Henry David Thoreau condenses his two-year stay at Walden Pond into one year.

3. Everyone who entered the contest was asked to proceed to the exit.

4. Only twenty minutes from Las Vegas which is famous for its noisy casinos one can visit Red Rock Canyon which is an oasis of tranquility.

5. Caesarean section is a surgical procedure named after Julius Caesar who was supposedly born by that method.

6. The crocodile that followed our rowboat made a strange ticking sound and even seemed to smile at us.

7. Oscar told us the story of the day when Leticia proposed to him.

8. She asked him to pass her the fish sauce that was on the table to his left.

9. Mongolia which is a country adjacent to China was the home of Genghis Khan who was the founder of the Mongol Empire.

10. Luisa was raised in Mexico City where she learned to speak both English and Spanish.

Appositives

Appositives give you another option for adding descriptive detail. An **appositive** is a noun or pronoun, along with any modifiers, that **renames** another noun or pronoun. The appositive almost always follows the word it refers to, and it is usually set off with commas.

Note how the following two sentences can be combined not only by adding an adjective clause but also by adding an appositive:

My neighbor plays the trombone all night long.

He is an insensitive man.

 EXAMPLES

(adjective clause)   My neighbor, **who is insensitive,** plays his trombone all night long.

(appositive)   My neighbor, **an insensitive man,** plays his trombone all night long.

In the appositive, the noun *man* renames the noun *neighbor.*

EXAMPLES

The wedding <u>ring</u>, **a** <u>symbol</u> **of eternal love,** dates back to 2800 BC in Egypt. (The noun *symbol* renames the noun *ring.*)

The huge <u>trout</u>, **the** <u>one</u> **still in the river,** would have made an impressive trophy on the wall of Harold's den. (The pronoun *one* renames the noun *trout.*)

The <u>honeymoon</u>, **a popular marriage** <u>custom</u>**,** comes from an ancient Northern European practice of stealing brides. (The noun *custom* renames the noun *honeymoon.*)

PRACTICE   Underline the appositives and circle the nouns or pronouns that the appositives rename.

1. The (modem,) a device for connecting to the Internet, has changed the way we communicate with each other.

2. Jay Gatsby, a wealthy but lonely man, stared at the green light at the end of the dock.

3. Jerome and Geena wanted to enroll in an MOOC, a massive open online course.

4. Martin, an opponent of online courses, counseled them to go to a real college.

5. One of the key figures of the American Revolution was Benjamin Franklin, the famous author, inventor, and diplomat.

6. Twitter, a medium through which one can let other people know that one has just sneezed, is now on the stock market.

7. High school teachers, an underpaid and stressed-out group of professionals, refuse to be blamed for all the problems of society.

8. Christopher picked up his favorite instrument, a handcrafted classical guitar, and began to play.

9. The recent storms damaged two of Esther's favorite trees, the eucalyptus in her front yard and the cypress right next to it.

10. Ophelia, an ophthalmologist practicing in Oman, offered her services to the oligarch.

 PRACTICE

Add an appositive or an adjective clause to each of the following sentences. Use commas when they are needed.

1. The bicycle was leaning against the tree.

   The bicycle that Josh had hit with his car was leaning against the tree.

2. Marie Antoinette had no idea that there was going to be a revolution.

   Nobody told Marie Antoinette, so she had no idea that there was going to be a revolution

3. Hosni Mubarak was equally surprised by the Arab Spring.

   I decided to go with Hosni Mubarak, and I was equally suprised by the Arab Spring

4. Ichabod Crane listened fearfully to the story about the strange rider.

   I told a scary story, and Ichabod listened fearfully to the story about the strange rider

5. Bombay is a city with a very large film industry.

   Bombay is a city in which I am told is a very large film industry.

6. The pilot flew fearlessly into the Bermuda Triangle.

   The pilot knew a storm was coming but he flew fearlessly into the Bermuda Triangle.

7. She was torn between the beef empanadas and the lamb kebab.

   She was torn between the beef empanadas and the lamb kebab, because they are both so good.

8. The librarian hopped into his car and drove to his favorite fishing spot.

   The librarian hopped into his car after a long day of work and drove to his favorite fishing spot.

9. Poseidon looked confused when the sailors started to call him Neptune.

   Poseidon looked confused after he had a big meal when the sailors started to call him Neptune.

10. Octavio Paz was listening to an old recording by Celia Cruz.

    Octavio Paz found an mp3 player and was listening to an old recording by Celia Cruz.

Section Two Review

1. **Adjective clauses** modify nouns and pronouns.

2. **Adjective clauses** follow the nouns or pronouns they modify.

3. **Adjective clauses** begin with *who, whom, whose, which, that* (and sometimes *when* or *where*).

4. **Adjective clauses** that contain information necessary to identify the words they modify are not set off with commas.

5. **Adjective clauses** that do not contain information necessary to identify the words they modify are set off with commas.

6. **Appositives** are words or word groups containing a noun or pronoun that renames another noun or pronoun in a sentence.

7. **Appositives** usually follow the nouns or pronouns they rename.

8. **Appositives** are usually set off with commas.

Exercise 2A

Get a local paper of any kind. That may be a campus newspaper, a city magazine, a neighborhood paper, or any paper readily available to you that contains at least some articles and not only advertisements. Find ten sentences in that paper that contain at least one adjective clause each and five sentences that contain appositives.

A. Ten adjective clauses:

1. _____

_____

2. _____

_____

3. _____

_____

4. _____

_____

5. _____

_____

6. _____

_____

7. _____

_____

8. _____

_____

9. _____

_____

10. _____

_____

Exercise 2A

continued

B. Five appositives:

11. _____

_____

12. _____

_____

13. _____

_____

14. _____

_____

15. _____

_____

Exercise 2B

Underline all adjective clauses and appositives. Circle the words they modify or rename. Indicate whether the modifier is an appositive (AP) or an adjective clause (Adj). Add commas where necessary.

___AP___ 1. *The Babe* is a contemporary movie about (Babe Ruth,) the famous baseball player.

_____ 2. Babe Ruth whose pictures usually show him to be somewhat overweight was famous for his appetite. _____ 3. There are rumors that he could eat more than twenty hot dogs and drink several beers before a game. _____ 4. The pin-striped uniforms a Yankee trademark were not adopted to make Ruth look thinner. _____ 5. The Yankees began wearing pinstripes in 1912 which was eight years before Babe Ruth joined the team.

_____ 6. *The Babe Ruth Story* an early black-and-white movie starred William Bendix.

_____ 7. Bendix who had been a batboy with the New York Giants knew Ruth well.

_____ 8. Once, before a game, Bendix brought Ruth twelve hot dogs and two quarts of soda which made the Babe sick and sent him to the hospital. _____ 9. It was a favor that caused the batboy to be fired. _____ 10. In 1930 and 1931 his top years Ruth made $80,000 per year in salary. _____ 11. Today, it is not unusual to see players who make several million dollars a year. _____ 12. Some players make hundreds of thousands of dollars a year just to wear items of equipment that sports companies give them. _____ 13. Another way baseball players earn additional money is to appear in TV commercials which are commonly about sports or personal hygiene products. _____ 14. Such TV commercials usually a form of product endorsement were not open to Babe Ruth, but the wealth he acquired by hitting a ball with a stick was considerable. _____ 15. Some people have come up with an estimate that Ruth's total earnings would be worth about $24 million today.

Exercise 2C

A. Add adjective clauses of your own to each of the sentences below. Make sure you use commas where necessary.

1. My brother always enjoyed riding his bicycle in the mountains.

   My brother, who loves the outdoors, always enjoyed

   riding his bicycle in the mountains.

2. Abraham Lincoln was responsible for the Emancipation Proclamation.

   _____

   _____

3. However, Abolitionists had been arguing against slavery for decades.

   _____

   _____

4. The polar bear was looking for an iceberg.

   _____

   _____

5. Lake Tahoe is famous for the clarity of its water.

   _____

   _____

6. A child stood in front of the shopping center with a big sign around his neck.

   _____

   _____

7. A lonely widow sent her life savings to the unscrupulous telemarketer.

   _____

   _____

8. Wole Soyinka won the Nobel Prize for Literature and went to Stockholm.

   _____

   _____

Exercise 2C

continued

B. Add appositives of your own to the sentences below. Make sure you use commas where necessary.

9. The car collided with the delivery van on the interstate freeway.

   The car, a late-model Ford, collided with the

   delivery van on the interstate freeway.

10. A blue basketball bounced onto the sidewalk and hit a pedestrian.

   _____

   _____

11. The musician smiled when she looked at her new instrument.

   _____

   _____

12. Esmeralda had just bought her ticket for spring break on a travel website.

   _____

   _____

13. Jonah was beginning to feel comfortable inside the whale.

   _____

   _____

14. The biologist developed a plan to clone a bug.

   _____

   _____

15. Without Enkidu, Gilgamesh was unsure what to do on a Sunday afternoon.

   _____

   _____

Underline all adjective clauses and circle the words they modify. Underline all appositives and circle the words they rename. Add commas where necessary.

1. Many (people) who are otherwise well informed are of the mistaken (opinion) that personal trainers, chefs on TV, or even doctors on TV are the best sources for information on nutrition. **2.** However, personal trainers who may otherwise be competent on a variety of subjects do not have the necessary scientific background to give nutritional advice. **3.** Chefs especially chefs on TV are sometimes the very people who cause other people to need nutritional advice. **4.** And doctors who are trained in a variety of medical fields often have very little information on nutrition as part of their curriculum in medical school. **5.** Unfortunately, the people who are most qualified to counsel the public on nutritional matters—nutritionists—are rarely seen on TV. **6.** People who actually study nutrition can become registered dietitians or go on and get their doctorates in nutrition. **7.** Typically, students of nutrition have to study several of the natural sciences—biology biochemistry and sometimes physics. **8.** In addition, they also have to study anatomy and physiology subjects studied by medical students as well. **9.** Besides these subjects, mathematics and statistics which are necessary both for individual nutritional assessments and for public health nutrition are also background fields for nutritionists. **10.** Nutritionists who decide to acquire a doctorate can specialize in many different fields. **11.** For example, diabetes and obesity diseases that are posing an ever-increasing threat to public health, are growing sub-specializations in the field of nutrition. **12.** Child nutrition a field that focuses on the specific dietary needs of children is another sub-specialization. **13.** With heart diseases being a major cause of death in the United States and elsewhere, many researchers study the foods that promote heart health. **14.** Some nutrition scientists focus on nutrition in the developing world to help combat malnutrition in poor countries that sometimes do not have the resources to engage in such kinds of research. **15.** In short, nutritionists do a wide variety of important work that deserves more attention and recognition than it currently gets.

Misplaced and Dangling Modifiers

In Chapter Two, when you combined clauses to form various sentence types, you learned that joining clauses improperly can lead to comma splices and fused sentences. As you can probably guess, adding modifiers to sentences leads to an entirely new set of problems. In some cases, these problems are a bit more complicated than those caused by comma splices and fused sentences, but with a little practice, you should have no trouble at all handling them.

Misplaced Modifiers

Misplaced modifiers are exactly what their name says they are—modifiers that have been "misplaced" within a sentence. But how is a modifier "misplaced"? The answer is simple. If you remember that a modifier is nearly always placed just before or just after the word it modifies, then a misplaced modifier must be one that has been mistakenly placed so that it causes a reader to be confused about what it modifies. Consider the following sentence, for example:

 EXAMPLE　　Albert said **quietly** to move away from the snake.

Does the modifier *quietly* tell us how Albert said what he said, or does it tell us how we should move away from the snake? Changing the placement of the modifier will clarify the meaning.

 EXAMPLES　　Albert **quietly** said to move away from the snake. (Here, the word modifies the verb *said*.)

Albert said to move **quietly** away from the snake. (Here the word modifies the verbal *to move*.)

Sometimes finding the correct placement of a modifier can be a bit difficult. Let's look at a few other typical examples.

Misplaced Words

Any modifier can be misplaced, but one particular group of modifiers causes quite a bit of trouble for many people. These words are *only, almost, just, merely,* and *nearly.* Consider, for example, the following sentences:

 EXAMPLES　　By buying her new computer on sale, Floretta **almost** saved $100.

By buying her new computer on sale, Floretta saved **almost** $100.

As you can see, these sentences actually make two different statements. In the first sentence, *almost* modifies *saved*. If you *almost* saved something, you did *not* save it. In the second sentence, *almost* modifies *$100*. If you saved *almost* $100, you saved $85, $90, $95, or some other amount close to $100.

Which statement does the writer want to make—that Floretta did *not* save any money or that she *did* save an amount close to $100? Because the point was that she bought her computer on sale, the second sentence makes more sense.

To avoid confusion, be sure that you place all of your modifiers carefully.

 EXAMPLES

(incorrect)	Her piano teacher encouraged her **often** to practice.
(correct)	Her piano teacher **often** encouraged her to practice.
(correct)	Her piano teacher encouraged her to practice **often**.
(incorrect)	Sophia **nearly** drank a gallon of coffee yesterday.
(correct)	Sophia drank **nearly** a gallon of coffee yesterday.

 PRACTICE

Underline and correct any misplaced words in the following sentences. Some of the sentences may be correct.

1. I have not finished all of my work because I ~~only~~ started it *only* an hour ago.

2. The poet standing at the curb sadly stared at the rejection letter in his hand.

3. After the battle, Tecumseh wished only that his Shawnee be left in peace.

4. The two men who had been arguing quietly reached a compromise.

5. By the time he had almost fallen ten thousand feet, the skydiver was wondering if he should open his chute.

6. Peyton Farquhar nearly crept to the edge of the trees before he saw the Union soldiers.

7. Because she had eaten a large lunch, Araceli just decided to order a small dinner salad.

8. The counselor advised Fred frequently to attend the meetings.

9. Richard and Keisha were surprised that the trendy restaurant only offered two vegan dishes.

10. The sportswriter criticized the game even though he nearly had missed the entire second half.

Misplaced Phrases and Clauses

The phrases and clauses that you studied earlier in this chapter are as easily misplaced as individual words. Phrases and clauses often follow the words they modify.

EXAMPLES

(prepositional phrase)	The driver **in the blue sports car** struck an innocent pedestrian.
(present participial phrase)	The dog **chasing the car** barked at the bewildered driver.
(past participial phrase)	They gave the bicycle **donated by the shop** to the child.
(adjective clause)	Lucia gave the money **that she had borrowed from her sister** to the homeless woman.

In each of the above sentences, the modifier follows the word it modifies. Notice what happens when the modifier is misplaced so that it follows the wrong word.

EXAMPLES

The driver struck an innocent pedestrian **in the blue sports car.**

The dog barked at the bewildered driver **chasing the car.**

They gave the bicycle to the child **donated by the shop.**

Lucia gave the money to the homeless woman **that she had borrowed from her sister.**

Obviously, misplaced phrases and clauses can create rather confusing and sometimes even humorous situations. Of course, not all phrases and clauses follow the words they modify. Many occur before the word they refer to.

EXAMPLES

| (past participial phrase) | **Angered by the umpire's poor call,** Dana threw her bat to the ground. |
| (present participial phrase) | **Hoping to win the debate,** Cyrus practiced three hours every day. |

Regardless of whether the modifier appears before or after the word it modifies, the point is that you should place modifiers so that they clearly refer to a specific word in the sentence.

◉ PRACTICE   Underline and correct any misplaced phrases and clauses in the following sentences. Some of the sentences may be correct.

1. The cat leaped at the canary <u>that had been hungrily eyeing it.</u>

   <u>*The cat that had been hungrily eyeing the*</u>

   <u>*canary leaped at it.*</u>

2. Vera gave a cake to her boyfriend soaked in rum.

   _____

   _____

3. Artemis shot the arrow at the frightened stag using her strong bow.

   _____

   _____

4. Lester set his suitcase next to the flight attendant that held his collection of dead watch batteries.

   _____

   _____

5. My German shepherd lunged at the skunk, which sleeps at the foot of my bed, when it entered our garage.

   _____

   _____

6. *Full Metal Jacket* has become a classic film about the Vietnam War directed by Stanley Kubrick.

   _____

   _____

7. *To Live*, an excellent movie by Zhang Yimou, depicts life during the
    Cultural Revolution in China, who is a famous Chinese director.

    _____

    _____

8. Gong Li plays the lead role in that movie, who stars in many of Zhang
    Yimou's early films.

    _____

    _____

9. The monkeys in the cage looked out at the tourists hanging from limbs
    by their tails.

    _____

    _____

10. Amber showed the koi to her kindergarten class, which had bright orange
    and black markings.

    _____

    _____

Dangling Modifiers

A **dangling modifier** is an introductory phrase (usually a verbal phrase) that
lacks an appropriate word to modify. Since these modifiers usually represent
some sort of action, they need a **doer** or **agent** of the action represented.

For example, in the following sentence the introductory participial phrase
"dangles" because it is not followed by a noun or pronoun that could be the
doer of the action represented by the phrase.

> **Driving madly down the boulevard,** the horse just missed being hit and
> killed.

The present participial phrase *Driving madly down the boulevard* should be followed by a noun or pronoun that could logically do the action of the phrase. Instead, it is followed by the noun *horse,* which is the subject of the sentence. Was the horse "driving"? Probably not. Therefore, the modifying phrase "dangles" because it has no noun or pronoun to which it can logically refer. Here are some more sentences with dangling modifiers.

 EXAMPLES

Nearly exhausted, the game was almost over.
(Was the *game* exhausted?)

After studying all night, the test wasn't so difficult after all.
(Did the *test* study all night?)

To impress his new girlfriend, Dominic's Chevrolet was polished.
(Did the *Chevrolet* want to impress Dominic's girlfriend?)

As you can see, you should check for dangling modifiers when you use introductory phrases.

 PRACTICE

In the following sentences, indicate whether the modifying phrases are correctly used by writing either "C" for correct or "D" for dangling modifier in the spaces provided.

_____D_____ **1.** Hurrying to work, Ofelia's briefcase fell into a puddle.

_____ **2.** Wiping tears from her eyes, the story of Hansel and Gretel always upset the old witch.

_____ **3.** Delighted by his graphic novel, Rocco grinned broadly.

_____ **4.** To become invisible, the enclosed disappearance cream must be applied to the body.

_____ **5.** Enthralled by the game, Nayeli's bowl of chips fell from the table.

Correcting Dangling Modifiers

You can correct a dangling modifier in one of two ways.

1. Rewrite the sentence so that the introductory modifier logically refers to the subject of the sentence it introduces.

EXAMPLES   Nearly exhausted, **I** hoped the game was almost over.
(*I* was nearly exhausted.)

After studying all night, **Lucilla** passed the test easily.
(*Lucilla* studied all night.)

To impress his new girlfriend, **Dominic** polished his Chevrolet.
(*Dominic* wanted to impress his girlfriend.)

2. Change the introductory phrase to a clause.

 EXAMPLES   **Because I was nearly exhausted,** I hoped the game was almost over.

After Lucilla had studied all night, she passed the test easily.

Dominic wanted to impress his girlfriend, so he polished his Chevrolet.

NOTE: Do not correct a dangling modifier by moving it to the end of the sentence or by adding a possessive noun or pronoun to a sentence. In either case, it will still "dangle" because it lacks a **doer** or **agent** that could perform the action of the modifier.

 EXAMPLES   (incorrect)   **After searching for three weeks,** the lost watch was finally found. (There is no doer for *searching*.)

(still incorrect)   The lost watch was finally found **after searching for three weeks.** (There still is no logical doer.)

(still incorrect)   **After searching for three weeks,** Alfredo's lost watch was finally found. (Adding the possessive form *Alfredo's* does not add a doer of the action.)

(correct)   **After searching for three weeks,** Alfredo finally found his watch. (The noun *Alfredo* can logically perform the action—*searching*—of the modifying phrase.)

(correct)   **After Alfredo had searched for three weeks,** he finally found his watch. (Here again, the doer of the action is clear.)

PRACTICE   Underline and correct any dangling modifiers in the following sentences. Some of the sentences may be correct.

1. To pass the time, another movie was watched.

To pass the time, we watched another movie.

2. Waiting for the game to begin, Michael's stomach was upset.

_____

_____

3. After drinking the magic potion, his disappointment was obvious.

_____

_____

4. Determined to die with dignity, the philosopher drank the cup of

hemlock.

_____

_____

5. After running swiftly up the hill, the flag was raised by the warrior.

_____

_____

6. Concerned about her students' dangling modifiers, Leanne's new lesson

plan began to take shape.

_____

_____

7. To watch the solar eclipse, sunglasses will protect your eyes.

_____

_____

8. Breathing hard, the Eiffel Tower seemed to have too many stairs.

_____

_____

9. Startled by the sudden explosion, the summer sky was filled with cranes and egrets.

_____

_____

10. To be certain, the test results were checked a third time.

_____

_____

Section Three Review

1. A **misplaced modifier** is a modifier that has been mistakenly placed so that it causes the reader to be confused about what it modifies.

2. Commonly misplaced words are *only, almost, just, merely,* and *nearly.*

3. Place modifying phrases and clauses so that they clearly refer to a specific word in a sentence.

4. A **dangling modifier** is an introductory phrase (usually a verbal phrase) that lacks an appropriate word to modify. Since these modifiers usually represent some sort of action, they need a **doer** or **agent** of the action represented.

5. You can correct a dangling modifier in one of two ways.

   a. Rewrite the sentence so that the introductory modifier logically refers to the subject of the sentence it introduces.

   b. Change the introductory phrase to a clause.

6. Do not correct a dangling modifier by moving it to the end of the sentence or by adding a possessive noun or pronoun.

Exercise 3A

A. Underline and correct any misplaced words in the following sentences. Some sentences may be correct.

1. After <u>nearly</u> working for a week, I finally finished planting my garden.

    After working for nearly a week, I finally finished

    planting my garden.

2. Clement only traded five of his defects for virtues.

3. We had expected a larger crowd, but half a dozen people merely showed up.

4. After she bought her electronic reading device, Britney almost read 30 percent fewer books than she had before.

5. Because Prince Myshkin just performed good deeds, people became suspicious of him.

B. Underline and correct any misplaced phrases or clauses in the following sentences. Some of the sentences may be correct.

6. Leon showed a chicken to his daughter <u>that had two heads.</u>

    Leon showed a chicken that had two heads to

    his daughter.

continued

7. My friend gave a rabbit to her new husband that had big floppy ears and a white tail.

_____

_____

8. The scientist took a side trip to see the dolphins arguing in favor of stem cell research.

_____

_____

9. Abbie watched the chicken cross the road pondering whether it was really worth the risk.

_____

_____

10. In calculus class the student did not notice the professor standing behind him texting his girlfriend.

_____

_____

C. Underline and correct any dangling modifiers in the following sentences. Some of the sentences may be correct.

11. Worried about the poor weather, a raincoat and an umbrella are advised.

If you are worried about the poor weather, we advise you to take a

raincoat and an umbrella.

12. Before leaving the desert, pick up all of those plastic water bottles.

_____

_____

continued

13. Surprised by the party for his fiftieth birthday, a heart attack was suffered by Homer.

_____

_____

14. To avoid being completely humiliated, one more try was necessary.

_____

_____

15. Thinking about the message from the ghost, a plan was devised by Hamlet.

_____

_____

Exercise 3B

Underline and correct any misplaced or dangling modifiers in the following sentences. Some of the sentences may be correct.

1. After driving for seven straight hours, all of the towns began to look the same.

   After I drove for seven straight hours, all of the towns began to look the same.

2. Marvin described the new board to his friend that he had bought at the surf shop.

3. The computer only crashes when an important assignment is due.

4. Looking at the territory from the mountaintop, Lewis and Clark discussed their progress so far.

5. Overwhelmed by the good news, Phoebe's eyes filled with tears.

6. The band member walked up to the microphone with a skull and crossbones tattoo and began to sing.

continued

7. Although at first I thought I had found a diamond in the sand, it merely turned out to be

   a piece of costume jewelry.

   _____

   _____

8. When returning merchandise, bring the receipt to the store with you.

   _____

   _____

9. The Girl Scouts stopped to look at the snake hiking down the mountain.

   _____

   _____

10. Hiding escaping slaves during the Civil War, Harriet Tubman's actions saved the lives of

    many men and women.

    _____

    _____

11. William Carlos Williams wrote about a red wheelbarrow in one of my favorite poems

    that was surrounded by white chickens.

    _____

    _____

12. To prepare for his Thanksgiving dinner, Homer almost bought all of the Spam in the

    store.

    _____

    _____

continued

13. After hiking for three days, my back began to ache.

_____

_____

14. Because the hike in the desert was so exhausting, Rashida almost drank a gallon of Gatorade.

_____

_____

15. A woman wielding a gun with green eyes threatened the bank teller.

_____

_____

Exercise 3C

Correct any dangling or misplaced modifiers in the following paragraph.

1. The trickster hero is common to the mythology and folklore of many cultures, <u>who</u>
<u>embodies a sense of mischief and insists upon the need for change.</u> 2. For example, the trickster
Loki is full of trickery and deceit, who is found in Norse mythology. 3. Serving the other gods as
legal counselor and advisor, mischief is always on his mind. 4. His nature forces action and
change upon the other gods, which is fiery and elusive. 5. At times Loki's actions almost seem
comical in the generally dark Norse myths. 6. Another trickster is the god Edshu, who is found in
West African folklore. 7. Loving to create trouble, one African story describes Edshu walking
through a farming area. 8. He is wearing a hat while he enjoys the walk that is red on one side,
white on the other, green in front, and black in back. 9. Later in the day, arguing about the color
of the hat, a fight is started among the farmers. 10. Two of the farmers are brought before a
judge, who tried to knife each other. 11. When the trial nearly is over, Edshu reveals what he has
done, saying, "They could not help but quarrel. I wanted it that way." 12. One of the most
common trickster figures is the rabbit. 13. Appearing as B'rer Rabbit in the American South, as
the Hare in African tales, and as a variety of rabbit heroes in Southeast Asia, Iran, and India,
quick thinking characterizes the trickster rabbit. 14. His large, dangerous opponents suffer
painfully when they deal with the rabbit, who are always outwitted by him. 15. The trickster
rabbit even appears in modern cartoons, whose quick wits protect him from all dangers, in the
form of Bugs Bunny. 16. In all cases, no matter what form the character takes, tricksters cut big
egos down to size and bring heroes and audiences down to earth.

Sentence Practice: Using Participial and Infinitive Phrases, Appositives, and Adjective Clauses

In this chapter, you have become aware of the many choices you have when you want to modify words in your sentences. Your options range from single-word modifiers to modifying phrases to subordinate clauses. Let's explore some of the possibilities with the following sentence.

> The beautiful Dalmatian looked hungrily at the thick steaks cooking on the grill and quietly begged the chef for a bite.

By changing various modifiers, you can express the sentence in several other ways. For instance, *The beautiful Dalmatian,* with its single-word modifier *beautiful* describing *Dalmatian,* could be changed into an appositive.

> The dog, **a beautiful Dalmatian,** looked hungrily at the thick steaks cooking on the grill and quietly begged the chef for a bite.

This version tends to emphasize the beauty of the dog.

If you change the part of the sentence that contains the verb *looked* to a present participial phrase, you will get a different effect.

> **Looking hungrily at the thick steaks cooking on the grill,** the beautiful Dalmatian quietly begged the chef for a bite.

This version places a bit more emphasis on the dog's hungry look.

Another alternative is to change the present participial phrase *cooking on the grill* to an adjective clause.

> The beautiful Dalmatian looked hungrily at the thick steaks **that were cooking on the grill** and quietly begged the chef for a bite.

As you can see, the choices are many, and good writers often try several versions of a sentence before deciding on the one that best expresses their ideas. Experimenting with your sentences in this way is part of the fun and the challenge of writing.

The exercises in this section are designed to give you practice in using various types of modifiers when you compose your sentences.

Sentence Combining Exercises

Using your knowledge of modifying phrases and clauses, combine the following lists of sentences according to the directions. Avoid dangling and misplaced modifiers. Add commas where necessary.

 EXAMPLE   Combine these sentences into one sentence. Use sentence a as a present participial phrase. Use sentence b as an appositive.

   a. Lupe felt good about her promotion to manager.
   b. Lupe was a generous person.
   c. Lupe invited her co-workers to dinner.
   d. The dinner would be at their favorite Thai restaurant.

Feeling good about her promotion to manager, Lupe, a

generous person, invited her co-workers to dinner

at their favorite Thai restaurant.

1. Combine the following sentences into one sentence. Combine sentences a and b into one adverb clause.

   a. A physician was from the ancient world.
   b. A physician wanted to relieve fever.
   c. The physician recommended the bark of the willow tree.

   _____

   _____

   _____

2. Combine the following sentences into one sentence. Use sentence b as an appositive. Use sentence e as an adjective clause.

   a. Aspirin is a variation of the old remedy.
   b. Aspirin is an acid.
   c. The remedy was rediscovered by a German chemist.
   d. It was rediscovered in 1853.
   e. He was looking for a cure for arthritis.

   _____

   _____

   _____

Sentence Combining Exercises

continued

3. Combine these sentences into one sentence. Use sentence a as an introductory past participial phrase. Use sentence d as an adjective clause.

   a. Aspirin was ignored for years.
   b. Aspirin is an extract from that ancient willow tree.
   c. It is also an extract from another plant.
   d. The other plant is a relative of the rose.

   _____

   _____

   _____

4. Combine these sentences into one sentence. Use sentences c and d as appositives.

   a. Goldfish swallowing was started by Lothrop Withington, Jr.
   b. It was started in 1939.
   c. It was one of the most unusual fads of the twentieth century.
   d. Lothrop Withington, Jr., was a Harvard first-year student.

   _____

   _____

   _____

5. Combine the following sentences into one sentence. Use sentence a as an introductory adverb clause. Use sentence b as an adjective clause. Use sentence d as an infinitive phrase.

   a. Withington boasted to friends that he had once eaten a live fish.
   b. His friends attended college with him.
   c. His friends dared him.
   d. The dare was to eat another one.

   _____

   _____

   _____

Sentence Combining Exercises

continued

6. Combine the following sentences into one sentence. Use sentence a as a present participial phrase. Use sentence d as an adjective clause.

    a. Withington accepted the challenge.
    b. He agreed to meet on March 3.
    c. He would meet them in the student dining hall.
    d. He would eat a live goldfish.

_____

_____

_____

7. Combine the following sentences into one sentence. Use sentence c as an appositive. Use sentence d as an adjective clause.

    a. The date arrived.
    b. Withington stood before a crowd of students.
    c. Withington was a natural actor.
    d. The students had heard about the challenge.
    e. Withington grabbed a goldfish from a bowl.

_____

_____

_____

8. Combine the following sentences into one sentence. Use sentence a as a present participial phrase.

    a. He held the fish by its tail.
    b. Withington slowly lowered it into his mouth.
    c. He chewed it for a moment.
    d. He then swallowed it.

_____

_____

_____

continued

9. Combine the following sentences into one sentence. Use sentence a as an infinitive phrase. Use sentence c as an adjective clause.

    a. He completed his performance.
    b. Withington pulled out a toothbrush.
    c. He used it to clean his teeth.
    d. Then he said, "The scales caught a bit on my throat."

_____

_____

_____

10. Combine these sentences into one sentence. Use sentence a as an introductory prepositional phrase. Use sentence c as a past participial phrase.

    a. It was that spring.
    b. College students across the country were gulping down goldfish.
    c. The students were worried about exams.
    d. They were ready for any diversion.
    e. They were gulping down as many as forty-two goldfish at one sitting.

_____

_____

_____

Essay and Paragraph Practice: Using Examples

Writing Assignment

In the first two chapters of this text, you have written paragraphs about an event and a place. Such writing is usually called "narrative" or "descriptive" because it either narrates (tells about) an event or describes a place. In this chapter you will write an **expository** paragraph or essay (your instructor will decide which one). Expository writing **explains** a topic or idea to a reader, or it **informs** the reader about a topic or idea. The topic of an expository paragraph or essay can range from explaining how to conduct an experiment in chemistry to analyzing the causes of World War II. In fact, most of the writing you will do in college classes will be expository.

One common type of expository writing is the paragraph or essay that relies upon examples to make its point. If you look at Exercises 1D (page 163), 2D (page 175), and 3C (page 192) of this chapter, you will see that they all rely on examples to support the statements made in the topic sentences. Exercise 1D gives examples of inaccurate historical stories, and Exercise 2D gives examples of false ideas about who are the best sources of nutritional information, and Exercise 3C gives examples of the trickster hero in mythology and folklore.

Supporting your ideas with examples is a powerful way to help your readers understand your point. Examples allow your readers to see your topic at work in real-life situations, and they show your readers that your topic is based on reality. Of course, examples are also important when you take tests. Your ability to back up general answers with specific examples can show an instructor that you have understood and mastered the material you have been studying.

For this chapter, your assignment is to write a paper that uses several *specific examples* to support a statement made in a topic sentence or a thesis statement. Develop your paper from one of the following prewriting suggestions or from an idea suggested by your instructor.

Reading Assignment

The reading selections in the "Using Examples" section of Chapter Six can help you see how professional writers include examples to illustrate their ideas. Read one or more of the selections, as assigned by your instructor, and use the questions that follow them to develop ideas for your own paper.

Prewriting to Generate Ideas

Whether you are writing a paragraph or an essay, the prewriting techniques are the same. Use freewriting, brainstorming, and clustering to develop ideas from the topic suggestions that follow. Look for topics that you can illustrate with specific, detailed examples of your own.

Prewriting Application: Finding Your Topic

Read the following topic suggestions before you begin to prewrite. Not all of them will apply to you. Find the suggestions that interest you the most and then spend five or ten minutes freewriting on each of them. Try not to settle for a topic that seems only mildly interesting. Instead, look for that "Aha!" experience, the emotional reaction that identifies a topic that really moves you.

1. Give examples of *one* particular personality characteristic of your own. Are you a hard-working, "Type A" personality? Do you overeat when you experience stress, anger, or boredom? Are you sometimes too outspoken? Are you overly impulsive? Choose *one* personality characteristic of your own and illustrate it with examples.

2. Do you know anyone whom you admire? Why do you admire that person? Give specific reasons why you admire him or her and examples of that person's admirable behavior.

3. Have you ever found that at times telling a lie is the ethical, responsible thing to do? Have you ever told a lie to protect someone from danger or from unnecessary pain? Use specific examples to illustrate times when lying seemed to you to be the correct, responsible behavior.

4. Take any simple statement that you know to be true and illustrate it with specific examples. Consider ideas like these:

   - A weather event in recent years has had a strong impact on a neighborhood or city in your state.

   - In recent years, everyone at public events has become more aware of the potential of danger.

   - When telling a joke, it is more important how one tells it than what the content of the joke is.

   - Keeping up with technological change is not easy.

   - Cats and dogs have fully developed individualities.

5. Have you ever experienced intolerance or bigotry because of your race, gender, religious beliefs, or age? Write a paper in which you use specific examples to illustrate what has happened to you.

6. It is sometimes said that we really value something only if we had to work for it. If you think that is true, give examples that illustrate the truth of that statement.

7. Choose a sport, activity, or hobby with which you are familiar. Use specific examples to illustrate something that you know to be true about it.

8. Use examples to illustrate the kinds of desserts that can be made from fruits.

9. Choose a statement that people commonly believe to be true and use examples to show why it is or is not true in your life. Here are some examples:

   ■ Whatever can go wrong will go wrong.

   ■ Sometimes help can come from the most unlikely places.

   ■ If you try hard enough, you will succeed.

   ■ You can't tell who your real friends are until you need help.

10. Choose a type of cell phone (one you own or hope to own) and explain with examples why that phone is useful or bothersome to you.

Choosing and Narrowing the Topic

As you choose your topic, remember that a more specific focus will result in a better paper than a more general focus. For example, don't try to give examples of a topic as general as *problems in the United States*. There are hundreds of possible examples of such a general topic, so all you would be able to do is briefly list a few of them, without going into detail about any. On the other hand, a more focused topic, such as *problems caused by my father's excessive drinking*, could certainly be supported by several detailed, descriptive examples.

Writing a Topic Sentence

If your assignment is to write a single paragraph, use your prewriting to decide upon a narrowed topic and a limited central point. Then write a topic sentence that can be supported with examples. Examine your topic sentence closely. Not all statements suggest that examples will follow. Consider the following sentences. Which would cause a reader to expect examples as support? Which would not?

EXAMPLES   **1.** I really like eating shrimp.

2. At a Korean BBQ restaurant I visited recently, I was served many types of raw meats and fish that were ready to be put on the table grill.

Sentence 1 merely states a fact. It does not cause one to expect examples. Sentence 2 would cause a reader to expect examples of the types of meats and fish served.

Prewriting Application: Working with Topic Sentences

Identify the topic sentences in Exercises 1D (page 163), 2D (page 175), and 3C (page 192). Then identify the topic and the central point in each topic sentence.

Prewriting Application: Evaluating Topic Sentences

Write "No" before each sentence that would not make a good topic sentence *for this assignment*. Write "Yes" before each sentence that would make a good one. Using ideas of your own, rewrite the unacceptable topic sentences into topic sentences that might work.

_____ **1.** I like a lot of different things.

_____

_____

_____ **2.** Computers are supposed to be convenient, time-saving machines, but mine has brought me nothing but trouble.

_____

_____

_____ **3.** People often talk about freedom, but one person's freedom can cause another person a lot of inconvenience.

_____

_____

_____ **4.** I love to watch and to play basketball.

_____

_____

_____ **5.** After having owned a turtle for more than five years, I am still not
sure whether he likes me.

_____

_____

_____ **6.** Whenever I go to a garage sale or a swap meet, I end up buying
some absolutely useless item.

_____

_____

_____ **7.** My paragraph will talk about why I like music so much.

_____

_____

_____ **8.** My best friend's parties always seem to turn into near riots.

_____

_____

_____ **9.** The economy is important, but there are many other important
things about a country, too.

_____

_____

_____ **10.** My father believes that we should never lie, but sometimes his honesty is so painful it is almost cruel.

_____

_____

Prewriting Application: Talking to Others

Once you have decided on a topic and a preliminary topic sentence, you need to develop your examples. A good way to do so is to tell three or four other members of your class why your topic sentence is true. Think of yourself as an attorney before a jury. You must provide the evidence—the examples—to support the central idea in your topic sentence.

For example, if your topic is that your father's honesty borders on cruelty, convince the other people in your group with brief, specific examples. Consider these questions as you discuss your topics.

1. Exactly where and when does each example occur? Have the place and time of each instance been clearly identified?

2. Can you visualize the examples? Are the people mentioned in the example identified by name or by relationship? Are physical features specifically named or described?

3. What point do these examples reveal? Should the topic sentence be revised to express that point more clearly?

4. Are you convinced? Have enough examples been provided to illustrate the topic idea? Should any of the examples be more convincing?

5. Which example should be used first in the paper? Last?

Organizing Examples

Examples can be organized in a number of ways. Sometimes a **chronological order** is best, arranging examples according to *when* they occurred. Sometimes a **spatial order** would work well, arranging examples by *physical location*. Many times an **emphatic order** should be used, arranging examples from *least to most important* (or, sometimes, from most to least important).

Prewriting Application: Organizing Examples

First, arrange the following examples in chronological order, numbering them 1, 2, 3, 4, 5. Next, arrange them in spatial order. Finally, arrange them in emphatic order. If you prefer one arrangement over another, explain why.

[MCL] Topic Sentence: My father thinks that the junk he buys at swap meets and garage sales makes terrific household decorations.

————   He bought a warped wooden tennis racket a few months ago for five dollars and nailed it above our front door. He thinks it makes our house look "sporty."

————   On the hallway wall is a cuckoo clock that he bought last Saturday. The bird is missing one of its wings, and the clock will not keep correct time anymore. He thought it was a real bargain because he got the clock for one dollar.

————   Upstairs in our guest bedroom is a faded velvet picture of Elvis Presley and another one of some dogs playing poker. He bought them last year for ten dollars each.

————   When we used to live in Big Bear, California, he spent $75 for a huge moth-eaten moose head that turned out to be crawling with bugs that infested our whole house. It's now mounted over the fireplace in the living room.

————   Two plastic pink flamingos are stuck into our front lawn. Dad bought them the weekend we moved into this house. He says they add "character" to our home.

Writing the Paragraph

Write the first draft of your paragraph. Your first sentence should be your preliminary topic sentence. After writing the topic sentence, write the examples that illustrate your point. Devote several sentences to each example and be as specific and as detailed as you can in each of those sentences.

Using Transitions

Transitions are words, phrases, or clauses that let the reader know when you are moving from one idea or example to another. They are essential for clear writing because they help your readers follow your train of thought. Since you will be writing several examples in one paragraph for this assignment, you need to let your readers know when one example has ended and another is beginning. Use common transitional phrases such as those below to introduce each new example:

for example   to illustrate
for instance   another example of

Notice how transitional words and phrases are used to introduce examples in Exercise 1D, page 163.

EXAMPLES   **For example,** many stories say that Christopher Columbus had trouble financing his voyage because people of his time thought that the world is flat.

Another example of inaccurate history is the story of the Liberty Bell cracking on July 4, 1776.

Finally, many people believe that Thomas Edison invented the first electric light, but he did not.

Writing Application: Identifying Transitional Sentences

Examine Exercise 3C (page 192). Identify the transitions that introduce each example.

Rewriting and Improving the Paragraph

1. Once your first draft is complete, read it over to determine how you can improve the examples you have used. In particular, try to make the examples as specific and as concrete as you can. Use actual names of people and places and refer to specific details whenever possible.

2. As you read your draft, make sure you can tell where each of your examples ends and the next begins. Revise your transitional sentences as needed to make them clearer.

3. If your preliminary topic sentence can be improved so that it more accurately states the central point of your paragraph, change it now.

4. Examine your draft for sentences that can be combined using participial phrases, appositives, infinitive phrases, or adjective clauses. Combine such sentences the way you did in the Sentence-Combining Exercises.

Rewriting Application: Responding to Writing

Read the following paragraph. Then respond to the questions following it.

I Enjoy H$_2$O to Relax

Whenever I feel stressed, I find that I can relax best if I am near the water. For example, as a teenager living in San Bernardino, I would drive many miles into the local foothills of the mountains, where a small river or a large stream called Lytle Creek was located in the little town of Applewhite. I would walk down between the trees and then over all of the rocks to find a place where I would sit for hours. I enjoyed watching the water rush by because it made me become very relaxed. Then, in the late 1980s, I moved to San Diego County. My first apartment was in Escondido, and times were troubled and stressful nearly every day, yet I was able to find comfort by driving to Lake Dixon. After several weekend trips I began taking this drive at all different times of the week. Usually alone, but sometimes with my boys, I would go to the lake and feed the ducks or just fish from the shore. Now, living in San Marcos, I prefer the ultimate water experience by relaxing at the beach. During most of my quick trips, I drive down Del Dios Highway and across the railroad tracks into Solana Beach parking lot. I walk down the large ramp and sit on the sand or walk along the shoreline to the cave. Watching the water really washes away any troubles that I brought with me. It seems to clear my head and to bring a warm feeling of contentment to my soul. In conclusion, no matter whether the water is a stream, lake, or ocean, its appearance and its soothing sounds take away all of my stress and troubles.

1. Identify the topic sentence. State its topic and central idea. Is it an effective topic sentence? Why or why not?

2. Identify the transitional sentences that introduce each example.

3. Are the examples specific? Point out which words in each example identify specific places or things.

4. Which words in each example would you make still more specific?

5. Which example is the most effective? Why? Which one would you improve? How?

Proofreading

Before you do the final editing of your paper, revise it one more time. If the topic sentence needs work, improve it now. Check the examples. Are they as specific and descriptive as they can be? Add transitional sentences between examples. Wherever you can, combine related sentences using subordinate clauses as well as participial and infinitive phrases.

Now edit the paper. Check your draft for any of the following errors:

- Sentence fragments
- Comma splices
- Fused sentences
- Misplaced modifiers
- Dangling modifiers
- Misspelled words

Prepare a clean final draft, following the format your instructor has requested. Before you turn in your final draft, proofread it carefully and make any necessary corrections.

Moving from Paragraph to Essay

All of the assignments so far have asked you to write single paragraphs, but most college classes will ask you to produce essays consisting of several paragraphs.

Writing an essay is not really much different from writing a paragraph. An essay focuses on and develops one central idea, just as a paragraph does. The central idea of an essay is called its **thesis statement.**

The main difference between an essay and a paragraph is that the supporting material in an essay is longer and more complicated, so it needs to be separated into different body paragraphs, each with its own **topic sentence.**

Recognizing Essay Form

An essay consists of an introductory paragraph, one or more body paragraphs, and a concluding paragraph.

- The *introductory paragraph* includes the **thesis statement** (usually as the last sentence of the first paragraph).

- Each *body paragraph* starts with a **topic sentence** that supports the thesis statement. The central idea of each body paragraph is supported with **facts, examples,** and **details.**

- The *concluding paragraph* brings the essay to a close, often by restating the central idea of the essay.

Introductory Paragraph

Introductory sentences
ending with a
thesis statement.

Body Paragraphs

Topic sentence
supported with
facts, examples, and details.

> **Topic sentence**
>
> supported with
>
> facts, examples, and details.

> **Topic sentence**
>
> supported with
>
> facts, examples, and details.

Concluding Paragraph

> Concluding sentences
>
> bringing the essay
>
> to a close.

Choosing and Narrowing a Thesis Statement

A **thesis statement** states the topic and the central idea of an entire essay, just as a topic sentence states the topic and central idea of a paragraph. Like a topic sentence, a thesis statement needs to be narrowed and focused so that it does not try to cover too much material in a short essay.

Consider the following sentences. Which is narrowed enough to function as a thesis statement in a brief essay?

 EXAMPLES

1. Many people have problems when they move to a new place.

2. Immigrants face many obstacles when they move to the United States.

3. Immigrants who do not yet speak English will encounter several obstacles when they try to get a job in the United States.

Sentence 1 is much too broad for any essay. Both sentences 2 and 3 could work as thesis statements, but sentence 3 will work better in a brief essay because it is narrowed to the topic of *Immigrants who do not yet speak English,* and its central point is focused on *obstacles when they try to get a job.* An essay with this thesis statement would devote a separate body paragraph to each obstacle to getting a job. Each body paragraph would then include examples of one or more immigrants who encountered that obstacle.

Writing the Essay

An essay takes more time to write than a paragraph, but the writing process itself is very similar.

- Generate topic ideas as well as supporting material by freewriting, brainstorming, and clustering.

- Focus your material on one central idea, expressed in a thesis statement.

- Divide your supporting material (examples, facts, details) into separate body paragraphs.

- Arrange your body paragraphs into a logical order, such as a chronological, spatial, or emphatic order.

- Write your first draft without worrying too much about the quality of your writing. Focus more on getting your ideas onto paper. You can improve them later.

Rewriting and Improving the Essay

Once you have a complete draft, consider these questions as you revise your paper.

- Do your opening sentences introduce the topic in a way that will interest a reader?

- Is your thesis sufficiently narrowed? Is it placed at the end of the introductory paragraph?

- Does each paragraph open with a topic sentence that clearly supports the thesis statement?

- Are the supporting facts and examples in each paragraph specific and clear?

- Does each paragraph contain enough examples?

- Are transitions used to move clearly from one idea to another?

- Does the conclusion close the essay in an interesting way?

Application: Working with Essay Form

Read the following student essay and answer the questions at the end.

Lying

My parents are two of the most honest people I have ever met. Ever since I can remember, they have told me that "Honesty is the best policy." My father says that lying leads to only more lying and that telling the truth is exactly the right thing to do. The problem is that I don't think they are right. There are times when the right thing to do is to tell a lie.

For example, sometimes lying can mean the difference between survival and disaster. I have a friend with two daughters, ages three and five. When her husband deserted her, she needed to find a job fast. But there was one problem: Every place where she applied asked if she had ever been convicted of a crime. She told the truth that she had been convicted of selling marijuana years ago, and she was politely shown out the door at Sears, Target, and Walmart. It didn't matter that she hasn't used drugs or alcohol now for over seven years. She needed to feed her children, so on her next job application she lied and got the job. I would have lied too.

Lying is also the right thing to do when you need to spare people any unnecessary pain in an emotional time. For instance, when I was in high school, a friend of mine named Melody died in a car accident, and the police believed drugs were involved. The parents refused to believe that their little girl would ever have taken drugs, but they didn't know everything about their daughter. Several of her friends and I knew that Melody had been using marijuana for a while. She had even tried cocaine a few times, but when her parents talked to us, we told them that she had never tried drugs. What good would telling the truth have done? It would only have hurt her parents more. So we lied.

I've also found that telling the truth can sometimes cause trouble among friends. There have been plenty of times when I have prevented a fight by not telling one friend what another one said about him or her. I've prevented these situations when I felt that the argument between the two was not worth fighting over.

I know that lying is not usually the right answer to a problem. But sometimes honesty isn't either. It seems to me that a person has to think about each situation and not live his or her life by general rules that don't always apply.

1. Underline the thesis statement. Is it sufficiently narrowed for a brief essay? Explain your response.

2. Now underline each topic sentence. Each topic sentence should clearly refer to and support the thesis statement. Explain how each one does so.

3. Look at the introductory sentences before the thesis statement. What function do they serve?

4. Look at the examples in each body paragraph. Which examples are the strongest? Why? Which are the weakest? Why?

5. Consider the organization of the three body paragraphs. Should it be changed at all? Explain why or why not.

6. Look at the concluding paragraph. Does it close the essay effectively? Why or why not?

Proofreading

As with all of your papers, proofread your essay carefully before you submit it.

Chapter 3 Practice Test

I. Review of Chapters One and Two

A. In the following sentences, identify the underlined words by writing one of the following abbreviations above the words: noun (N), pronoun (Pro), verb (V), adjective (Adj), adverb (Adv), conjunction (Conj), preposition (Prep).

1. The <u>soldiers</u> and marines in Iraq did not <u>dress</u> the same as their counterparts in Vietnam.

2. The soldiers and marines in Iraq <u>always</u> looked the same, <u>with</u> nothing extra added or written on their uniforms.

3. In Vietnam, the soldiers and marines were <u>blatantly</u> informal, with all kinds of things written on their <u>dirty</u> helmets and sweat-stained flak jackets.

4. The troops <u>in</u> Vietnam were mostly draftees, <u>so</u> many of them did not want to be there.

5. The troops in Iraq <u>were</u> an all-volunteer army <u>who</u> considered themselves professional.

B. In the following sentences, underline the subjects once and the complete verbs twice. Put parentheses around all prepositional phrases.

6. Two foxes moved silently into the forest.

7. Will Queequeg or Tashtego learn how to harpoon in time?

8. The Grangerfords entered the church and sat a few pews behind the Shepherdsons.

9. The Hopi lived in stable villages, but the Apache tended to migrate.

10. Before Apollo entered his chariot, he covered himself with sunscreen.

C. Compose sentences of your own according to the instructions.

11. Write a simple sentence with two subjects, one verb, and at least one prepositional phrase.

   _____

   _____

12. Write a compound sentence. Use a semicolon, a transitional word, and a comma to join the two clauses.

   _____

   _____

continued

13. Write a complex sentence that ends with a subordinate clause.

_____

_____

14. Write a complex sentence that starts with the subordinator *while*.

_____

_____

15. Write a compound-complex sentence. Use the conjunction *but* and the subordinator *if*.

_____

_____

D. Identify the following items as being correct (C), fused (F), comma splice (CS), or fragment (Frag). Then correct the errors. If a sentence is correct, do nothing to it.

_____ **16.** The little mermaid stared at the menu, she ordered a seafood salad.

_____

_____

_____ **17.** Alexander Skarsgard, who played one of the main characters in an HBO series.

_____

_____

_____ **18.** Iris believed in telling the truth she always admitted her mistakes.

_____

_____

continued

_____ **19.** Although Justin Bieber is not a particularly talented singer.

_____

_____

_____ **20.** Sacagawea showed Lewis and Clark the way, then she regretted having done so.

_____

_____

Chapter 3 Practice Test

II. Chapter Three

A. Underline all infinitive and participial phrases and circle the words they modify.

1. Crossing the English Channel, the Normans conquered England in 1066.

2. Agent 007 could not decide which secret decoder ring to give Agent 99.

3. Not everyone was happy for the man elected president.

4. The sword hanging on the wall once belonged to King Arthur.

5. The package to give to the mail carrier is sitting by the front door.

B. Add infinitive or participial phrases to the following sentences at the places indicated. Use the verbs in parentheses.

6. The puppy ^ belongs to the woman around the block. (find)

   _____

   _____

7. ^ Blanche dimmed all of the lights. (conceal)

   _____

   _____

8. The commercials ^ cost a great deal of money. (broadcast)

   _____

   _____

9. ^ Always check your equipment carefully and always dive with at least one other person. (be)

   _____

   _____

10. ^ Chantal called the police. (alarm)

   _____

   _____

continued

C. Underline the adjective clauses and appositives in the following sentences and circle the words they modify.

11. Dr. Nguyen, a well-known physicist, will discuss quantum mechanics tonight in the auditorium.

12. The arrow that William Tell shot split the apple.

13. *The Catcher in the Rye,* which is a novel by J. D. Salinger, is a classic tale of rebellious youth.

14. Dolores Huerta, an effective organizer, improved the lives of many farmworkers.

15. *The Life of Pi,* which contains many computer-animated scenes, is based on a novel by Yann Martel.

D. Add adjective clauses or appositives to the following sentences and punctuate them correctly.

16. Juliet drove her new car to the costume party.

_____

_____

17. *Scandal* must have made some people in Washington very nervous.

_____

_____

18. The police officer watched the three men enter the bank.

_____

_____

19. Even though many other puppets encouraged him, Elmo refused to go near the garbage can.

_____

_____

continued

20. Plato often discussed the nature of love.

_____

_____

E. Underline and then correct any dangling or misplaced modifiers in the following sentences. Do nothing if a sentence is correct.

21. Rocco read the story to his creative writing class that he had found in his attic.

_____

_____

22. Running out the door, Ruth almost forgot her briefcase.

_____

_____

23. Standing at the top of the hill, the view was magnificent.

_____

_____

24. To get from here to there, asking Mark Twain for directions is recommended.

_____

_____

25. Ms. Schmidt only bought the 1999 Mercedes for two thousand dollars.

_____

_____

26. Thinking it was a peace offering, the giant wooden horse was wheeled into the city.

_____

_____

continued

27. The column of army ants terrified Ricardo and Amanda, swarming over the sweet

potato pie.

_____

_____

28. Frightened by the angry crowd, Moira's hand covered her mouth.

_____

_____

29. Roaming the empty city streets, the zombies were beginning to get seriously bored.

_____

_____

30. The two young boys who were whispering to each other quietly crept toward their

unsuspecting sister.

_____

_____

Lining Up the Parts of a Sentence

The Careful Writer

As you have probably already noticed, effective writing is less a matter of inspiration and more a matter of making innumerable choices and paying careful attention to detail. Strictly speaking, every word in each of your sentences represents a specific choice on your part. Good writers carefully choose words and their positions in sentences, not only to be grammatically correct but also to make their writing clear and concise.

Although close attention to detail alone will not ensure good writing, it does have a number of advantages. The most important reason for you to take care in your writing is to make certain that you communicate your ideas clearly. As you can see from having worked through the last chapter, if your sentences contain misplaced or dangling modifiers, your reader will sometimes be confused about what you mean. In addition, a clear and careful piece of writing in itself creates a good impression, just as a well-tended lawn does. You have probably already found that people are often judged by their writing. If your writing is carefully thought out and presented with an attention to correctness and detail, it will be taken seriously.

Making sure that your sentences are correctly constructed and checking to see that your modifiers clearly and logically modify the right words are two ways of taking care in your writing. In this chapter we will discuss a few others: paying attention to the special relationship between those two most important parts of your sentences, the subjects and verbs; making sure that the pronouns you use are in their correct forms; and checking the connection between your pronouns and the words they stand for.

Subject–Verb Agreement

One reason you need to be able to identify subjects and verbs accurately is that the form of the verb often changes to match the form of its subject. If the subject of your sentence is singular, your verb must be singular. If the subject is plural, your verb must be plural. This matching of the verb and its subject is called **subject–verb agreement.**

You need to pay special attention to subject–verb agreement when you use present tense verbs. **Most present tense verbs that have singular subjects end in "s." Most present tense verbs that have plural subjects do not end in "s."** Here are some examples.

Singular	*Plural*
The dog bark**s**.	The dogs bark.
He walk**s**.	They walk.
It i**s**.	They are.
The man ha**s**.	The men have.
She doe**s**.	They do.

Notice that in each case the verb ends in "s" when the subject is singular. This rule can be confusing because an "s" at the end of a <u>noun</u> almost always means that the noun is plural, but **an "s" at the end of a <u>verb</u> almost always means it is singular.**

 PRACTICE

Change the subjects and verbs in the following sentences from singular to plural or from plural to singular. You may need to add *a, an,* or *the* to some of the sentences.

1. A few days before Halloween, the store runs low on candy.

   A few days before Halloween, the stores run low on candy.

2. The mattress inflates easily.

   _____

3. Every Christmas Eve, my sisters decorate the tree.

   _____

4. In the field, the workers were raising the pole for the circus tent.

   _____

5. My neighbor's car makes too much noise.

Identifying Subjects: A Review

1. Make sure you accurately identify the subject. Sentences usually contain several nouns and pronouns.

 EXAMPLE   The **girls** from the private **school** on the other **side** of **town** often use our **gymnasium**.

This sentence contains five nouns, but only *girls* is the subject.

2. Remember that a noun or pronoun that is part of a prepositional phrase cannot be the subject.

 EXAMPLE   **Each** of the children takes a vitamin with breakfast.

The subject is *Each*, not *children*, because *children* is part of a prepositional phrase.

3. Indefinite pronouns can be subjects. The indefinite pronouns are listed on page 5.

 EXAMPLE   **Everyone** sitting at the tables under the trees has a picnic lunch.

Subject–Verb Agreement: Points to Know

1. Two subjects joined by *and* are plural.

 EXAMPLES
         S   S   V
The **boy** <u>and</u> his **dog** **were** far from home.

    S   S   V
Ham <u>and</u> **rye** **make** a delicious combination.

2. However, if a subject is modified by *each* or *every*, it is singular.

 EXAMPLES
             S   S   V
<u>Every</u> **boy** and **girl** at the party <u>**was**</u> given a present to take home.

             S   S   V
<u>Each</u> **envelope** and **piece** of paper <u>**has**</u> the name of the company on it.

3. The following indefinite pronouns are singular.

anybody	either	neither	one
anyone	everybody	nobody	somebody
anything	everyone	no one	someone
each	everything	nothing	something

 EXAMPLES

S   V
Each of the band members **has** a new uniform.

S   V
Everyone sitting under the trees **is** part of my family.

4. A few nouns and indefinite pronouns, such as *none, some, all, most, more, half,* or *part,* may sometimes be considered plural and sometimes singular, depending on the prepositional phrases that follow them. If the object of the preposition is singular, treat the subject and verb as singular. If the object of the preposition is plural, treat the subject and verb as plural.

 EXAMPLES

                    S   V
(singular)   **None** of the cake **is** left.

                    S   V
(plural)   **None** of the people **are** here.

 PRACTICE   Place an "S" above the subjects and underline the correct verb form in parentheses.

                    S   S
1. A trumpet player and a trombonist (was <u>were</u>) warming up together.

2. The weathered cross with its peeling paint (give gives) visitors to the church a bad impression.

3. Each demerit and low grade (cause causes) a cadet to receive punishment.

4. Forgiveness and compassion (seems seem) to be personal qualities worth cultivating.

5. Some of the citizens of Rome (believes believe) the Visigoths are nomadic, peaceful people.

6. At the summit of the mountain, everyone who arrives (sign **signs**) a logbook.

7. Each winter, the churches in our town (**provide** provides) shelter for homeless people.

8. The murder of a king and the appearance of his ghost (create **creates**) interest during the first scene of the play.

9. A few of the clues for the crime (**lead** leads) to the housekeeper.

10. Marie, as well as her traveling companions, (**is** are) unwilling to face the troll.

---

5. **When subjects are joined by *or* or *nor,* the verb agrees with the closer subject.** If one subject is singular and one is plural, place the plural subject closer to the verb to avoid awkwardness.

 EXAMPLES

                                           S   S   V

(singular subjects)   Neither **Alberto** nor his **sister knows** what to do.

                                     S   S   V

(plural subjects)   Either the **actors** or the **screenwriters have decided** to strike.

                                     S   S   V

(singular and)   Neither **Alberto** nor his **sisters were** at last night's
(plural subjects)   concert.

NOTE: When you have helping verbs in a sentence, the helping verb—not the main verb—changes form.

 EXAMPLES

    HV   S   S   MV

Does Alberto or his **sister** want to go fishing?

    HV   S   S   MV

Have the **actors** or **screenwriters** decided to strike?

6. **Collective nouns usually take the singular form of the verb.** Collective nouns represent groups of people or things, but they are considered singular. Here are some common collective nouns.

audience	crowd	herd
band	family	jury
class	flock	number
committee	government	society
company	group	team

EXAMPLES

> S   V
> The **audience was delighted** when the curtain slowly rose to reveal the orchestra already seated.

> S   V
> My **family goes** to Yellowstone National Park every summer.

7. The relative pronouns *that, which,* and *who* may be either singular or plural. When one of these pronouns is the subject of a verb, you will need to know which word it refers to before you decide whether it is singular or plural.

 EXAMPLES

(singular)	I bought the <u>peach</u> **that was** ripe.
(plural)	I bought the <u>peaches</u> **that were** ripe.
(plural)	Colleen is one of the <u>students</u> **who are** taking flying lessons.
(singular)	Colleen is the only <u>one</u> of the students **who is** taking flying lessons.

 PRACTICE

Place an "S" above the subjects and underline the correct verb form in parentheses.

1. Either pasta or potatoes (goes <u>go</u>) well with veal.

2. A pack of wolves (has have) made a den in our foothills.

3. Either Sandy or her daughters (leave leaves) some fruit at our backdoor each week.

4. Neither my best friend nor my worst enemy (was were) involved in the prank played on the principal.

5. Her trip to Disneyland or her vacation to Nepal (is are) all Amanda thinks about.

6. In that society a jury of one's peers (makes make) the decision.

7. Don is my only friend who still (eat eats) a sirloin steak every three times a week.

8. (Has Have) Mr. Ed or Private Francis said anything to you?

9. A troop of Boy Scouts (meet meets) at our church on Thursdays.

10. Van Gogh is one of the impressionist painters who (is are) currently

featured at the Getty Museum.

---

8. A few nouns that end in "s" are usually considered singular, so they take the singular form of the verb. These nouns include *economics, gymnastics, mathematics, measles, mumps, news, physics,* and *politics.*

 EXAMPLES

         S   V

World **economics** <u>has</u> **been** an important international issue for years.

   S   V

Gymnastics <u>is</u> one of the most popular events in the Olympics.

9. When units of measurement for distance, time, volume, height, weight, money, and so on are used as subjects, they take the singular verb form.

 EXAMPLES

        S   V

Two **teaspoons** of sugar **was** all that the cake recipe called for.

     S V

Five **dollars** **is** too much to pay for a hot dog.

10. In a question or in a sentence that begins with *there* or *here,* the order of the subject and verb is reversed.

 EXAMPLES

   V   S

Was the **bus** on time?

   V   S

Is there a squeaking **wheel** out there somewhere?

        V   S

There **is** an **abundance** of wildflowers in the desert this spring.

      V   S

Here **are** the **keys** to your car.

11. The verb must agree only with the **subject.**

 EXAMPLE

                    S   V

Our biggest **problem is** termites in the attic.

The singular verb form *is* is correct here because the subject is the singular noun *problem.* The plural noun *termites* does not affect the form of the verb.

PRACTICE Place an "S" above the subjects and underline the correct verb form in parentheses.

1. Gymnastics (<u>has</u> have) always been Chelsea's favorite sport.

2. Thirty-six inches of two-by-four boarding (is are) required for the job.

3. The manager's main concern (was were) the players who chewed tobacco during the game.

4. Carlos has found that mathematics (confuses confuse) him, especially if he doesn't study the textbook.

5. (Has Have) economics caused people to avoid talking about the issue?

6. Ten miles of a tortuous trail (winds wind) up that mountain.

7. (Does Do) some of the users seem unable to install Apple's new operating system?

8. There, next to the St. Bernard, (sits sit) a hamster and a gecko.

9. The main topic at Anthony's table (was were) the mosquitos that seemed to be everywhere.

10. Here (goes go) my first attempt to cook a dark chocolate cake.

Section One Review

1. In the present tense, when the subject is a singular noun or a singular pronoun, the verb form usually will end in "s."

2. Subject–verb agreement: points to know

   a. Two subjects joined by *and* are plural.

   b. If a subject is modified by *each* or *every*, it is singular.

   c. Indefinite pronouns are usually singular.

   d. Sometimes nouns and indefinite pronouns like *some, half,* or *part* are considered plural, depending on the prepositional phrases that follow them.

   e. When subjects are joined by *or* or *nor*, the verb agrees with the closer subject. If one subject is singular and one is plural, place the plural subject closer to the verb to avoid awkwardness.

   f. When a collective noun, such as *family* or *group*, is the subject, the singular form of the verb is used.

   g. The relative pronouns *that, which,* and *who* may be either singular or plural, depending upon the word the pronoun refers to.

   h. A few nouns, such as *economics* or *news*, end in "s" but are considered singular.

   i. When the subject is a unit of measurement, such as distance, weight, or money, the singular form of the verb is used.

   j. In a question or in a sentence that begins with *there* or *here*, the verb will often come before the subject.

   k. The verb must agree only with the subject.

Exercise 1A

Circle the subjects and underline the correct verb form in parentheses.

1. (Someone) outside the theater (<u>was</u> were) selling his tickets.

2. Neither the huge rat in the kitchen nor the bats in the upper floors (bothers <u>bother</u>) (Usher) very much.

3. On the Fourth of July, the (Optimists and the Rotary Club) (has <u>have</u>) always presented a patriotic fireworks display.

4. (My family) from the Paris suburbs always (visit <u>visits</u>) our relatives in Mexico on the Day of the Dead.

5. Near the counter at the rear of the store (wait <u>waits</u>) (my brother and his girlfriend) with their new iPhones.

6. A picnic for (kindergarteners) and a subsequent slumber party (<u>takes</u> take) much planning and imagination.

7. (<u>Does</u> Do) a (fifty-pound piece of lead) fall as fast as a (fifty-pound ball of cotton candy?)

8. The sighting of (a wolf and its cubs) (occur <u>occurs</u>) sometimes in the country north of Nome, Alaska.

9. (<u>Has</u> Have) the band of (Mescalero Apaches) met with the governor yet?

10. Each boulder and tree (was <u>were</u>) unique to (John Muir) and (Ansel Adams.)

11. According to the report, (high school gymnastics) (cause <u>causes</u>) more injuries than football.

12. (One of the pigs) in the upcoming truffle-sniffing contest (<u>seems</u> seem) overly aggressive.

13. Three hundred pounds of weight (<u>is</u> are) how much (Natalie) was practicing to lift.

14. Either the (ogre) next door or the (warlock) around the block (<u>owns</u> own) a thumbscrew that you may borrow.

15. Half of the (spectators) in the arena (has <u>have</u>) been booing.

Exercise 1B

Correct any subject–verb agreement errors in the following sentences. If a sentence is correct, do nothing to it. To check your answers, circle the subjects.

1. For the last month, neither my (physician) nor my (acupuncturist) ~~were~~ *was* able to ease the pain in my spine.

2. Everyone in my humanities classes seem to know about the myth of Sisyphus.

3. Each violinist and cellist in the orchestra were trying to get the attention of the conductor.

4. The high cost of airline tickets and hotels cause many of my friends to delay their trips to Greece.

5. She is one of the few rap singers who never uses foul language.

6. That pride of lions are being diminished by poachers.

7. Have the explanation from the president or the newsletter from the faculty helped you make your decision?

8. A student from Mr. Axle's class and another one from Ms. Olsen's class usually places somewhere in the top three.

9. At the site of the bombing, each of the spectators were being interviewed.

10. Homer and his cowchip pitching team helps clean the barn out each month.

11. In Fellini's film somebody with two dogs on a motorcycle race around the town square each night.

12. Fifty tons of crushed rock have been used to fill each hole in the dam.

13. His decision to paint both of his cars black and orange really surprise me.

14. Everything about the Civil War and World War I interest Bob Grant.

15. Here, in good shape, is the Corvette and the Thunderbird I borrowed from your garage last week.

Exercise 1C

Correct all subject–verb agreement errors.

   1. Even though football and wrestling are both physically demanding sports, each one ~~differ~~ *differs* from the other in several ways. 2. For example, both sports requires different ways to train. 3. Football is one of the sports that demand a great deal of size and strength. 4. As a result, most football players I know runs sprints rather than long distances. 5. A player on a football team do not seem to need as much endurance as a wrestler because he is able to rest between plays. 6. In addition, in football a professional player or a college player usually try to gain weight, so he eats as much as he can. 7. Wrestlers, on the other hand, requires more flexibility and definition than mass. 8. And, in contrast to a football player, a wrestler often run long distances to build endurance. 9. Of course, both wrestling and football involves a great deal of contact, but in different ways. 10. There is a lot of bumps and bruises in football. 11. In wrestling, however, a contestant turn and twist his opponent like a pretzel. 12. Finally, a football team act as a group, while wrestlers are individualistic. 13. If the football team fail to score during a game, there is usually several people who can be blamed. 14. If someone loses a wrestling match, there are nobody to blame but the wrestler. 15. So while football and wrestling resembles each other in their physicality, they differ in key details.

Pronoun Agreement and Reference

Pronoun–Antecedent Agreement

Because pronouns stand for or take the place of nouns, it is important that you make it clear in your writing which pronouns stand for which nouns. The noun that the pronoun takes the place of is called the **antecedent. Pronoun–antecedent agreement** refers to the idea that a pronoun must match or "agree with" the noun that it stands for in **person** and in **number**.

Person

Person in pronouns refers to the relationship of the speaker (or writer) to the pronoun. There are three persons: **first person, second person,** and **third person.**

1. **First person** pronouns refer to the person speaking or writing:

Singular	*Plural*
I	we
me	us
my, mine	our, ours

2. **Second person** pronouns refer to the person spoken or written to:

Singular	*Plural*
you	you
your	your
yours	yours

3. **Third person** pronouns refer to the person or thing spoken or written about:

Singular	*Plural*
he, she, it	they
him, her, it	them
his, her, hers, its	their, theirs

Because nouns are always in the third person, pronouns that refer to nouns should also be in the third person. Usually this rule poses no problem, but sometimes writers mistakenly shift from third to second person when they are referring to a noun.

EXAMPLE   When a new **student** first enters the large and crowded registration area, **you** might feel confused and intimidated.

In this sentence, *you* has mistakenly been used to refer to *student*. The mistake occurs because the noun *student* is in the third person, and the pronoun *you* is in the second person. There are two ways to correct the sentence:

1. You can change the second person pronoun *you* to a third person pronoun.

EXAMPLE   When a new **student** first enters the large and crowded registration area, **he or she** might feel confused and intimidated.

2. You can change the noun *student* to the second person pronoun *you*.

EXAMPLE   When **you** first enter the large and crowded registration area, **you** might feel confused and intimidated.

Here's another incorrect sentence.

EXAMPLE   Most **people** can stay reasonably healthy if **you** watch **your** diet and exercise several times a week.

One way to correct this sentence is to change *you* to *they* and *your* to *their* so that they agree with *people*.

EXAMPLE   Most **people** can stay reasonably healthy if **they** watch **their** diets and exercise several times a week.

PRACTICE   Correct any errors in pronoun person in the following sentences. When you correct the pronoun, you also may need to change the verb.

1. Whenever anyone passes the Sweet and Crispy donut shop, ~~you~~ *he or she* will want to stop and enter it.

2. Many people today are worried about their weight, so ~~you~~ *They* watch those diet ads on television.

3. When a person signs up for one of those miracle diets, ~~you need~~ *He or she needs* to check the cost of it carefully.

4. Nevertheless, people can find diets that will effectively cause ~~you~~ *Them* to lose some weight.

5. A prospective dieter should be aware that an exercise program is also needed to help ~~you~~ *Them* lose weight in a healthful way.

Number

Errors in number are the most common pronoun–antecedent errors. To make pronouns agree with their antecedents in **number,** use singular pronouns to refer to singular nouns and plural pronouns to refer to plural nouns. The following guidelines will help you avoid errors in number.

1. Uses plural pronouns to refer to words joined by *and* unless the words are modified by *each* or *every.*

 EXAMPLE

General Ulysses S. Grant and General Dwight D. Eisenhower led **their** armies to victory.

2. Use singular pronouns to refer to the following.

anybody	either	neither	one
anyone	everybody	nobody	somebody
anything	everyone	no one	someone
each	everything	nothing	something

 EXAMPLES

Everything was in **its** place.

Neither of the girls wanted to give up **her** place in line.

One of the fathers was yelling loudly at **his** son throughout the game.

NOTE: In spoken English, the plural pronouns *they, them,* and *their* are often used to refer to the antecedents *everyone* or *everybody.* However, in written English the singular pronoun is still more commonly used.

 EXAMPLE

Everybody at the game cheered for **his** favorite team.

3. In general, use singular pronouns to refer to collective nouns.

 EXAMPLE

The **troop** of soldiers had almost reached **its** camp when the blizzard started.

4. When antecedents are joined by *or* or *nor,* use a pronoun that agrees with the closer antecedent.

 EXAMPLE

Neither **Chris** nor **Craig** wanted to spend **his** Saturday mowing the lawn.

NOTE: If one antecedent is singular and one is plural, place the plural antecedent last to avoid awkwardness. If one antecedent is female and one is male, rewrite the sentence to avoid awkwardness.

EXAMPLES

(awkward)   Either the **members** of the council or the **mayor** will send **his** regrets.

(rewritten)   Either the **mayor** or the **members** of the council will send **their** regrets.

(awkward)   Either **Mary** or **Ruben** will lend you **his** watch.

(rewritten)   You may borrow a watch from either Mary or Ruben.

PRACTICE

Correct any pronoun–antecedent errors in the following sentences. When you correct a pronoun, you may also need to change the verb. Not all sentences will contain errors.

1. If an employee wants to get ahead at that company, ~~you have~~ *he or she has* to be very competent and aggressive.

2. Anyone starting a car should not forget to check their rear view mirror.

3. When parents read a story by the Brothers Grimm, ~~you~~ *They* might scare ~~your~~ *Their* children.

4. The team from Atlanta was surprised when a fan objected to their "tomahawk chop."

5. Each police officer and sheriff has turned on their siren.

6. Everyone was laughing at the dog that was trying to catch its own tail.

7. After a patient sees that doctor a few times, ~~you~~ *They* might consider changing clinics.

8. Wolf Blitzer asked the camera operator to quit popping their gum.

9. When people drive on our street, ~~you~~ *They* need to watch out for children.

10. Neither Juanita nor Donna wanted to get their flu shot.

Sexist Language

In the past it was traditional to use masculine pronouns when referring to singular nouns whose gender could be either masculine or feminine. A good example is the sentence *A **person** should stop delivery of **his** newspaper before **he** leaves on a trip of more than a few days*. Although the noun *person* could be either masculine or feminine, masculine pronouns like *he* or *his* tended to be used in a case like this one.

Because women make up over 50 percent of the English-speaking population, they have been justifiably dissatisfied with this tradition. The problem is that the English language does not contain a singular personal pronoun that can refer to either sex at the same time in the way that the forms of *they* can.

The solutions to this problem can prove awkward. One of the solutions is to use feminine pronouns as freely as masculine ones to refer to singular nouns whose gender could be masculine or feminine. Either of the following sentences using this solution is acceptable.

> A **person** should stop delivery on **her** newspaper before **she** leaves on a trip of more than a few days.

> A **person** should stop delivery on **his** newspaper before **he** leaves on a trip of more than a few days.

Another solution is to change *his* to *his or her* and *he* to *he or she*. Then the sentence would look like this:

> A **person** should stop delivery on **his or her** newspaper before **he or she** leaves on a trip of more than a few days.

As you can see, this solution does not result in a very graceful sentence. An alternative is to use *her/his* and *she/he*, but the result would be about the same. Sometimes a better solution is to change a singular antecedent to a plural one and use the forms of *they*, which can refer to either gender. That would result in a sentence like this:

> **People** should stop delivery of **their** newspapers before **they** leave on a trip of more than a few days.

This sentence is less awkward and just as fair. Finally, in some situations, the masculine pronoun alone will be appropriate, and in others the feminine pronoun alone will be. Here are two such sentences:

> Each of the hockey players threw **his** false teeth into the air after the victory. (The hockey team is known to be all male.)

> The last runner on the relay team passed **her** opponent ten yards before the finish line. (All members of the relay team are female.)

Whatever your solutions to this problem, it is important that you be logical and correct in your pronoun–antecedent agreement in addition to being fair.

Unclear Pronoun Reference

Sometimes, even though a pronoun appears to agree with an antecedent, it is not clear exactly which noun in the sentence is the antecedent. And sometimes a writer will use a pronoun that does not clearly refer to any antecedent at all. The following two points will help you use pronouns correctly.

1. A pronoun should refer to a specific antecedent.

 EXAMPLE

Mr. Mellon told **Larry** that **he** could take a vacation in late August.

In this sentence, *he* could refer to *Mr. Mellon* or to *Larry.* To correct this problem, you can eliminate the pronoun.

EXAMPLE

Mr. Mellon told Larry that **Larry** could take his vacation in late August.

Or you can revise the sentence so that the pronoun clearly refers to only one antecedent.

EXAMPLES

Mr. Mellon told **Larry** to take **his** vacation in late August.

OR

Mr. Mellon told Larry, "Take your vacation in late August."

Here is another example:

EXAMPLE

Every time **Patricia** looked at the **cat, she** whined.

In this sentence, the pronoun *she* could refer to *Patricia* or the *cat.* The pronoun reference needs to be clarified.

EXAMPLES

Patricia whined every time **she** looked at the cat.

OR

The **cat** whined every time Patricia looked at **her.**

PRACTICE

Revise the following sentences so that each pronoun refers to a specific antecedent.

1. Franco told his father that he needed to shave before going out to dinner.

   Franco told his father to shave before going out to dinner.

2. General Eisenhower and Field Marshall Montgomery met to discuss his plans for the invasion.

3. No matter how many times Sheila tried to talk to her mother, she always cried.

   _____

   _____

4. The children spoke rudely to their mother and then gave her their report cards; later, she discussed them with her husband.

   _____

   _____

5. Susie received a kitten from her aunt and a puppy from her mother at

   Christmas, but she refused to play with it.

   _____

   _____

---

2. <u>Pronouns should not refer to implied or unstated antecedents.</u> Be especially careful with the pronouns *this, that, which,* and *it.*

EXAMPLE   My baseball coach made us go without dinner if we lost a game; **this** was unfair.

In this sentence, there is no specific antecedent for the pronoun *this* to refer to. The following sentence clarifies the pronoun reference.

EXAMPLE   My baseball coach made us go without dinner if we lost a game; **this punishment** was unfair.

Sometimes a pronoun refers to a noun that is only implied in the first part of the sentence.

EXAMPLE   Mrs. Brovelli is a poet, **which** she does some of every day.

In this sentence, *which* apparently stands for "writing poetry," which is implied in the noun *poet;* however, there is no specific noun for the pronoun *which* to stand for. The faulty pronoun reference can be cleared up in several ways.

EXAMPLES   Mrs. Brovelli is a poet, and **she writes** poetry every day.

Mrs. Brovelli is a poet **who writes** poetry every day.

PRACTICE   Revise the following sentences so that each pronoun refers to a specific, not an implied or unstated, antecedent. To correct the sentence, you may have to eliminate the pronoun altogether.

1. Karen has always refused to eat the sweet potatoes at Thanksgiving dinner, which has insulted her grandmother.

   Karen's grandmother feels insulted when Karen refuses to eat the sweet

   potatoes at Thanksgiving dinner (Other correct answers are possible.)

2. Bertha disliked visiting her uncle, and this made him unhappy.

   _____

   _____

3. Tar was getting all over his motorcycle, and its windshield had cracked, but Randy said he was not worried about it.

   _____

   _____

4. Dr. Freud daydreamed as he smoked his cigar, which caused him to worry.

   _____

   _____

5. Southern California has beaches for summer surfing and mountains for winter skiing. This is why I want to move there.

   _____

   _____

Reflexive and Intensive Pronouns

The reflexive and intensive pronouns are those that end in *self* or *selves*. The singular pronouns end in *self,* and the plural ones end in *selves.*

Singular	*Plural*
myself	ourselves
yourself	yourselves
himself	themselves
herself	
itself	
oneself	

These are the only reflexive and intensive forms. Avoid nonstandard forms like *hisself, ourselfs, theirselves,* or *themselfs.*

The **reflexive pronouns** are used to reflect the action of a verb back to the subject.

 EXAMPLE   Amos gave **himself** a bloody nose when he tried to slap a mosquito.

The **intensive pronouns** emphasize or intensify a noun or another pronoun in the sentence.

 EXAMPLE   Let's have **Estella Cordova herself** show us how to cross-examine a witness in court.

To help you use intensive and reflexive pronouns correctly, remember these three points.

1. Do not use a reflexive pronoun unless it is reflecting the action of a verb back to a subject.

2. Do not use an intensive pronoun unless the sentence contains a noun or pronoun for it to emphasize or intensify.

3. In general, do not use a reflexive or intensive pronoun where a personal pronoun is called for. For example, reflexive and intensive pronouns are never used as subjects.

EXAMPLES   (incorrect)   Tim's mother and **myself** often go shopping together on Saturdays.

(correct)   Tim's mother and **I** often go shopping together on Saturdays.

(incorrect)   The other employees at the restaurant gave Carmen and **myself** large bouquets of flowers on the anniversary of our first year there.

(correct)   The other employees of the restaurant gave Carmen and **me** large bouquets of flowers on the anniversary of our first year there.

⊚ **PRACTICE**   Correct any errors in the use of reflexive or intensive pronouns in the following sentences.

1. The teacher and his students cleaned up the spilled water by ~~theirself~~. *themselves*

2. Paris and ~~myself~~ *I* chose the apple to give to the most beautiful goddess.

3. We argued ~~among ourselfs~~ *with eachother* about what choice Paris would make.

4. The Republicans ~~and himself~~ could not agree on the budget.

5. The principal gave the awards to ~~the third graders and myself.~~ *myself and the third graders*

⊚ **PRACTICE**   Correct any errors in pronoun reference or in the use of reflexive and intensive pronouns in the following sentences. Not all sentences will contain errors.

1. I once ate out at least five times a week, but I don't go to ~~them~~ *restaurants* very much

    anymore.

2. As finals approached, Burt and ~~myself~~ *I* started drinking many bottles of

    ~~those energy~~ *Redbull* drinks a day.

3. The stars were aligned in never-before-seen formations, and Pluto was

    no longer considered a planet; this bothered many astrologers.

4. Katrina asked Paula to go rock climbing with Stephanie and ~~her~~ *them* even

    though Paula doesn't really like her.

5. Dickson himself stood up and told Sandra that All Night Fitness would be

    the best choice.

6. Terry wanted to play reggae music for his pool party, but he couldn't get

    it to work.

7. The instructor droned on for two hours about unclear pronouns, which bored the entire class.

8. Oprah and the ~~people in her~~ audience agreed among ~~theirself~~ themselves that Dr. Phil had not been very wise for a change.

9. When Ken bought a new car and ~~then~~ a new GPS system, Barbie decided to buy one for herself.

10. Although he was ill with the flu and ~~most~~ likely contagious, Sam shook hands with Leon.

Section Two Review

1. The **antecedent** is the word a pronoun stands for.

2. A pronoun must agree with its **antecedent** in **person** and in **number.**

3. Use a plural pronoun to refer to antecedents joined by *and.*

4. Use a singular pronoun to refer to an **indefinite pronoun.**

5. Use a singular pronoun to refer to a **collective noun.**

6. When you refer to two antecedents that are joined by *either/or, neither/nor, or, nor,* or *not only/but also,* your pronoun usually should agree with the closer word.

7. Make sure a pronoun refers to a specific antecedent in its sentence or in the previous sentence.

8. Be sure that your pronoun does not refer to an implied or unstated antecedent.

9. A **reflexive pronoun** reflects the action of a verb back to the subject.

10. An **intensive pronoun** emphasizes or intensifies a noun or pronoun in the sentence.

11. Do not use a reflexive or intensive pronoun when a personal pronoun is called for.

Exercise 2A

Underline the correct pronouns in parentheses.

1. The stand-up comedian told a lot of crass jokes, but we didn't appreciate (it / <u>them</u>) at all.

2. Each participant at the symposium smiled because (he or she / they) liked the subject being discussed.

3. When the team arrived in New York, (it / they) headed for the nearest hotel.

4. Either the first grade or the second grade will have (its / their) classroom painted this summer.

5. A person in the audience at the concert had lost (his or her / their) car keys.

6. Trying to fix our computer problem, we found (ourself / ourselfs / ourselves) unable to understand the magnitude of the problem.

7. As a person passes through the entrance to Japan's new Olympic stadium (you / he or she / they) will be astonished at the imaginative design.

8. We have spent hours training our dogs, yet neither the rat terrier nor the papillon will come when we call (it / them).

9. Although all of the witnesses had told the judge that Jesse was innocent, the judge would not take (his or her / their) testimony seriously.

10. Every woman in the city had (her / their) opinion about the wooden horse.

11. The Trojans asked (themselves / themselves / theirselfs) whether they should trust this gift from the Greeks.

12. When customers enter that electronics store, (you / he or she / they) will see a giant aquarium.

13. Each citizen in the city expected (his or her / their) opinion to be respected.

14. Most of the triathletes found that (he or she / they) had underestimated the difficulty of the course.

15. The bee outside my window or the spider on the wall will soon find (its / their) way into my new story.

Exercise 2B

Correct all errors in pronoun usage in the following sentences. Do nothing if the sentence is correct.

1. When a skier approaches the lip of a double-diamond slope, ~~you~~ *he or she* might have second

   thoughts about continuing.

2. The firefighters' union was able to bargain for a raise for their membership.

3. Anybody who wants to protect their skin from cancer should use sunblock.

4. At the faculty gathering, a committee representing the concerns of the nonfaculty employees

   presented their ideas.

5. Either the two Doberman pinschers next door or the Labrador retriever down the street

   barks whenever they hear a car drive by.

6. If a person wants to visit Niagara Falls, you should bring along a raincoat.

7. Since our neighbors did not want to participate in a block party, we had a barbecue in our

   backyard by ourselfs.

8. My sister and I went to Pollos Maria restaurant yesterday, which is my favorite food.

9. Whenever Mr. Ed and myself go for a ride, we have a long conversation.

10. Mr. Miyamoto removed his Picasso from the wall and then sprayed it with green paint.

11. Many neighbors complained about his messy yard, but this did not bother Makayla.

12. When someone vandalized the local church, the minister said that we should forgive them.

13. Marianne knew that Sylvia and herself would have to work hard if they planned to become

    famous poets.

14. Susan stopped smoking because she found out she was pregnant, which pleased her friends.

15. Anyone who regularly drives through the Mojave Desert knows that you should always

    carry a supply of extra water.

Exercise 2C

In the following paragraph, correct any errors in pronoun agreement or reference or in the use of intensive and reflexive pronouns.

1. When I moved from the suburban city of Brea to the rural community in Poway, ~~you~~ *I* could immediately tell the two places were very different yet also similar in some respects. **2.** In Brea, houses sit right next to each other on small lots, and many kids of the same age live on the same street, and this makes it easy to meet people. **3.** Almost every family in the neighborhood have young children of similar ages. **4.** They all play out in the street, so you can easily make friends. **5.** In Poway, however, each home is built on a one-acre lot, and they are set back from the street. **6.** In spite of this isolation, the kids welcomed my brother and myself when we arrived. **7.** I soon discovered that the neighborhood kids are extremely nice. **8.** There is a neighborhood touch football team with their own t-shirts. **9.** I have joined them, and you compete against a team from another street. **10.** So I have found that people in Poway are as friendly as in the Brea neighborhood. **11.** In addition, even though the Brea school I attended has 500 students and the Poway school has 1,500, this did not matter very much. **12.** At both schools, every teacher goes out of their way to help all students. **13.** One surprising similarity between Poway and Brea, one that many people might not expect, concerns its wildlife. **14.** In Brea, coyotes will come from the canyon at night looking for food, sometimes hunting for neighborhood cats, so if residents leave a cat outside, they might be killed. **15.** Similarly, since Poway is located in the country, a coyote pack often roams the streets at night, and they also have taken many cats. **16.** Brea and Poway, therefore, are different, but not as different as you might think as first.

Pronoun Case

Pronouns, like verbs, can appear in a variety of different forms, depending on how they function in a sentence. For example, the pronoun that refers to the speaker in a sentence may be written as *I, me, my,* or *mine*. These different spellings are the result of what is called **pronoun case.**

The three pronoun cases for English are the **subjective,** the **objective,** and the **possessive.**

Subjective Case

Singular	Plural
I	we
you	you
he, she, it	they
who	who

Objective Case

Singular	Plural
me	us
you	you
him, her, it	them
whom	whom

Possessive Case

Singular	Plural
my, mine	our, ours
your, yours	your, yours
his, her, hers, its	their, theirs
whose	whose

Subjective Pronouns

The subjective pronouns are *I, we, you, he, she, it, they,* and *who*. They are used in two situations.

1. Subjective pronouns are used as subjects of sentences.

 EXAMPLES

    s
I will return the car on Monday.

    s
They are trying to outwit me.

2. Subjective pronouns are used when they follow linking verbs. Because the linking verb <u>identifies</u> the pronoun after it with the subject, the pronoun must be in the same case as the subject.

 EXAMPLES

s
It was **she** who won the award for being the best-dressed mud wrestler. (The subjective pronoun *she* is <u>identified</u> with the subject *it* by the linking verb *was*.)

s
That was **I** you saw rowing across the lake yesterday.

s
It was **they** who caused the huge traffic jam.

Objective Pronouns

The **objective pronouns** are *me, us, you, him, her, it, them,* and *whom*. They are used in three situations.

1. Objective pronouns are used as objects of prepositions.

 EXAMPLES

Sally loved the chrysanthemums that Mr. Kim had given <u>to **her.**</u>

The difficulties <u>between Samantha and **me**</u> continued into the fall.

2. Objective pronouns are used as direct objects of action verbs. The noun or pronoun that receives the action of the action verb is called the **direct object.**

For example, in the simple sentence *Tuan visited Serena yesterday,* the verb is *visited,* an action verb. The direct object of *visited* is *Serena* because *Serena* receives the action of the verb *visited.* If you substitute a pronoun for *Serena,* it must be the objective pronoun *her—Tuan visited **her** yesterday.*

 EXAMPLES

Brenda married **him** on March 7, 1987.

Last summer Joan beat **me** at tennis every time we played.

Both classes helped clean up the park, and the city rewarded **them** with a picnic.

3. Objective pronouns are used as indirect objects. The **indirect object** indicates **to whom** or **for whom** (or **to what** or **for what**) **an action is directed,** but the prepositions *to* and *for* are left out.

 EXAMPLES

(prepositional phrase)   He threw the ball **to her.**

(indirect object)   He threw **her** the ball.

In the first sentence, *her* is the object of the preposition *to*. In the second sentence, the *to* is omitted and the pronoun is moved, making *her* the indirect object. In both sentences, the direct object is *ball*. Here are other examples.

 EXAMPLES

She had already given **me** two chances to make up for my mistakes.

The architect showed **them** a picture of how the new city hall would look.

PRACTICE

In the blanks, identify the underlined pronouns as subjective (Sub) or objective (Obj).

Sub   **1.** Last night <u>I</u> read the first chapter of *The Inferno*.

_____   **2.** Bill Gates told <u>me</u> that I could borrow his beach house at Malibu.

_____   **3.** Has <u>he</u> returned your new Audi yet?

_____   **4.** They fired <u>him</u> for telling racist jokes.

_____   **5.** The Cretan stranger told <u>them</u> that they would need a string for the labyrinth.

_____   **6.** Lily Tomlin knew as a girl that <u>she</u> could make people laugh.

_____   **7.** When he chose the wrong woman, the goddess told him <u>he</u> would regret it.

_____   **8.** Gina showed <u>her</u> how to use the iTunes Radio feature.

_____   **9.** <u>I</u> was glad to hear my brother was returning from Afghanistan.

_____   **10.** My professor told <u>me</u> why John Wilkes Booth had assassinated President Lincoln.

Possessive Pronouns

The **possessive pronouns** are *my, mine, our, ours, your, yours, his, her, hers, its, their, theirs,* and *whose*. They are used in two situations.

1. <u>Possessive pronouns are used as adjectives to indicate possession.</u>

 EXAMPLES

The old sailor had turned up **his** collar against the wind.

The weary travelers shuffled off to **their** rooms.

The polar bear constantly paced up and down **its** enclosure.

NOTE: The contraction *it's* means "it is." The word *its* is the only possessive form for *it*. (In fact, you do not use apostrophes with any of the possessive pronouns.)

2. Some possessive pronouns indicate possession without being used as adjectives. In this case, they may be used as subjects or objects.

EXAMPLE   I had to borrow Zan's flashlight because **mine** was lost.

Here the possessive pronoun *mine* is the subject of its clause.

EXAMPLE   The Chin house is large, but **yours** is cozy.

In this example, *yours* is the subject of its clause.

EXAMPLE   He didn't have any change for a phone call because he had given **his** to the children begging on the street.

Here the possessive pronoun *his* is a direct object.

Common Sources of Errors in Pronoun Case

Compound Constructions

Compound subjects and objects often cause problems when they include pronouns. If your sentence includes a compound construction, be sure to use the correct pronoun case.

EXAMPLES

(compound subject)	**Sandra and <u>she</u>** will return the car on Monday.
(compound after linking verb)	That was **my friend and <u>I</u>** whom you saw on the news.
(compound object of a preposition)	They awarded first place trophies **to both Dolores and <u>me</u>.**
(compound direct object)	Julio's boss fired **Mark and <u>him</u>** yesterday.
(compound indirect object)	She had already given <u>**him and me**</u> two chances to make up our minds.

In most cases, you can use a simple test to check whether you have chosen the right pronoun case when you have a compound construction. Simply remove one of the subjects or objects so that only one pronoun is left. For example, is this sentence correct? *Our host gave **Erin and I** a drink.* Test it by dropping *Erin and. Our host gave **I** a drink.* Now you can see that the *I* should be *me* because it is an object (an indirect object). The correct sentence should read: *Our host gave **Erin and me** a drink.*

PRACTICE   Underline the correct pronoun in parentheses.

1. The other science teacher and (<u>I</u> me) will take our students to the Museum of Science and Industry in Chicago.

2. Sergeant Ayers told my friends and (I me) that Norman Mailer had died.

3. A disagreement arose between the other contestants and (she her).

4. Before the Battle of Bull Run, Roderick and (he him) argued over the drum.

5. Fergal offered to take pictures of the tour guide and (they them) kissing the Blarney Stone.

6. Guinevere told Arthur that she wanted to repair the friendship between Lancelot and (he him).

7. Zeus and Hera have invited you and (I me) for a feast of ambrosia, the nectar of the gods.

8. Henry Ford insisted that it was (he him) who developed the assembly line.

9. Flora and (I me) discussed the impasse between the Republicans and Democrats over the budget.

10. The guide showed the other travelers and (she her) the site of Harriet Tubman's home.

Who and *Whom*

When to use *who* or *whom* is a mystery to many writers, but you should have no problem with these pronouns if you remember two simple rules.

1. Use the subjective pronoun *who* or *whoever* if it is used as the subject of a verb.

2. Use the objective pronoun *whom* or *whomever* if it is not used as the subject of a verb.

 EXAMPLES   After leaving the airport, I followed the man **who** had taken my bags. (*Who* is the subject of *had taken*.)

The letter was sent to the person **whom** we had decided to hire. (*Whom* is not the subject of a verb.)

Please give the money to **whoever** needs it. (*Whoever* is the subject of *needs*.)

PRACTICE   Underline the correct pronoun in parentheses.

1. The corporals wondered (who <u>whom</u>) the lieutenant would promote to sergeant.

2. The commander of the Spanish explorers asked the Aztecs (who whom) had greeted him if he could speak to their leader.

3. The head of the CSI unit wanted to speak to anyone (who whom) the suspect had threatened.

4. They took DNA samples of (whoever whomever) had been near the scene.

5. The investigator gave a lie detector test to (whoever whomever) she suspected of the crime.

Comparisons

When a pronoun is used in a comparison, you often need to supply the implied words in order to know what pronoun case to use. For example, in the sentence *My brother cannot skate as well as I*, the implied words are the verb *can skate: My brother cannot skate as well as I [can skate]*.

 EXAMPLE   The police officer allowed my friend to leave the scene sooner than **me.**

You can tell that *me* is the correct case in this sentence when you supply the implied words:

 EXAMPLE   The police officer allowed my friend to leave the scene sooner than **[she allowed]** me **[to leave].**

 PRACTICE   Underline the correct pronoun in parentheses.

1. Myra was better than (<u>I</u> me) in the Internet game *Words with Friends*.

2. After Brad spoke to the director, the director chose (I me) over Rebecca.

3. Sylvester Stallone told the two weightlifters that he could lift more weight than (they them).

4. The teacher gave Lana a higher course grade than (I me) even though we had both received the same test scores.

5. Irving went as Frankenstein, and Ernestine went as Cruella DeVille, but he was not nearly as scary as (she her).

Appositives

As you will remember from Chapter Three, an appositive is a word group containing a noun or pronoun that renames another noun or pronoun. When the appositive contains a **pronoun** that does the renaming, be sure that the pronoun is in the same case as the word it renames.

 EXAMPLE   Some team members—Joe, Frank, and **I**—were late for practice.

Here *I* is in the subjective case because the appositive *Joe, Frank, and I* renames the word *members,* the subject of the sentence.

 EXAMPLE   When the show is over, please send your review to the producers, Mark and **her.**

Here *her* is in the objective case because the appositive *Mark and her* renames *producers,* the object of the preposition *to.*

 PRACTICE   Underline the correct pronoun in parentheses.

1. Joan gave the trick-or-treaters—Robert, Finn, and (I <u>me</u>)—some cookies.

2. The bouncers stared at the two people who had just walked in, Rambo and (I me).

3. The outraged customers, Mick and (he him), left the pub and headed home.

4. The veterinarian selected the best puppy for his favorite friends, Maria and (she her).

5. The finalists in the lottery—Tessie, Old Man Warner, and (I me)—did not act very excited.

PRACTICE   Underline the correct pronoun form in parentheses.

1. The TV commentator wanted to interview the woman (<u>who</u> whom) had given first aid to the bomb victim.

2. Zerkon knew that no one had as many magical powers as (he him).

3. The practical jokers—Campbell, Vera, and (I me)—hid behind the bushes to see who would try to pick up the wallet.

4. Have the other coaches and (she her) been warned about the approaching storm?

5. The princess would give the silver key to (whoever whomever) was wearing the pink soccer jersey.

6. The wound to Achilles' heel was a horrible blow to two people, Athena and (I me).

7. Send the Mad Hatter and (she her) to the Queen's palace for the beheading.

8. Because Cyndy always arrives at work early, it was (she her) who received the raise.

9. In the chewing tobacco section of the store, we saw the bluegrass fiddler (who whom) we had heard on the radio.

10. Since she practices more than (he him), the concert committee offers her more first positions than (he him) during performances.

Section Three Review

1. The **subjective pronouns** are used in two ways:

   a. As the subjects of sentences

   b. After linking verbs

2. The **objective pronouns** are used in three ways:

   a. As objects of prepositions

   b. As direct objects of action verbs

   c. As indirect objects

3. The **possessive pronouns** are used in two ways:

   a. As adjectives to modify nouns to indicate possession

   b. As subjects and objects

4. Some common sources of errors in pronoun case:

   a. Pronouns in compound constructions

   b. The use of the pronouns *who, whom, whoever,* and *whomever*

   c. Pronouns in comparisons

   d. Pronouns in appositives

Exercise 3A

Underline the correct pronoun form in parentheses.

1. Batman was worried about the Batcycle because (<u>its</u> it's) back tire was low.

2. My father is concerned about the troublesome issue between you and (I me).

3. Irene gave Pavlov and (she her) a bloodhound as a wedding gift.

4. Was it (he him) (who whom) threw rotten tomatoes when Barry Manilow stepped on stage?

5. Kelly's new pet rat seems to like Danny more than (she her).

6. Dr. Jekyll told no one except Dr. Bruce Banner and (we us) about his amazing formula.

7. The physicist (who whom) the anthropologist detested would not stop talking about quarks.

8. Can Dulcinea and (she her) help Don Quixote choose a better horse?

9. The orca was sheltering (it's its) newborn from the white shark.

10. Mireya types on her laptop much faster than (I me).

11. The gold medals will go to two people—(whoever whomever) makes more points and (whoever whomever) shows the most creativity.

12. Otto will be showing his World War II mementos to you and (I me).

13. Henny Penny told only two others, the frog and (she her), about the sky.

14. When the moon rover started (its it's) journey over the crater, Sara and (I me) smiled.

15. The three goddesses—Aphrodite, Venus, and (she her)—were amazed at how much they resembled each other.

Exercise 3B

Correct any pronoun errors in the following sentences. Some sentences may not contain errors.

1. Our parents always wanted my brother Chad and ~~I~~ *me* to have happy lives.

2. Have Maya and her decided which track event to compete in?

3. Has Little Bo Peep divulged who she saw sneaking around her sheep?

4. Inside the walls of Fort Sumter, Beauregard and me could see the men were nervous.

5. General Custer asked two scouts, Prairie Bob and he, to check around Little Big Horn.

6. It's true that Aphrodite looked at the apple in Paris's hand and admired it's shine.

7. The butler smiled at the sculptor and I when we asked him about the missing parts of

   the statue.

8. The Australian aborigines and we went looking for koalas.

9. The old rock star who we recognized at the café was glad to give us autographs.

10. After taking square dance lessons, Tex and Lynette could do-si-do and allemande-left better

    than them.

11. The river was between the Spartans and us before the battle.

12. Because it's looking old and faded, the aircraft carrier USS *Midway* will be repainted at it's

    berth in San Diego Harbor.

13. Roberto told Camilla that the spacecraft him and her were looking at could not be real.

14. The server was insulted because whomever had eaten at the table had not left a tip.

15. Billie turned and walked away when Miles asked an unknown singer rather than her to join

    him on stage.

Correct any errors in pronoun case in the following paragraph.

1. There is such a big difference between the life my partner and ~~me~~ *I* live now and the one we lived five years ago. **2.** People whom knew us back then do not even recognize us now. **3.** Its hard to believe that just five years ago we were fully into our drug addiction. **4.** Nobody knows better than me that I looked pretty bad, and my partner looked even worse. **5.** In fact, there were times when my partner and me would not bathe for weeks. **6.** Its accurate to say that us as well as all of our crack-addict friends looked bad and smelled bad. **7.** Today, though, us former addicts—especially my partner and me—really are "clean" and sober. **8.** We dress like respectable citizens rather than like someone who a person would want to avoid. **9.** We also live in a clean, three-bedroom house with a well-kept yard. **10.** When we were drug addicts, few people in our town lived worse than my partner and me. For a while we were homeless, so some other addicts let us live in a tent in a canyon with they and their dog. **11.** We befriended whoever we could, usually people just like we. **12.** Of course, my poor parents didn't know what to say. **13.** Sometimes my dad would offer help, but they—both my mom and him—were afraid of how I would react if they criticized us. **14.** After a while, them as well as my brothers and sisters wouldn't even invite us over for Thanksgiving. **15.** All that has changed, however. Ever since my partner and me finally entered a twelve-step program and got clean and sober, our lives have completely turned around. **16.** People whom used to avoid us now invite my partner and I into their homes. **17.** We both love our sobriety, and we are grateful for it's many blessings.

Sentence Practice: Using Transitions

Writers use certain words and phrases to indicate the relationships among the ideas in their sentences and paragraphs. These words and phrases provide links between ideas, leading a reader from one idea to another smoothly. They show relationships like time, addition, or contrast. Consider this paragraph from Rachel Carson's *Edge of the Sea*:

> **When** the tide is rising the shore is a place of unrest, with the surge leaping high over jutting rocks **and** running in lacy cascades of foam over the landward side of massive boulders. **But** on the ebb it is more peaceful, **for then** the waves do not have behind them the push of the inward pressing tides. There is no particular drama about the turn of the tide, **but presently** a zone of wetness shows on the gray rock slopes, **and** offshore the incoming swells begin to swirl **and** break over hidden ledges. **Soon** the rocks that the high tide had concealed rise into view and glisten with the wetness left on them by the receding water.

Because she is writing about a process, most of Rachel Carson's transitional words indicate a relationship in time (*when, then, presently, soon*). But she also uses transitional words that indicate contrast (*but*), cause (*for*), and addition (*and*). As you can see, she uses these expressions to lead her readers smoothly from one idea to another.

The sentence combining exercises in this chapter are designed to give you practice in using transitional words and phrases to link your ideas. Try to use as many different ones as you can. For your convenience, here is a list of commonly used transitional words and phrases.

- Time: *then, soon, first, second, finally, meanwhile, next, at first, in the beginning*

- Contrast: *yet, but, however, instead, otherwise, on the other hand, on the contrary*

- Addition: *and, also, besides, furthermore, in addition, likewise, moreover, similarly*

- Cause–effect: *for, because, consequently, so, therefore, hence, thus, as a result*

- Example: *for example, for instance, that is, such as*

- Conclusion: *thus, hence, finally, generally, as a result, in conclusion*

⊙ **PRACTICE**   Add transitions to the following sentences.

1. My good friend Jaime dislikes many spices. _____, he cannot

   stand coriander.

2. Daniel saw a bear in the middle of the trail. _____, he reached for his

   flintlock rifle.

3. Cher excels at dancing. _____, she acts and sings well.

4. Fidel kept interrupting his teacher in his humanities class. _____,

   he was dropped from the class.

5. Brigitte thought that she should choose the Chardonnay. _____,

   she preferred red wines.

Sentence Combining Exercises

Combine the following sentences, using transitions as indicated in the directions.

 EXAMPLE   Combine these sentences into two sentences. Use transitions that indicate contrast, example, and addition. Underline your transitions.

   a. Herman knows he needs to lose weight.
   b. He is unable to resist the urge to eat ice cream.
   c. Yesterday he drank a low-fat fiber shake for lunch.
   d. After work he stopped at a 31 Flavors ice cream store.
   e. He ate a large chocolate sundae.

   Herman knows he needs to lose weight, but he is unable to resist the urge to eat ice cream. For example, yesterday he drank a low-fat fiber shake for lunch, but after work he stopped at a 31 Flavors ice cream store and ate a large chocolate sundae.

1. Combine the following sentences into three sentences. Use transitions that indicate example and addition. Underline your transitions.

   a. Bella has many interesting pursuits.
   b. She enjoys listening to jazz at small clubs in Chicago.
   c. For fun and extra income, she raises peacocks.
   d. She really likes a chocolate doughnut and a latte while sitting on the sea wall.

   _____

   _____

   _____

   _____

2. Combine the following sentences into three sentences. Use transitions that indicate example, cause–effect, and addition.

   a. New technologies have improved our ways of communicating in many marvelous respects.
   b. It is easy to watch a recent film on a sixty-inch screen right in our homes.
   c. Cell phones keep us in touch whenever or wherever we are.
   d. We have the choice of talking to or texting one another.
   e. We can even see each other as we converse on our phones, tablets, or computers.

   _____

   _____

   _____

   _____

Sentence Combining Exercises

continued

3. Combine sentences a and b using a cause–effect transition. Then combine sentences c, d, e, and f. Underline your transitions.

    a. The symbol of barbers is a red and white striped pole.
    b. In the twelfth century barbers had the job of bleeding people who were sick.
    c. The red stripes represent blood.
    d. The white stripes represent bandages.
    e. The gold knob at the end represents a basin.
    f. The barber used the basin to catch blood.

_____

_____

_____

_____

4. Combine the following sentences into three sentences. Use transitions that indicate cause–effect and addition. Underline your transitions.

    a. In Roman mythology, Janus is one of the most interesting gods.
    b. He has two faces.
    c. He is the god of beginnings and transitions.
    d. He presided over the beginnings and endings of wars and other conflicts.
    e. The month of January is named after Janus
    f. The start of January marks the end and beginning of the year.

_____

_____

_____

_____

Sentence Combining Exercises

continued

5. Combine the following sentences into two or three sentences, using transitions that show cause–effect and time. Underline your transitions.

   a. Silvio Perro always loved to be around animals.
   b. He worked as a veterinarian nurse during college.
   c. At college he earned a BS degree in biology.
   d. He was accepted to the UC Davis School of Veterinary Medicine.
   e. He became a veterinarian.
   f. He accomplished his dream.

   _____

   _____

   _____

   _____

6. Combine the following sentences into three sentences. Use transitions that indicate relationships of time and addition. Underline your transitions.

   a. The bubonic plague starts out as a bacterial disease in rats.
   b. The bubonic plague is known as the Black Death.
   c. Fleas become infected when they bite the rats.
   d. Fleas spread the plague from rat to rat.
   e. Fleas spread the plague from human to human.
   f. Humans spread the plague to each other.
   g. Humans spread the plague when they speak, cough, or sneeze.

   _____

   _____

   _____

   _____

continued

7. Combine the following sentences into three or four sentences, using transitions that show addition and example. Underline your transitions.

   a. The common shirt has almost twenty parts.
   b. Each part has its own name.
   c. The face of the shirt has a front placket for the buttonholes.
   d. Each sleeve has its own placket.
   e. The shirt has a neckband.
   f. The shirt has a shirttail, a breast pocket, and a lapel.
   g. The back has a yoke and sometimes a tailor's loop.

   _____

   _____

   _____

   _____

8. Combine the following sentences into two sentences. Join the two sentences with a transition that indicates cause–effect. Underline your transitions.

   a. Periodically the weather in Scandinavia may become too hot for the lemmings.
   b. Periodically the lemmings' food supply may change.
   c. Periodically the lemmings may feel overcrowded.
   d. Thousands of Scandinavian lemmings travel for miles.
   e. They throw themselves into the sea.
   f. They swim until they are exhausted and drown.

   _____

   _____

   _____

   _____

Sentence Combining Exercises

continued

9. Combine the following sentences into three sentences, using transitions that show time relationships. Underline your transitions.

   a. Brenda finished reading *Romeo and Juliet*.
   b. Brenda folded her laundry.
   c. Brenda made a list of tasks she had to complete by Monday.
   d. Brenda worked on her poem.
   e. It was very late.
   f. Brenda watched *Late Show with David Letterman*.

   _____

   _____

   _____

   _____

10. Combine the following sentences into three sentences. Use transitions that indicate example and addition. Underline your transitions.

    a. Hundreds of English words have found their way into other languages.
    b. In the Ukraine, people visit the barber.
    c. They want a *herkot*.
    d. In Spain, people become chilly.
    e. They put on a *sueter*.
    f. One might need to place a phone call in the Netherlands.
    g. He or she asks for the *telefoon*.
    h. In China, one asks for the *te le fung*.

    _____

    _____

    _____

    _____

Essay and Paragraph Practice: Comparing and Contrasting

Writing Assignment

Comparing or contrasting two topics is an activity that you participate in nearly every day. When you recognize that two people have much in common, you have observed similarities between them. When you decide to take one route rather than another, you have noticed differences between the two routes. Even something as simple as buying one toothpaste rather than another involves some sort of comparison and contrast. In fact, recognizing similarities and differences affects every part of our lives. How could you know if you were looking at a tree or a bush if you were not able to see their differences as well as their similarities?

Much college writing involves comparing or contrasting two topics. You may be asked to compare (show similarities between) the results of two lab experiments in a biology class or to contrast (show differences between) the religious beliefs of two cultures in an anthropology class. In addition, in many classes you may be asked to write papers or reports or to take essay exams in which you show both the similarities and the differences between two related topics.

Exercises 1C (page 230), 2C (page 245), and 3C (page 257) in this chapter are comparison/contrast paragraphs. Exercise 1C contrasts the sports of football and wrestling; Exercise 2C compares and contrasts a city and a more rural community; and Exercise 3C contrasts life before and after sobriety. Note that each of these paragraphs opens with a topic sentence that makes a statement about similarities or differences.

Your assignment is to write an essay or a paragraph (whichever your instructor assigns) that compares and/or contrasts two related topics. Develop your paper from the ideas that follow.

Reading Assignment

The reading selections in the "Comparing and Contrasting" section of Chapter Six can help you see how several writers examine similarities or differences. Read one or more of the selections, as assigned by your instructor, and use the questions that follow them to develop ideas for your own paper.

Prewriting to Generate Ideas

Prewriting Application: Finding Your Topic

As you read the following topics, remember that the one that looks the easiest may not result in the best paper for you. Use the techniques of freewriting, brainstorming, and/or clustering to develop your reactions to several of these ideas before you choose one of them. Look for the topic idea that interests you the most, the one you have an emotional or personal reaction to.

1. Compare and/or contrast your city or neighborhood with one you used to live in.

2. Compare and/or contrast a place as it is today with the way it was when you were a child.

3. Compare and/or contrast what you expected college to be like before you enrolled in your first class with what you found it to be like later on.

4. If you are returning to school after several years' absence, compare and/or contrast your last school experience with your current one.

5. Compare and/or contrast the characteristics of someone you know with the stereotype of that type of person. For example, if you know an athlete or a police officer, compare and/or contrast that person's actual personality with the stereotype people have of athletes or police officers.

6. Compare and/or contrast your latest vacation or trip with your vision of the ideal vacation or trip.

7. Compare and/or contrast two sports, two athletes, or two teams.

8. Compare and/or contrast the person you are today with the person you were several years ago.

9. Compare and/or contrast any two places, persons, or events that you remember well.

10. If you have a background in two cultures, compare and/or contrast a few specific characteristics of both cultures.

Choosing and Narrowing the Topic

Once you have settled on several possible topics, consider these points as you make your final selection.

- Choose the more limited topic rather than the more general one.

- Choose the topic about which you could discuss several, not just one or two, similarities or differences.

- Choose the topic about which you have the most experience or knowledge.

- Choose the topic in which you have the most personal interest. Avoid topics about which you do not really care.

Writing a Thesis Statement or Topic Sentence

If your assignment is to write a single paragraph, you will open it with a topic sentence. If you are writing a complete essay, you will need a thesis statement at the end of your introductory paragraph. In either case, you will need a clear statement of the topic and central idea of your paper.

Prewriting Application: Working with Topic Sentences

Identify the topic sentences in Exercises 1C (page 230), 2C (page 245), and 3C (page 257). Then identify the topic and the central point in each topic sentence. Finally, state whether the topic sentence is introducing a paragraph that will examine similarities or differences.

Prewriting Application: Evaluating Thesis Statements and Topic Sentences

Write "No" before each sentence that would not make an effective thesis statement or topic sentence for a comparison or contrast paper. Write "Yes" before each sentence that *would* make an effective one. Determine whether each effective sentence is introducing a comparison paper or a contrast paper. Using ideas of your own, rewrite each ineffective sentence into one that might work.

_____ **1.** I had not seen my hometown of Monroe, South Dakota, for over fifteen years, so when I visited it last summer, I was amazed at how little it had changed.

_____

_____

_____ **2.** My father and mother love to watch the Kentucky Derby.

_____

_____

_____ **3.** Many holidays that are common to both Mexico and the United States are celebrated in very different ways.

_____

_____

_____ **4.** Our society is much worse in this day and age than it used to be.

_____

_____

_____ **5.** This years San Diego Padres is a better team than last year's in several key areas.

_____

_____

_____ **6.** *Roxanne,* a 1980s movie starring Steve Martin, contains many similarities to the play *Cyrano de Bergerac.*

_____

_____

_____ **7.** About the only thing that snowboarders and skiers have in common is that they share the same mountain.

_____

_____

_____ **8.** While walking down the Las Vegas Strip last year, I was amazed at how bright and colorful everything was, even at two o'clock in the morning.

_____

_____

_____ **9.** Although both the San Diego Zoo and the San Diego Zoo Safari Park feature exotic animals, the two places are not at all similar.

_____

_____

_____ **10.** Many things have happened to me in the past few years to make me a more tolerant person.

_____

_____

Prewriting Application: Talking to Others

Form a group of three or four people and discuss the topics you have chosen. Your goal here is to help each other clarify the differences or similarities that you are writing about. Explain your points as clearly as you can. As you listen to the others in your group, use the following questions to help them clarify their ideas.

1. Is the paper focusing on similarities or on differences?

2. Exactly what similarities or differences will be examined in the paper? Can you list them?

3. Which similarities or differences need to be explained more clearly or fully?

4. Which points are the most significant or most interesting? Why?

5. Which similarity or difference should the paper open with? Which should it close with?

Organizing Similarities and Differences

Point-by-Point Order

One of the most effective ways to present your ideas when you compare or contrast two topics is called a **point-by-point** organization. Using this method, you cover one similarity or difference at a time. For example, if you were contrasting snowboarders and skiers, one of the differences might be the general age level of each group. The first part of your paper would then contrast the ages of most snowboarders with the ages of most skiers. Another difference might be the clothing worn by the two groups. So you would next contrast the clothing of snowboarders with the clothing of skiers. You might then contrast the physical activity itself, explaining what snowboarders do on the snow that is different from what skiers do. Whatever points you cover, you take them one at a time, point by point. An outline of this method for a single paragraph would look like this:

Point by Point—Single Paragraph

> *Topic Sentence:* About the only thing that snowboarders and skiers have in common is that they share the same mountain.
>
> I. Ages
>
>   A.   Snowboarders
>
>   B.   Skiers
>
> II. Clothing
>
>   A.   Snowboarders
>
>   B.   Skiers
>
> III. Physical Activity
>
>   A.   Snowboarders
>
>   B.   Skiers
>
> *Concluding Sentence*

Point by Point—Essay

If you are writing a complete essay, the point-by-point pattern changes only in that you devote a separate paragraph to each point. Develop each paragraph with details and examples to illustrate the differences or similarities you are discussing.

Introductory Paragraph

> Introductory sentences
>
> ending with a
>
> **thesis statement**
>
> *Thesis Statement:* About the only thing that snowboarders and skiers have in common is that they share the same mountain.

1st Body Paragraph

> I. *Topic sentence* about the difference in ages
>
>   A.   Snowboarders
>
>   Examples
>
>   B.   Skiers
>
>   Examples

2nd Body Paragraph

> II. *Topic sentence* about the difference in clothing
>
> A.   Snowboarders
>
>   Examples
>
> B.   Skiers
>
>   Examples

3rd Body Paragraph

> III. *Topic sentence* about the difference in technique
>
> A.   Snowboarders
>
>   Examples
>
> B.   Skiers
>
>   Examples

Concluding Paragraph

> Concluding sentences
>
> bringing the essay
>
> to a close

Subject-by-Subject Order

Another method of organization presents the topics **subject by subject.** Using this method, you cover each point of one topic first and then each point of the second topic. Be careful with this organization. Because the points are presented separately rather than together, your paper might end up reading like two separate descriptions rather than like a comparison or contrast of the two topics. To make the comparison or contrast clear, cover the same points in the same order, like this:

Subject by Subject—Single Paragraph

Topic Sentence: About the only thing that snowboarders and skiers have in common is that they share the same mountain.

I. Snowboarders

    A.   Ages

    B.   Clothing

    C.   Technique

II. Skiers

    A.   Ages

    B.   Clothing

    C.   Technique

Concluding Sentence

Subject by Subject—Essay

The following example illustrates a paper with two body paragraphs—one for each subject. Depending on the complexity of your topic or assigned length of your paper, you may need to write more than one body paragraph per subject.

Introductory Paragraph

Introductory sentences

ending with a

thesis statement

Thesis Statement: About the only thing that snowboarders and skiers have in common is that they share the same mountain.

1st Body Paragraph

I. *Topic sentence* about characteristics of snowboarders

    A.   Ages

                Examples

    B.   Clothing

                Examples

    C.   Technique

                Examples

2nd Body Paragraph

> II. *Topic sentence* about characteristics of skiers
>
>   A.   Ages
>
>   Examples
>
>   B.   Clothing
>
>   Examples
>
>   C.   Technique
>
>   Examples

Concluding Paragraph

> Concluding sentences
>
> bringing the essay
>
> to a close

Prewriting Application: Organization of the Comparison/Contrast Paragraph

Examine Exercise 1C (page 230), Exercise 2C (page 245), and Exercise 3C (page 257). Outline the paragraph in each exercise to determine its point-by-point or subject-by-subject organization.

Writing the Paper

Now write the rough draft of your paper. Pay particular attention to transitions as you write. If you are using a point-by-point organization, use a clear transition to introduce each point of comparison or contrast. For subject-by-subject organizations, write a clear transition as you move from the first subject of your paper to the second. In addition, as you write the second half of a subject-by-subject paper, use transitional words and phrases that refer to the first half of the paper in order to emphasize the similarities or differences.

Writing Application: Identifying Transitional Words, Phrases, and Sentences

Examine Exercises 1C (page 230), 2C (page 245), and 3C (page 257).

1. Identify the organizational pattern of each as point-by-point or subject-by-subject.

2. Identify transitional sentences that introduce each point of comparison or contrast in a point-by-point paper or that move from one subject to another in a subject-by-subject paper.

3. In the subject-by-subject paper, identify transitions in the second half of the paper that emphasize the comparison or contrast by referring to the subject of the first half.

4. Identify any other transitions that serve to connect ideas between sentences.

Rewriting and Improving the Paper

1. Revise your sentences so that they include specific and concrete details. As much as possible, use actual names of people and places, and refer to specific details whenever possible.

2. Add or revise transitions wherever doing so would help clarify movement from one idea to another.

3. Improve your preliminary thesis statement (if you are writing an essay) or your preliminary topic sentence (if you are writing a single paragraph) so that it more accurately states the central point of your paper.

4. Examine your draft for sentence variety. If many of your sentences tend to be of the same length, try varying their length and their structure by combining sentences using the techniques you have studied in the Sentence Practice sections of this text.

Rewriting Application: Responding to Paragraph Writing

Read the following paragraph. Then respond to the questions following it.

Romeo and Juliet—Then and Now

The 1968 movie version of William Shakespeare's play *Romeo and Juliet* contrasts with the updated version of 1996 in a number of ways. First, the 1968 director had the characters battle each other with swords. That is the way they fought back then, but today's youth couldn't really relate to that kind of situation. In the 1996 version the director wanted to show a weapon that the audience had seen on TV shows and in other movies. Swords were replaced with shiny, artistic-looking handguns. Another contrast between the '68 version and the '96 one is the style of costumes. The '68 designers kept the clothing as it would have looked during Shakespeare's time, making the male actors wear puffy-sleeved shirts, tights, and little beanie hats. The women had to endure much worse attire, such as long, heavy dresses. The designers in the updated version knew that today's youth wouldn't sit through a movie about guys wearing tights or women wearing clothes that hid everything. Instead, they had the men wear shirts that were colorful, comfortable, and modern. They also wore basic black and dark blue pants. I felt I could take the characters more seriously in normal clothes than in the old English attire. Although both versions did keep the original words of the play, I am glad that the new version changed the music of the earlier one. For instance, the boring love song "A Time for Us" was replaced by a touching, romantic tune called "Kissing You." The new music helped me follow the plot a little better. When I watched the old version, there wasn't very much background music at all. I really had to follow what was going on by watching the actors, and even then the movie was hard to follow. In conclusion, I think the director of the '96 version did a wonderful job making *Romeo and Juliet* into a movie that appeals to the young people of today.

1. Identify the topic sentence. State its topic and central idea. Is it an effective topic sentence? Can you tell whether the paper will focus on similarities or differences?

2. Is this a point-by-point or subject-by-subject organization? How many points of contrast are covered in this paper? Identify them.

3. Identify the transitional sentences that introduce each major section of the paragraph. What other transitions are used between sentences?

4. Consider the organization of the paragraph. Would you change the order of the contrasts? Explain why or why not.

5. Consider the sentence variety. What sentences would you combine to improve the paragraph?

Rewriting Application: Responding to Essay Writing

Read the following essay. Then respond to the questions at the end of it.

Guamuchil

I was born in Guamuchil, Mexico, which is a small town near the Gulf of California. It is about six hundred miles south of the border in the state of Sinaloa. I have wonderful memories of growing up there, and I have wanted to visit it for many years. Therefore, I was really excited my husband and I decided to return to my hometown in 1994. Unfortunately, I found many changes there.

The very first difference I saw was the bridge that we crossed to enter the city from north to south. It used to be an attractive green bridge that crossed a wide, flowing river. It had brightly painted rails that protected sidewalks on each side of it. In contrast to what I had described to my husband, the bridge now looked old and rundown. The paint on the rails was peeling off, and in some places the rails were crushed into the sidewalk because they had been hit by cars and never fixed. Even the river that I used to see every time I went across the bridge was almost gone. A very small stream was all that we could see.

Another thing that I had told my husband was that, even though the city was small, it had good streets and was well kept. I had even mentioned that many new stores with large, clean parking lots were being built when I had left. Unfortunately, the streets and stores now were very different. From the entrance of the city to the middle of it, we kept finding streets where the pavement was cracked and broken. In some streets as well as in parking lots, there were many big holes. And the stores were even worse. They looked run-down, and many of them were out of business. I was very unhappy at the sight.

Finally, when I lived in Guamuchil, it was a lively place, but now all that had changed. When I was young, I knew that we were not the richest town in the state, but the houses, shops, and cars remained well painted at all times, so the overall appearance of the city was presentable. However, when I visited it in 1994, everybody seemed to have lost hope for a better future, and they did not have the will or perhaps the money to fix the things they owned or to maintain a lively city instead of an old, run-down town.

I have not been back to Guamuchil since 1994, but I think I will visit it again soon. I know it will not be the way it was when I was young, but it is still my hometown, and I will never forget that.

1. Identify the thesis statement. State its topic and central idea. Is it an effective thesis statement? Can you tell whether the paper will focus on similarities or differences?

2. Identify each topic sentence. State its topic and central idea. Does each topic sentence clearly introduce one specific similarity or difference?

3. What transitional words introduce each new body paragraph?

4. Does the essay use a point-by-point or a subject-by-subject organization? Would you change the order of the paragraphs? Why or why not?

5. Is each similarity or difference explained clearly and fully? If you would improve any, explain how you would do so.

Proofreading

When proofreading your paper, watch for the following errors:

- Sentence fragments, comma splices, and fused sentences
- Misplaced modifiers and dangling modifiers
- Errors in subject–verb agreement
- Errors in pronoun case, pronoun–antecedent agreement, and pronoun reference
- Errors in comma use
- Errors in the use of periods, question marks, exclamation points, colons, semicolons, and quotation marks
- Errors in capitalization, titles, and numbers
- Misspelled words

Prepare a clean final draft, following the format your instructor has requested.

Chapter 4 Practice Test

I. Review of Chapters One, Two, and Three

A. Underline all subjects once and complete verbs twice. Place all prepositional phrases in parentheses.

1. Either the freezer or the stove in our church kitchen malfunctions at least once every

   three months.

2. In Shakespeare's time, the people in the audience sometimes talked to the actors

   during the plays.

3. The monks and nuns assisted the sick people and tried to ease their pain.

4. Serfs and peasants lived in poverty; however, the royalty were well off.

5. When the apple fell from the tree, it helped Isaac Newton to formulate the law of gravity.

B. Correct any fragments, fused sentences, or comma splices in the following sentences. Do nothing if the sentence is correct.

6. Orville looked at Wilbur then Orville gave the signal.

   _____

   _____

7. Orson Welles, wondering if anyone would believe his radio broadcast.

   _____

   _____

8. Over the moon leaped the cow, and it landed in the river.

   _____

   _____

9. Awarding the prize for the muddiest pig at the fair.

   _____

   _____

continued

10. Katniss stared at the white rose on her plate, later she told Peeta about it.

_____

_____

C. At the places indicated, add adjective clauses, appositives, infinitive phrases, or participial phrases to the following sentences as directed in parentheses. Use commas where they are needed.

11. Michelle's water dragon ^ looked at her with beady eyes. (adjective clause)

_____

_____

12. The astrophysicist ^ was on her way to the Jet Propulsion Laboratory. (appositive)

_____

_____

13. ^ George Washington scratched his head and laughed at Benjamin Franklin. (participial phrase)

_____

_____

14. The psychic said that John Lennon wanted him ^ before the end of the year. (infinitive phrase)

_____

_____

15. Emma stared at the ants ^ and started to scream. (participial phrase)

_____

_____

continued

D. Correct any dangling or misplaced modifiers in the following sentences. Do nothing if the sentence is correct.

16. Feeling tired after working thirty-six straight hours, Ofelia almost drank four bottles of Red Bull.

_____

_____

17. Alonso offered a piece of the wedding cake to his bride that he had just frosted.

_____

_____

18. Worried about his upcoming interview, Jose's Ford slowed to a stop.

_____

_____

19. Paula saw that Jim had only put two roses in the bouquet he gave her.

_____

_____

20. Preparing to talk to her daughter, a short prayer was said by Pearl.

_____

_____

Chapter 4 Practice Test

II. Chapter Four

A. Underline the correct verb form in parentheses.

1. Every one of the hotel guests (was were) presented with a fruit basket in his or her room.

2. Politics along with a ready smile (was were) easy for Grantham.

3. The most important item on the town council's agenda (concerns concern) mosquitoes.

4. A bear with two cubs (appear appears) in our backyard around dusk almost every day.

5. Here (is are) the staple gun and paper cutter that you need for your project.

B. Correct any subject–verb agreement errors in the following sentences. Do nothing if the sentence is correct.

6. The cockatiel in the cage by the window and the African gray parrot near it has made a huge mess.

7. The colonel believed that none of the soldiers under his command were afraid.

8. Neither Roderick Usher nor his sister Madeline feel like going for a picnic.

9. Have Thor or any of the other gods ever interfered in human affairs?

10. A den of Cub Scouts were being shown around the ship by the docent.

C. Underline the correct pronoun in parentheses.

11. Each one of the Vikings (was were) drinking a tankard of mead.

12. Before a new member is accepted into the gang, (you he or she they) must be tattooed with a skull and crossbones.

13. The class was looking forward to (its their) trip to the marching band competition.

14. Neither the teacher nor the students knew whether (her their) experiment was a success yet.

15. After the tsunami, the Parkers and their son Calvin were determined to rebuild their home by (theirselves themself themselves theirselfs).

continued

D. Correct any pronoun errors in the following sentences. Do nothing if the sentence is correct.

16. After a dieter has lost those first five pounds, you have to avoid eating too many carbohydrates.

17. Mack told Todd that he needed to shave before dinner.

18. The people in the club chatted loudly, and the air conditioner had stopped working, which made the saxophone player angry.

19. The Benningtons and ourselfs enjoyed a weekend hiking in the nearby woods.

20. Before he left for Yale, he wanted to kiss his girlfriend goodbye, but this was impossible.

E. Underline the correct pronouns in parentheses.

21. That morning Hemingway, Faulkner, and (I me) wanted to go fishing, but Ernest had left his manuscript on the train.

22. The rest of the soldiers had retreated except for Dodson and (he him).

23. Eminem doesn't sing as well as (she her), but he is much more well known.

24. When I looked back, the woman with (who whom) I had been talking had disappeared.

25. The first members of the volleyball team to arrive, Victor and (he him), worried about the rest of the team.

F. Correct any pronoun errors in the following sentences. Do nothing if the sentence is correct.

26. Mr. Marx asked John Lenin and I to help him write his book.

27. When the Sundance Kid looked out the door, he knew that Butch and him were in serious trouble.

28. Even though I had more tattoos, the crowd enjoyed Sheila more than me because she had a snake on a leash.

29. My Australian shepherd could not stop scratching it's fleas, so Paul and I went to the vet to get some medicine.

30. Do Ms. Cyrus and her approve of the costume we designed?

Using Punctuation and Capitalization

When we speak to people face to face, we have a number of signals, aside from the words we choose, to let them know how we feel. Facial expressions—smiles, frowns, grimaces—convey our emotions and attitudes. Tone of voice can tell a listener whether we feel sad or lighthearted or sarcastic about what we are saying. Hand gestures and other body language add further messages to the communication. In fact, experts tell us that these nonverbal communications make up over 80 percent of the messages in a conversation.

When we write in order to communicate with a reader, we must make up for that 80 percent of lost, nonverbal communication by using the writing signals that we know. Some of the most important signals in writing are the punctuation marks. They signal whether we are making a statement or asking a question. They indicate the boundaries of our sentences. They determine much of the rhythm and emotion of our writing.

If you are able to use punctuation effectively, you have a powerful tool to control how your writing affects your readers. If you do not know the basic rules of punctuation, you run the risk of being misunderstood or of confusing your readers. In this chapter we will discuss the essential rules of punctuation, not just so that your writing will be correct but, more important, so that you will be able to express your ideas exactly the way you want them to be expressed.

Using Commas

The comma gives writers more trouble than any of the other punctuation marks. Before printing was developed, commas came into use to tell readers when to put in a slight pause when they were reading aloud. Now, although the placement of the comma does affect the rhythm of sentences, it also conveys many messages that are more important than when to pause. Because the comma is such an important punctuation mark and because it can be troublesome to you if you don't know how to use it correctly, we take it up first. You are already familiar with several of its uses.

Comma usage can be explained by four general rules:

1. Use commas before coordinating conjunctions that join main clauses to form a compound sentence.

2. Use commas between elements in a series.

3. Use commas after introductory elements.

4. Use commas before and after interrupters.

Commas in Compound Sentences

1. When you join two main clauses with one of the coordinating conjunctions to form a compound sentence, use a comma before the conjunction.

 EXAMPLES

I don't know her, **but** I like her already.

The tableware in the restaurant was exquisite, **and** the food was some of the best I have ever tasted.

We had to remove the huge eucalyptus tree, **or** its encroaching roots would have undermined our happy home.

2. When conjunctions join other parts of a sentence, such as two words, two phrases, or two subordinate clauses, do not put commas before the conjunctions.

 EXAMPLE

Every morning that scoundrel **has** a drink <u>and</u> then thoroughly **beats** his poor dog.

No comma is needed before *and* because it does not join two main clauses. Instead, it joins the verbs *has* and *beats*.

 EXAMPLE

I decided to visit France because I had never had a chance to see that country <u>and</u> because my travel agent was able to offer me a special discount on the trip.

No comma is needed before *and* because it joins two subordinate clauses, not two main clauses.

 PRACTICE   Add commas to the following sentences where necessary.

1. Zeus loved Hera, but he was not always faithful to her.

2. Bonnie Parker loved Clyde Barrow but all he cared about was robbing banks.

3. Romeo loved Juliet and did not care what his family thought.

4. Penelope loved Odysseus so she kept on fighting off other suitors.

5. Rhett loved Scarlett for her passion and for her strength and independence.

Commas with Elements in a Series

1. When listing three or more elements (words, phrases, clauses) in a series, separate them by commas. When the last two elements are joined by a coordinating conjunction, a comma before the conjunction is optional.

 EXAMPLES

(words)	The gazpacho was **cold, spicy, and fresh.**
(phrases)	In the mountains, he had been **thrown by his horse, bitten by a snake, and chased by a bear.**
(clauses)	To rescue the koala, **the firefighters brought a ladder, the police brought a rope, and the mayor brought a speech.**

2. When using two or more adjectives to modify the same noun, separate them with commas if you can put *and* between the adjectives without changing the meaning or if you can easily reverse the order of the adjectives.

 EXAMPLES

She eagerly stepped into the **comforting, cool water.**

A **stubborn, obnoxious** boll weevil is ruining my cotton patch.

Note that you could easily use *and* between the above adjectives. (The water is *comforting* and *cool*; the boll weevil is *stubborn* and *obnoxious*.) You could also reverse the adjectives (the *cool, comforting water* or the *obnoxious, stubborn* boll weevil).

3. On the other hand, if the adjectives cannot be joined by *and* or are not easily reversed, no comma is necessary.

EXAMPLE

A bureaucrat wearing a **black leather jacket** and a smirk strode into the auditorium.

Notice how awkward the sentence would sound if you placed *and* between the adjectives (*a black and leather jacket*) or if you reversed them (*a leather black jacket*).

 PRACTICE

Insert commas between main clauses joined by a coordinating conjunction and between items in a series.

1. I like the group Hootie and the Blowfish, so I think I will order their CD.

2. We studied the gods of the Greeks the goddesses of Norse mythology, and the heroes of the Native Americans in our mythology class.

3. Spiderman sewed up a tear in his suit repaired his webcaster, and went to look for someone who needed help.

4. The server brought us a delightful, delicious chablis.

5. The professor could see that the wrinkled sloppy paper had been carefully researched, but the quality of its writing was atrocious.

6. Delilah sharpened her shears for two hours, and then she began cutting.

7. Gatsby was generous with his money, but careless about his moral behavior.

8. Carlos Santana might arrive an hour early for his performance, or he could be two hours late.

9. LaVere bought some flowers visited her sick friend caught the trolley, and went to work.

10. The rancid, bitter honey disappointed Pooh.

Commas with Introductory Elements

When you begin a sentence with certain introductory words, phrases, or clauses, place a comma after the introductory element.

1. Use a comma after the following introductory words and transitional expressions.

Introductory Words		*Transitional Expressions*
next	similarly	on the other hand
first	nevertheless	in a similar manner
second	therefore	in other words
third	indeed	for example
moreover	yes	for instance
however	no	in fact
		in addition
		as a result

 EXAMPLES

First, we will strike at the heart of the matter and then pursue other clichés.

For example, let's all stand up and be counted.

2. Use a comma after introductory prepositional phrases of five or more words. However, you may need to use a comma after shorter introductory prepositional phrases if not doing so would cause confusion.

 EXAMPLES

After a long and thrilling nap, Buster went looking for a cat to chase.

After dinner we all went for a walk around the lake.

In spring, time seems to catch up with small furry animals.

Without the comma, this last sentence might look as if it begins *In springtime.*

3. Use a comma after all introductory infinitive and participial phrases.

 EXAMPLES

Blackened with soot, the little boy toddled out of the smoldering house.

Begging for her forgiveness, Homer assured Hortense that they would never run short of Spam again.

To break in your new car properly, drive at varying speeds for the first one thousand miles.

4. Use a comma after introductory adverb subordinate clauses.

 EXAMPLES

Because Umberto played the tuba so well, he was awarded a music scholarship.

As soon as he arrived on shore, Columbus claimed the land for Spain.

Although it was raining furiously, Freida ran six miles anyway.

 PRACTICE

Insert commas after introductory elements.

1. Indeed, Columbus told Queen Isabella that the earth was round.

2. Taking Cheetah by the hand, Tarzan kissed Jane goodbye.

3. Teetering dangerously at the top of the hill, the large stone might have rolled down and crushed Sisyphus.

4. Before they left for the trip to the space station, the crew of the shuttle emailed their families.

5. Yes, I have always wanted to have a wisdom tooth pulled without any anesthetic.

6. Pledging his undying devotion, Popeye asked Olive Oyl to marry him.

7. As Hester walked through town, Pearl was always beside her.

8. After Jack Reacher thought long and hard, he decided to pull the trigger.

9. For instance, my mother had never heard of the Kardashians.

10. To impress Daisy, Jay Gatsby threw his beautiful shirts onto the table.

Commas with Interrupters

Sometimes certain words, phrases, or clauses will interrupt the flow of thoug
in a sentence to add emphasis or additional information. These interrupters ar
enclosed by commas.

1. Use commas to set off parenthetical expressions. Common parenthetical
   expressions include *however, indeed, consequently, as a result, moreover, of
   course, for example, for instance, that is, in fact, after all, I think,* and
   therefore.

 EXAMPLES

The answer, **after all,** lay right under his left big toe.

That big blue bird by the feeder is, **I think,** one of those unruly Steller's
jays.

She is, **moreover,** a notorious misspeller of the word *deceitful.*

NOTE: Whenever a parenthetical expression introduces a second main
clause after a semicolon, the semicolon takes the place of the comma in
front of it. (See page 302 for a review of this rule.)

 EXAMPLE

Yes, you may eat your snails in front of me; **after all,** we are old friends.

 PRACTICE

Use commas to set off any parenthetical elements in the following sentences.

1. Vice President Biden, in fact, admired the good taste of President
   Obama's daughters.

2. During World War I for instance more men died of influenza than from
   bullets or artillery.

3. Dexter felt bad about stealing the money; however he did it anyway.

4. Maria agreed to attend I think because she admires you so much.

5. Ms. Mendoza's main fear moreover is that an airplane will crash into
   her house.

2. Use commas to set off nonrestrictive elements. Nonrestrictive elements are
   modifying words, phrases, or clauses that are not necessary to identify the
   words they modify. They include adjective subordinate clauses, appositives,
   and participial phrases.

djective Clauses

(See pages 164–165 if you need to review adjective clauses.) If the information in an adjective clause <u>is not necessary to identify the word it modifies</u>, it is called a **nonrestrictive clause**, and it is enclosed in commas.

EXAMPLE   Ms. Erindira Sanchez, **who is president of that company,** began twenty years ago as a secretary.

Because the name of the person is used, the adjective clause is not necessary to identify which woman began twenty years ago as a secretary, so the commas are needed.

However, if her name is not used, the adjective clause is a **restrictive** one <u>because the woman is not already identified</u>. In this case, the commas are not necessary.

EXAMPLE   The woman **who is president of that company** began twenty years ago as a secretary.

The following are additional examples of nonrestrictive clauses.

EXAMPLE   My oldest brother, **who is a park ranger,** showed me his collection of arrowheads.

Because a person can have only one oldest brother, the brother is already identified, and the adjective clause is <u>not needed to identify him</u>, making it nonrestrictive.

EXAMPLE   His hometown, **which is somewhere in northeastern Indiana,** wants him to return for its centennial celebration.

A person can have only one hometown, so the adjective clause is nonrestrictive.

PRACTICE   In the following sentences, set off all nonrestrictive clauses with commas.

1. Abraham Lincoln was assassinated at Ford's Theater, which has been preserved as a national historic site.

2. Penelope who was a very faithful wife, kept finding ways to delay her decision.

3. Tranquility Base, which was the name of the first lunar landing site was established in 1969.

4. The man who wrote *Huckleberry Finn,* was quite eccentric.

5. "Stopping by Woods on a Snowy Evening" which was written by

Robert Frost is one of the most well-known American poems.

Participial Phrases

(See pages 154–156 if you need to review participial phrases.) Participial phrases that <u>do not contain information necessary to identify the words they modify</u> are nonrestrictive and are therefore set off by commas. Restrictive participial phrases do not require commas.

 EXAMPLE   (nonrestrictive)   The president, **seeking to be reelected,** traveled throughout the country making speeches and kissing babies.

Because we have only one president, the participial phrase *seeking to be reelected* is nonrestrictive. It is not necessary to identify who is meant by *president*.

 EXAMPLE   (restrictive)   The woman **sitting by the door** is a famous surgeon.

Sitting by the door is a restrictive participial phrase because it is necessary to identify which woman is the famous surgeon.

 EXAMPLE   Foxworth, **discouraged by years of failure,** decided to buy a pet chimpanzee.

Discouraged by years of failure is a nonrestrictive past participial phrase. It is not necessary to identify Foxworth.

 PRACTICE   In the following sentences, set off nonrestrictive participial phrases with commas.

1. One of Sharon's business associates, disgusted by the company's tactics, resigned yesterday.

2. The cute boy, standing on the right in the photograph is my grandson.

3. Leonard Cohen trying not to show his despair, kept singing in front of the three beautiful women in black.

4. Roxanne trained always to be polite, tried not to giggle at the sight of such a large nose.

5. Howard attempting to stifle his yawns, fell asleep while watching the home movies.

Appositives

(See pages 166–168 if you need to review appositives.) Appositives usually contain information <u>not necessary to identify the words they modify</u> and are therefore nonrestrictive. Set them off with commas.

 EXAMPLES

Natalie's mother, **a lawyer in Boston,** will be coming to visit her soon.

Kleenex, **a household necessity,** was invented as a substitute for bandages during World War I because of a cotton shortage.

Parker took his stamp collection to Mr. Poindexter, **a noted stamp expert.**

 PRACTICE

In the following sentences, set off all nonrestrictive appositives with commas.

1. Mammoth Lakes, a beautiful mountain resort, is about a five-hour drive from my home.

2. Mercutio one of the most interesting characters in *Romeo and Juliet* is killed early in the play.

3. Gary an avid hiker did not mind being called a tree hugger.

4. We were married on July 19 a day before the first man stepped onto the moon.

5. The Australian shepherd an intelligent dog was introduced into Australia to herd sheep.

3. <u>Use commas to separate most explanatory words from direct quotations.</u>

 EXAMPLES

Mr. Jones asked, "Where are you going?"

"I will arrive before dinner is over," **he remarked.**

"Tonight's dinner," **he said,** "will be delayed."

NOTE: Do not use commas to separate explanatory words from a partial direct quotation.

EXAMPLE

He described the clouds as "ominous, dark, and threatening."

4. <u>Use commas to set off words of direct address.</u> If a writer addresses someone directly in a sentence, the word or words that stand for that person or persons are set off by commas. If the word or words in direct address begin the sentence, they are followed by a comma.

EXAMPLES

And now, **my good friends,** I think it is time to end this conversation.

Mr. Chairman, I rise to a point of order.

I would like to present my proposal, **my esteemed colleagues.**

5. <u>Use commas to set off dates and addresses.</u> If your sentence contains two, three, or more elements of the date or address, use commas to set off these elements. The following sentences contain two or more elements.

 EXAMPLES

We visited Disneyland on **Monday, June 5,** in order to avoid the weekend rush.

We visited Disneyland on **Monday, June 5, 2013,** in order to avoid the weekend rush.

Celia has lived at **3225 Oliver Street, San Diego,** for five years.

Celia has lived at **3225 Oliver Street, San Diego, California,** for five years.

Celia has lived at **3225 Oliver Street, San Diego, California 92023,** for five years.

NOTE: The zip code is not separated from the state by a comma.

The following sentences contain only one element.

 EXAMPLES

We visited Disneyland on **Monday** in order to avoid the weekend rush.

Celia has lived at **3225 Oliver Street** for five years.

 PRACTICE

In the following sentences, use commas to set off words in direct address or dates and addresses that have two or more elements.

1. Ernest, is your address 1500 Fitzgerald Boulevard, Oak Park, Illinois?

2. Lee Harvey Oswald changed the course of history on November 22 1963 when he pulled the trigger.

3. Michelle what is your favorite breed of dog?

4. Send this order of trout to Harbor House 2978 South First Street Seattle Washington by noon tomorrow.

5. Tell Adam that I am grateful Katie.

PRACTICE Use commas to set off parenthetical expressions, nonrestrictive elements, explanatory words for direct quotations, words in direct address, and dates and addresses that have two or more elements.

1. An asp, by the way, is the kind of viper that killed Cleopatra.

2. Edgar Allan Poe sat down at the table and said "Sister we have got to quit meeting like this."

3. *Dracula* a novel by Bram Stoker has scared many readers and has been the subject of many movies.

4. Ahab how do you like my new wide-wale corduroy pants?

5. The events of June 28 1914 started World War I.

6. At Hiroshima Japan and Nagasaki Japan tragic events occurred on August 6 1945.

7. Our famous performing arts center designed by Frank Lloyd Wright recently underwent a renovation.

8. Bill has watched *Big Night* his favorite film at least fifteen times.

9. Samson of course didn't wake up while his hair was being cut.

10. Gawain give this note to Guinevere who will hide it from Arthur.

Section One Review

1. <u>Use a comma before a coordinating conjunction that joins two main clauses.</u>

2. <u>Use commas to separate elements in a series.</u>

    a. Elements in a series may be words, phrases, or clauses.

    b. Two or more adjectives that modify the same noun may need to be separated with commas.

3. <u>Use a comma after an introductory element.</u> Introductory elements include:

    a. Introductory words

    b. Transitional expressions

    c. Prepositional phrases

    d. Verbal phrases

    e. Adverb clauses

4. <u>Use commas to separate interrupters from the rest of the sentence.</u> Interrupters include:

    a. Parenthetical expressions

    b. Nonrestrictive clauses

    c. Nonrestrictive participial phrases

    d. Appositives

    e. Explanatory words for direct quotations

    f. Words in direct address

    g. Dates and addresses with two or more elements

Exercise 1A

Add commas to the following sentences where necessary.

1. Coleen had run the whole marathon, and her body felt like it.

2. Furthermore Calvin thought the accommodations were quite adequate.

3. Arachna had long thin arms and legs but never considered herself unattractive.

4. Bertrand Lee Grant a Civil War expert shared some interesting details about the Battle of Shiloh.

5. Of course the swan did not like Zeus's idea at all.

6. My dentist who is also a lepidopterist has pictures of butterflies on his office walls.

7. Looking at her sullen disapproving demeanor Dimmesdale was not at all encouraged.

8. Shirley Temple dancing happily across the stage had a big grin on her face.

9. Exhilarated by the experience of flying Icarus the son of Daedalus flew higher and higher.

10. Narcissus will you stop looking into the pool of water?

11. Unable to stop staring at his reflection in the pool Narcissus eventually wasted away and died.

12. On March 5 2014 the attack began but the sunny warm weather favored the enemy.

13. Hannibal loved his personal elephant; however he found the trek over the mountains rather tedious and bumpy.

14. No Moby Dick did not appear at the Sea World in Boston Massachusetts in the 1800s.

15. Apple which has yearly earnings in the billions is in fierce competition with Samsung.

Exercise 1B

Add commas to the following sentences where necessary.

1. After eating all of the pepperoni and anchovy pizza, Terence asked for an antacid.

2. Many people for example dislike Ernest Hemingway's writing style.

3. Irritated and tired Willy Wonka soon became tired of children always asking him for candy.

4. The boxer got off the mat at the count of eight but she was unable to resume the fight.

5. Lieutenant Henry and Nurse Barkley escaping the war took a rowboat to Switzerland.

6. Vylani was proud of her proficiency at origami the ancient Japanese art of paper folding.

7. Darwin did not like the condition of the HMS *Beagle* his ship nor was he encouraged by the approaching weather front.

8. To get some money for supplies Bird sold his saxophone and then he had to borrow one for his new gig.

9. The Maze restaurant opened on May 5 2013 when its owner Paul Icarus moved from Labyrinthine Maine to Crete New Hampshire.

10. U. S. Grant lit a cigar went into his tent wrote a letter to Robert E. Lee and left for Appomattox.

11. Jubilant that he had finally escaped the Land of the Lotus Eaters Odysseus gave his sailors an extra ration of wine.

12. Lizzie Borden who supposedly killed her mother with an ax was actually acquitted of the crime.

13. Because Lance Armstrong was sanctioned for doping violations he was stripped of all his medals.

Exercise 1B

continued

14. King Midas who had all the gold he needed seemed to be a greedy ruthless leader.

15. "Do you know" asked Rocco "where I can find a paper clip a stapler and a three-hole

punch?"

Exercise 1C

In the following paragraph, add commas wherever they are needed.

1. Although students in public colleges and universities cost the taxpayers a great deal of money, there is a way for them to return the favor—doing volunteer work in their communities. **2.** When I attended Arizona State University in Tempe Arizona the tuition was about $3,500 per semester which was much less than it actually cost the state to educate me. **3.** On October 8 2013 I watched the documentary *Students Have a Responsibility to Their States and Country* which suggested several ways students could help defray the cost of their educations. **4.** The program sponsored by a non-profit organization proposed that one way students could help would be to perform community service. **5.** For instance while they are attending college students could volunteer at soup kitchens or at local charities like Goodwill. **6.** According to the documentary students could participate in programs such as environmental awareness community cleanup or recycling. **7.** In addition young people could help care for citizens who are aging disabled or unable to care for themselves. **8.** For example a friend of mine a current student at ASU goes once or twice a week to swim with people who are undergoing rehabilitation for strokes injuries or disabilities caused by aging. **9.** Some of his classmates shelve check out or repair books at public libraries. **10.** As college students become educated they can help teach elementary or high school students some of the things they have learned. **11.** College students have made it through the educational system to college; therefore they could counsel troubled or discouraged students who may have dropped out of school. **12.** To help alleviate the juvenile delinquency problem they might visit kids who have been sent to local or state institutions. **13.** Some students might complain that their study workload is too much; therefore they wouldn't have the time to spend time outside of school. **14.** However some colleges have given students credit for community service and some students have written about these experiences in their English or social studies classes. **15.** As I see it a required bit of community service would impress the taxpayers; more importantly it would make students more aware of the responsibility for and rewards of volunteerism.

Other Punctuation Marks

Punctuation would be simple if we could just include a page of punctuation marks at the end of a piece of writing and invite readers to sprinkle them about anywhere they choose. But if you want to be an effective writer, it helps a great deal to know how to use not only those troublesome commas but also all of the other marks of punctuation. In this section, we will take up end punctuation and the other punctuation marks.

The placement of punctuation marks can affect the meaning of a sentence profoundly. Here are a few examples.

In this sentence, the dog recognizes its owner.

EXAMPLE   A clever dog knows **its** master.

In this one, the dog is in charge.

EXAMPLE   A clever dog knows **it's** master.

In this sentence, we find a deliberately rude butler.

EXAMPLE   The butler stood by the door and called the **guests** names as they entered.

In this sentence, he is more mannerly.

EXAMPLE   The butler stood by the door and called the **guests'** names as they entered.

And in this sentence, we find a person who doesn't trust his friends.

EXAMPLE   Everyone **I know** has secret ambitions.

Add two commas, and you change the meaning.

EXAMPLE   Everyone, **I know,** has secret ambitions.

As you can see, punctuation marks are potent tools.

End Punctuation

The Period

1. <u>The period is used at the end of a sentence that makes a statement or gives a command.</u>

EXAMPLES   This rule is probably the easiest of all.

Circle the subject in the above sentence.

2. The period is used with most abbreviations.

 EXAMPLES   Mr., Mrs., Dr., A.D., Ph.D., U.S., min., sec., tsp., Sgt., Lt.

The Question Mark

1. The question mark is used at the end of sentences that ask questions.

 EXAMPLES   Where have all the flowers gone?

Is the water hot yet?

2. A question mark is not used at the end of an indirect question.

 EXAMPLES   (direct question)   Why is Emile going to the dance?

(indirect question)   I wonder why Emile is going to the dance.

The Exclamation Point

1. The exclamation point is used after words, phrases, and short sentences that show strong emotion.

 EXAMPLES   Rats!

Not on your life!

Watch it, Buster!

Ouch! That hurt!

2. The exclamation point is not often used in college writing. For the most part, the words themselves should express the excitement.

 EXAMPLE   Chased by a ravenous pack of ocelots, Cedric raced through the forest to his condo, bolted up his stairs, swiftly locked the door, and threw himself, quivering and exhausted, onto his beanbag chair.

 PRACTICE   Use periods, question marks, and exclamation points in the following sentences.

1. Santa wondered whether Rudolph's red nose meant that he had a cold.

2. Who is on first

3. The kitchen's on fire

4. Brent wondered if a boa constrictor could swallow a mature tiger

5. Does Roscoe want to visit the Liberace Museum

6. How does Dante get out of hell

7. Stop it immediately

8. Rosemary studied for her Ph D at Yale

9. Has Dr Payne agreed to treat you

10. Hamlet asked why it all had to end this way

Internal Punctuation

The Semicolon

1. A semicolon is used to join two main clauses that are not joined by a coordinating conjunction. Sometimes a transitional word or phrase follows the semicolon.

 EXAMPLES   Thirteen people saw the incident; each one described it differently.

All tragedies end in death; on the other hand, all comedies end in marriage.

2. A semicolon can be used to join elements in a series when the elements require further internal punctuation.

 EXAMPLE   Before making his decision, Elrod consulted his banker, who abused him; his lawyer, who ignored him; his minister, who consoled him; and his mother, who scolded him.

3. Do not use a semicolon to separate two phrases or two subordinate clauses.

 EXAMPLE   (incorrect)   I will pay you for the work when you return the tape deck that was stolen from our car; and when you repair the dented left fender.

The Colon

1. A colon is used to join two main clauses when the second clause is an example, an explanation, or a restatement of the first clause.

 EXAMPLES   The past fifty years had been a time of turmoil: war, drought, and famine had plagued the small country.

The garden was a delight to all insects: aphids abounded in it, ladybugs exulted in it, and praying mantises cavorted in it.

2. A colon is used when a complete sentence introduces an example, a series, a list, or a direct quotation. Often a colon will come after the words *follows* or *following*.

 EXAMPLES

The paper explored the comic elements of three Melville novels: *Moby Dick, Mardi,* and *Pierre.*

The list of complaints included the following items: leaky faucets, peeling wallpaper, and a nauseous green love seat.

3. A colon is generally not used after a verb.

 EXAMPLES

(incorrect)   At the store I bought: bread, eggs, and bacon.

(correct)   At the store I bought bread, eggs, and bacon.

 PRACTICE   In the following sentences, add semicolons and colons where necessary.

1. Check on the cobra; I'll look for the mongoose.

2. Homer bought the following items: bag balm, cow chip hardener, and an okra peeler.

3. Nessie was seldom seen in the loch; however, today would be an exception.

4. This summer, Beauregard is going to visit Gettysburg, Shiloh, and Manassas.

5. Every night Wilbur had the same dream: he saw himself flying through the air in some strange machine.

Quotation Marks

1. Quotation marks are used to enclose direct quotations and dialogue.

 EXAMPLES

"When a stupid man is doing something he is ashamed of, he always declares that it is his duty."

—George Bernard Shaw

Woody Allen said, "If my film makes one more person miserable, I've done my job."

2. Quotation marks are not used with indirect quotations.

 EXAMPLES

(direct quotation)   Alexandra said, "I will be at the airfield before dawn."

(indirect quotation)   Alexandra said that she would be at the airfield before dawn.

3. Place periods and commas inside quotation marks.

 EXAMPLES

Flannery O'Connor wrote the short story "A Good Man Is Hard to Find."

"Always forgive your enemies—nothing annoys them so much," quipped Oscar Wilde.

4. Place colons and semicolons outside quotation marks.

EXAMPLES

Priscilla was disgusted by the story "The Great Toad Massacre": it was grossly unfair to toads and contained too much gratuitous violence.

Abner felt everyone should read the essay "The Shocking State of Okra Cookery"; he had even had several copies made just in case he found someone who was interested.

5. Place the question mark inside the quotation marks if the quotation is a question. Place the question mark outside the quotation marks if the quotation is not a question but the whole sentence is.

EXAMPLES

The poem asks, "What are patterns for?"

Did Mark Twain say, "Never put off until tomorrow what you can do the day after tomorrow"?

6. Place the exclamation point inside the quotation marks if the quotation is an exclamation. Place it outside the quotation marks if the quotation is not an exclamation but the whole sentence is.

EXAMPLES

"An earwig in my ointment!" the disgusted pharmacist proclaimed.

Please stop saying "It's time to leave"!

PRACTICE   Add semicolons, colons, and quotation marks to the following sentences.

1. Bill said, "Gwyneth Paltrow is the most attractive actress"; however, he had not yet seen Roxanne Barr.

2. "It was the best of times; it was the worst of times" are the opening lines of what novel by Charles Dickens?

3. Starbuck looked at Ishmael and said, "Pass the half and half" however, Ishmael refused.

4. Paul kept repeating the following words to himself "One if by land, and two if by sea."

5. Clint Eastwood spoke into his cell phone and said, Play that dangerous song for me again.

6. Would you like to hear a riddle? asked the Sphinx.

7. The San Diego Chargers fan got up at halftime and started to leave, shouting, Never again!

8. When Sisyphus rolled the stone to the top of the hill, why did he say, Please don't roll back down?

9. Ambrose Bierce said, A bore is someone who talks when you wish him to listen.

10. Marc Antony said, I come to bury Caesar, not to praise him however, he really had much more to say.

The Apostrophe

1. <u>Apostrophes are used to form contractions.</u> The apostrophe replaces the omitted letter or letters.

I am	I'm	did not	didn't
you are	you're	is not	isn't
it is	it's	were not	weren't
they are	they're	will not	won't
does not	doesn't	cannot	can't

2. <u>Apostrophes are used to form the possessives of nouns and indefinite pronouns.</u>

   a. Add *'s* to form the possessive of all singular nouns and all indefinite pronouns.

 EXAMPLES

(singular nouns)	The **girl's** hair was shiny.
	Charles's car is rolling down the hill.
(indefinite pronouns)	**Everyone's** watch was affected by the giant magnet.
(compound words)	Mr. Giuliano left on Monday to attend his **son-in-law's** graduation.
(joint possession)	**Vladimir and Natasha's** wedding was long and elaborate.

b. Add only an apostrophe to form the possessive of plural nouns that end in *s*. However, add *'s* to form the possessive of plural nouns that do not end in *s*.

 EXAMPLES

(plural nouns that end in *s*)

The **Joneses'** cabin had been visited by an untidy bear.

We could hear the three **friends'** conversation all the way down the hall.

(plural nouns that do not end in *s*)

During the storm the parents were concerned about their **children's** safety.

3. Expressions referring to time or money often require an apostrophe.

EXAMPLES

Please give me one **dollar's** worth.

Two **weeks'** vacation is simply not enough.

4. Do not use apostrophes with the possessive forms of personal pronouns.

Incorrect	*Correct*
her's	hers
our's	ours
their's	theirs

NOTE: *It's* means "it is." The possessive form of *it* is *its*.

PRACTICE Add apostrophes (or *'s*) to the following sentences where necessary.

1. Ajaxs back hurt, but he couldnt put the world down.

2. James idea was to write a modern novel based on the *Odyssey*.

3. Didnt you enjoy Jennifer Lawrences performance in *The Hunger Games*?

4. When I quit, I was given a months salary.

5. Charles son couldnt believe how beautiful his sisters new baby was.

6. Its time for Persephones return from Hades.

7. As he rode in the back of his managers car, the boxer said, "I couldve been a contender!"

8. My sister-in-laws children will have only three weeks vacation this year.

9. Roy Lees eating habits disgusted his parents and in-laws.

10. Its a shame that the bobcats territory hasnt been protected.

 PRACTICE

Write sentences of your own according to the instructions.

1. Write a complete sentence in which you use the possessive form of *men*.

The men's room is being remodeled.

_____

2. Write a complete sentence in which you use the possessive form of *Louis*.

_____

_____

3. Write a complete sentence in which you use the possessive form of *father-in-law*.

_____

_____

4. Write a complete sentence in which you use the possessive form of *children*.

_____

_____

5. Write a complete sentence in which you use the possessive form of *Mr. Andrews* and the contraction for *does not*.

_____

_____

Section Two Review

1. Use a **period** at the end of sentences that make statements or commands.

2. Use a **period** to indicate most abbreviations.

3. Use a **question mark** at the end of sentences that ask questions.

4. Do not use a **question mark** at the end of an indirect question.

5. Use an **exclamation point** after exclamatory words, phrases, and short sentences.

6. Use the **exclamation point** sparingly in college writing.

7. Use a **semicolon** to join two main clauses that are not joined by a coordinating conjunction.

8. Use a **semicolon** to separate elements in a series when the elements require further internal punctuation.

9. Do not use a **semicolon** to separate two phrases or two subordinate clauses.

10. Use a **colon** to join two main clauses when the second main clause is an example, an explanation, or a restatement.

11. Use a **colon** to introduce an example, a series, a list, or a direct quotation.

12. Do not use a **colon** to introduce a series of items that follows a verb.

13. Use **quotation marks** to enclose direct quotations and dialogue.

14. Do not use **quotation marks** with indirect quotations.

15. Place periods and commas inside **quotation marks.**

16. Place colons and semicolons outside **quotation marks.**

17. If a quotation is a question, place the question mark <u>inside</u> the **quotation marks**. If the quotation is not a question, but the whole sentence is, place the question mark <u>outside</u> the quotation marks.

18. If the quotation is an exclamation, place the exclamation mark <u>inside</u> the **quotation marks**. If the quotation is not an exclamation, but the whole sentence is, place the exclamation point <u>outside</u> the quotation marks.

19. Use **apostrophes** to form contractions.

20. Use **apostrophes** to form the possessives of nouns and indefinite pronouns.

Exercise 2A

Add periods, question marks, exclamation points, semicolons, colons, quotation marks, and apostrophes (or 's) to the following sentences as necessary.

1. Carlos yelled, "Help me!"

2. Bonnie wondered why Clyde was spending so much time in the bank

3. Isnt Dad ever coming home asked Telemachus

4. Each of these ideas has affected the history of the Western world democracy, Marxism, Freudianism, existentialism, capitalism, and Protestantism

5. Ishmael asked for all of his shipmates attention

6. Mark Twain said, Never put off till tomorrow what you can do the day after tomorrow just as well

7. Butch looked at Sundance and asked, Shall we jump?

8. The weather was good therefore, NASA launched the shuttle

9. Did Ogden Nash say, Candy is dandy, but liquor is quicker

10. Dr Bolden A Bloodworthy, PhD, wouldn't rule out the existence of vampires

11. The CEO of Apple walked onto the stage then he introduced the companys new iPads

12. Boyds mother brought asparagus wine to the reception however, no one would drink it because of its olive green tint

13. What did you think of the zombies in Brad Pitts latest movie

14. The admiral looked at the bay and yelled, Damn the torpedoes Full speed ahead

15. Arlene Mitchell, M D, looked at the X-rays and then asked, Have you been eating paper clips

Exercise 2B

Add periods, question marks, exclamation points, semicolons, colons, quotation marks, apostrophes (or 's), and commas to the following sentences where necessary.

1. Deliver this package to the old mansion with all of its windows broken at 203 Pierce Boulevard, Concordia, California.

2. Get away yelled Harker when he saw the mans teeth

3. Did you spill your popcorn in the theater, or was that your brother

4. The wound on the side of his head was painful however it didnt deter Vincent from painting his self-portrait

5. Irene used the whole bottle of Vietnamese hot sauce on her burrito of course we had a case of antacid pills just for good measure

6. It takes seventeen muscles to smile and it takes forty-three to frown, said Alfred E Newman

7. You cant fold a piece of paper in half more than seven times luckily the note with the secret code fit into my watch pocket after only six times

8. Did you actually go backstage to ask Ben Affleck for his autograph after his brothers play was over

9. Juanitas mother asked the herpetologist Do all snakes shed their skins

10. Hit he deck shouted Popeye at 4 34 am

11. Harley Starling stated When I sell my poem Ill acquire the following a black cloak with a scarlet lining a floor-length scarf a beret a mysterious girlfriend and a battered typewriter

12. Jane Austen wondered if Mr. Darcys aloof personality would cause her readers to dislike him

13. Where have all the flowers gone asks a well-known folk song

14. My cousins relay team was disqualified when its star sprinters grades were proven to be falsified

15. Ophelia returned Hamlets gifts in addition she accused him of not loving her

Exercise 2C

In the following paragraph, correct any errors in the use of periods, exclamation points, question marks, semicolons, colons, quotation marks, or apostrophes.

1. Some people oppose any type of competition but I think that self-directed competition (i.e. competing against ones own personal standard) can bring many benefits. **2.** Karl Marx for example insisted The capitalist system fosters competition and egoism in all its members and thoroughly undermine's all genuine forms of community. **3.** In addition Ghandi had misgivings about competition **4.** He felt it came from the ego: and could undermine some of our most favorable virtues mutual love cooperation and sacrifice for the well-being of humanity **5.** Although unchecked competition can lead to war poverty and divisiveness it can also have many "positive effects" especially in the form of self-directed competition **6.** For example it has affected how well I play classical guitar **7.** When I started I played the guitar very poorly therefore I decided to play at least one piece or perform one technique more effectively than the week before. **8.** I began on October 10 2012 and as each week passed I competed against myself. **9.** Now only two year's later I have accepted the invitation to play before the Chamber of Commerce in Santa Barbara California. **10.** I have also applied the concept of self-competition to the sport of snow skiing. **11.** Last year while I was skiing in Utah one of my friends turned to me and asked; "Dont you want to try to the black diamond run? **13.** Because I knew my own limitations I decided to keep practicing on the intermediate runs **14.** Once I had mastered them I moved on to the more difficult slopes **15.** By the end of the ski season there were only three slopes all double diamond expert runs that I could not ski well. **16.** Finally self-directed competition has made me a better student **17.** When I am in a class I can choose to compare myself with the other students but I dont instead I try to improve what I have done **18.** My first essay was on a quotation from Henry David Thoreaus *Walden* Most men lead lives of quiet desperation. **19.** When I received only a C I knew that by applying self-competition I could do much better. **20.** By the end of the semester my A essays far outnumbered any others so I achieved an A in the class **21.** Self-directed competition may not be for everyone however I have found that its' a good way to enjoy getting better at what I do

Titles, Capitalization, and Numbers

The rules regarding titles, capitalization, and numbers are not, perhaps, as critical to clear writing as the ones for the punctuation marks discussed in the previous two sections. In fact, you can forget to capitalize at all without losing the meaning of what you are writing. So why should you learn to apply these rules correctly? The answer is simple. You should know how to apply them for the same reason you should know whether it is appropriate to slap a person on the back or to kiss him on both cheeks when you are first introduced. **How people write** says as much about them as **how they act**. Your ability to apply the rules presented in this section, as well as in other sections, identifies you as an educated person.

Titles

1. Place in italics the titles of works that are published separately, such as books, periodicals, and plays.

   - Books: *Huckleberry Finn, Webster's Dictionary*
   - Plays: *Hamlet, Death of a Salesman*
   - Pamphlets: *How to Paint Your House, Worms for Profit*
   - Websites: *CNN.com, Poetry Daily*
   - Long musical works: Beethoven's *Egmont Overture,* Miles Davis's *Kind of Blue*
   - Long poems: *Paradise Lost, Beowulf*
   - Periodicals: *The New York Times, Rolling Stone*
   - Films: *The Artist, Catching Fire*
   - Television and radio programs: *American Idol, Morning Edition*
   - Works of art: Rembrandt's *Night Watch, Venus de Milo*

 EXAMPLES   Hortencia has subscriptions to *Time* and *The New Yorker.*

   The Los Angeles Chamber Orchestra played Bach's *Brandenburg Concerto Number Five.*

2. Use quotation marks to enclose the titles of works that are parts of other works, such as articles, songs, poems, and short stories.

   - Songs: "Honeysuckle Rose," "Yesterday"
   - Poems: "Stopping by Woods on a Snowy Evening," "The Waste Land"

- Articles in periodicals or on websites: "Texas Air's New Flak Attack," "Of Planets and the Presidency"

- Episodes of radio and television programs: "Tolstoy: From Rags to Riches," "Lord Mountbatten: The Last Viceroy"

- Subdivisions of books: "The Pulpit" (Chapter Eight of *Moby Dick*)

 EXAMPLES

The professor played a recording of Dylan Thomas reading his poem "After the Funeral."

Many writing textbooks include Jonathan Swift's essay "A Modest Proposal."

 PRACTICE

In the following sentences, correct any errors in the use of titles. Indicate the need for italics in a title by underlining it.

1. Casey went online and ordered Pat Conroy's <u>The Death of Santini</u>.

2. In Nathaniel Hawthorne's short story <u>Young Goodman Brown</u>, the main character loses his faith in the goodness of people.

3. When I opened my mailbox, I found my current issues of <u>Time</u> and <u>The New Yorker</u> magazines.

4. Billy Collins's poem <u>Absence</u> uses the game of chess as a metaphor.

5. Two current films, <u>Great Expectations</u> and <u>The Great Gatsby</u>, are based on classic novels.

Capitalization

1. <u>Capitalize the personal pronoun *I*.</u>

 EXAMPLE

In fact, **I** am not sure **I** like the way you said that.

2. <u>Capitalize the first letter of every sentence.</u>

EXAMPLE

The road through the desert was endlessly straight and boring.

3. <u>Capitalize the first letter of each word in a title except for *a*, *an*, and *the*, coordinating conjunctions, and prepositions.</u>

NOTE: The first letter of the first word and the first letter of the last word of a title are always capitalized.

- Titles of books: *Moby Dick, Encyclopaedia Britannica*
- Titles of newspapers and magazines: *People, Cosmopolitan, Los Angeles Times*
- Titles of stories, poems, plays, and films: "The Lady with the Dog," "The Road Not Taken," *Othello, Gone with the Wind*

4. <u>Capitalize the first letter of all proper nouns and adjectives derived from proper nouns.</u>

- Names and titles of people: Coretta Scott King, Mr. Birch, Mayor Golding, President Roosevelt, Cousin Alice, Aunt Bea
- Names of specific places: Yosemite National Park, Albuquerque, New Mexico, London, England, Saudi Arabia, Rockefeller Center, London Bridge, Elm Street, Venus, the Rio Grande, the Rocky Mountains, the Midwest

NOTE: Do not capitalize the first letter of words that refer to a direction (such as "north," "south," "east," or "west"). Do capitalize these words when they refer to a specific region.

 EXAMPLES

Texas and Arizona are in the **Southwest.**

The police officer told us to drive **east** along the gravel road and turn **north** at the big pine tree.

- Names of national, ethnic, or racial groups: Indian, Native American, Spanish, Irish, Italian, African American
- Names of groups or organizations: Baptists, Mormons, Democrats, Republicans, American Indian Movement, Boy Scouts of America, Indianapolis Colts, U.S. Post Office
- Names of companies: Ford Motor Company, Target, Coca-Cola Bottling Company
- Names of the days of the week and months of the year but not the seasons: Thursday, August, spring
- Names of holidays and historical events: Memorial Day, the Fourth of July, the French Revolution, the Chicago Fire
- Names of specific gods and religious writings: God, Mohammed, Talmud, Bible

5. The names of academic subjects are not capitalized unless they refer to an ethnic or national origin or are the names of specific courses. Examples include mathematics, political science, English, History 105.

PRACTICE

Correct any errors in the use of titles or capitalization. Indicate the need for italics in a title by underlining it.

1. ȯn friday, september 2, the los angeles philharmonic will present beethoven's symphony number five.

2. A morning for flamingos, a novel by james lee burke, takes place in the south.

3. sierra magazine always gives me good articles on traveling, like the one titled georgia's len foote hike inn.

4. in the old bar, john prine's old folks was playing.

5. several prominent citizens of sioux falls, south dakota, are veterans of the war in iraq.

6. every new year's eve, which occurs on tuesday this year, juan volunteers to be the designated driver.

7. the people in the philippines are suffering through the worst typhoon in history.

8. every actor wants a chance to play the leading role in william shakespeare's play hamlet.

9. as professor kelber sat in the airliner, a flight attendant offered her copies of time, american pilot, and the new yorker magazines.

10. the thrift store run by the episcopal church on state street has decided to move three blocks north this summer.

Numbers

The following rules about numbers apply to general writing rather than to technical or scientific writing.

1. Spell out numbers that require no more than two words. Use numerals for numbers that require more than two words.

EXAMPLES

Last year it rained on only **eighty-four** days.

In 1986 it rained on more than **120** days.

2. Always spell out a number at the beginning of a sentence.

EXAMPLE

Six hundred ninety miles in one day is a long way to drive.

3. In general, use numerals in the following situations:

- Dates: August 9, 2014   30 AD   110 CE
- Sections of books and plays: Chapter 5, page 22
  Act 1, scene 3, lines 30–41
- Addresses: 1756 Grand Avenue
  Hemostat, ID 60047
- Decimals, percentages, and fractions: 75.8   30%, 30 percent   1/5
- Exact amounts of money: $7.95 $1,300,000
- Scores and statistics: Padres 8 Dodgers 5   a ratio of 6 to 1
- Time of day: 3:05   8:15

NOTE: Round amounts of money that can be expressed in a few words can be written out: twenty cents, fifty dollars, one hundred dollars. Also, when the word *o'clock* is used with the time of day, the time of day can be written out: *seven o'clock*.

4. When numbers are compared, are joined by conjunctions, or occur in a series, either consistently use numerals or consistently spell them out.

EXAMPLES

For the company picnic we need **25** pounds of fried chicken, **15** pounds of potato salad, **125** cans of soda, **85** paper plates, **230** napkins, and **85** sets of plastic utensils.

OR

For the company picnic we need **twenty-five** pounds of fried chicken, **fifteen** pounds of potato salad, **one hundred twenty-five** cans of soda, **eighty-five** paper plates, **two hundred thirty** napkins, and **eighty-five** sets of plastic utensils.

PRACTICE   Correct any errors in the use of numbers in the following sentences.

1. After the terrible typhoon that hit the Philippines, ~~six thousand~~ *6,203* ~~two hundred and three~~ children were rescued.

2. *The Secret Life of Walter Mitty* was showing at twelve o'clock and at 2:15.

3. For the class party, Suzette bought 10 boxes of plastic knives and forks, one hundred forty-five paper plates of various sizes, 55 plastic cups, one hundred ten paper coffee cups, and three hundred fifty paper napkins.

4. May eighth, nineteen forty-five is commonly known as V-E Day.

5. Mr. Johnson told 5 of his students to read Act One, scene four of the play.

Section Three Review

1. Underline or place in italics the **titles** of works that are published separately, such as books, plays, and films.

2. Use quotation marks to enclose the **titles** of works that are parts of other works, such as songs, poems, and short stories.

3. **Capitalize** the personal pronoun *I*.

4. **Capitalize** the first letter of every sentence.

5. **Capitalize** the first letter of each word in a title except *a, an, the,* coordinating conjunctions, and prepositions.

6. **Capitalize** all proper nouns and adjectives derived from proper nouns.

7. **Do not capitalize** names of academic subjects unless they refer to an ethnic or national origin or are the names of specific courses.

8. Spell out **numbers** that require no more than two words. Use numerals for numbers that require more than two words.

9. Always spell out a **number** at the beginning of a sentence.

10. In general, use **numerals** for dates, sections of books and plays, addresses, decimals, percentages, fractions, exact amounts of money, scores, statistics, and time of day.

11. When **numbers** are compared, are joined by conjunctions, or occur in a series, either consistently use numerals or consistently spell them out.

Exercise 3A

The following sentences contain errors in the use of titles, capitalization, and numbers. Correct any errors you find. Indicate the need for italics in a title by underlining it.

1. After the film was released, the theme music from *C*hariots of *F*ire became popular.

2. In the movie mccabe and mrs. miller, starring warren beatty and julie christy, music by leonard cohen was used, including the song sisters of mercy.

3. The population of lonestar, south carolina, has been reduced by 2 thousand lately because of a shortage of grits.

4. Our reading club, which is now reading police by jo nesbo, met last wednesday at ten o'clock at wilbur's country chicken house.

5. Last night our softball team, which is called comedy of errors, defeated the defending league champs by a score of twenty-five to twenty.

6. tennessee Williams's play the glass menagerie is being presented by the plutarch university drama club at bob dylan auditorium.

7. donna tart donated an autographed edition of her new novel the goldfinch to the st. bart's episcopal church book sale.

8. the workers at ralphs supermarket were on strike, so the managers had to stock the shelves with two hundred cases of soda, one hundred twenty-four boxes of cereal, 728 pounds of cheese and meat, and 429 cartons of ice cream.

9. Sometimes the powdermilk biscuit company sponsors a portion of the weekly radio program a prairie home companion.

10. The tune I play the most on miles davis's CD kind of blue is freddie freeloader.

11. an hour before the jimmy kimmel live show, his producer reads through the new york times newspaper.

Exercise 3A

continued

12. According to the magazine world weekly news, eight out of ten people who shop at supermarkets buy one of those gossip newspapers like national enquirer.

13. jenna's favorite professor, who teaches history 101 every year, told us that johnny appleseed really did exist.

14. jackson pollock's painting white light is a good example of the school of art called abstract expressionism.

15. The essay titled spam: text and subtext won first place and a prize of 15 ripe avocados in rocco's health 101 class.

Exercise 3B

Compose sentences of your own according to the instructions. (Indicate the need for italics in a title by underlining it.)

1. Write a sentence that includes the author and title of a book.

   During his vacation, Rafael read Tom Clancy's novel

   Patriot Games.

2. Write a sentence that describes a song you like and the musician who wrote it or performs it.

   _____

   _____

3. Tell what movie you last saw in a theater and how much you paid to see it.

   _____

   _____

4. Write a sentence that tells what school you attend and what classes you are taking.

   _____

   _____

5. Write a sentence that tells the number of people in your family, the number of years you have gone to school, the number of classes you are taking, and the approximate number of students at your school.

   _____

   _____

6. Write a sentence that mentions a website you have looked at lately. If possible, include the title of an article from that website.

   _____

   _____

continued

7. In a sentence, describe your favorite television program.

_____

_____

8. Tell where you would go on your ideal vacation. Be specific about the name of the place and its geographical location.

_____

_____

9. Write a sentence that includes your age and address. (Feel free to lie about either one.)

_____

_____

10. Write a sentence that names a musician or musical group or CD that you like.

_____

_____

11. Write a sentence that includes the name of a local newspaper, its approximate circulation, and the average number of pages during the week.

_____

_____

12. Write a sentence that includes a work of art that you know about and the name of the artist. If you need to, make up the name of a work of art and its artist.

_____

_____

Exercise 3B

continued

13. Write a sentence that includes the score of the last baseball, football, or basketball game you were aware of. If you are not a sports fan, make up a score.

_____

_____

14. Write a sentence that tells what time you get up on Mondays, what time your first class starts, what time you have lunch, and what time you usually have dinner.

_____

_____

In the following paragraph, correct any errors in the use of capitalization, numbers, or titles.

1. Although I believe that the beaches in my hometown ~~p~~oseidon, ~~o~~regon, are some of the most beautiful on the ~~C~~oast, I also know that they have some problems that need to be addressed. **2.** For example, on any given weekend between may and september, it is extremely difficult to find a parking place at sea cloud beach after seven-thirty in the morning. **3.** Of course, on any weekend along the pacific coast in the Summer, one can expect the beaches to be crowded, but it is ridiculous when one cannot find a space from Dawn to Nightfall. **4.** Just last weekend, after studying for my Math class on friday night, I rose early saturday morning and drove along the coast down highway 120 from neptune avenue to trident boulevard without finding even 1 parking place. **5.** I was so disappointed that by eight forty-five I gave up and drove South into lake county so I could do some Kayaking. **6.** Another problem with our beaches is the litter. **7.** Last year, when the arapaho film company was using our town as a location for its film called "The Last Time I Met You," I was embarrassed to see all the litter, especially along brandy beach. **8.** Out-of-town visitors can't walk along our beaches without stepping on 3 empty Soft Drink cans or on a gooey pile of paper litter from denny's or from local Concession stands. **9.** Just last monday, as I was reading a local newspaper article called *beaches*, a family picnicking near me neglected to put its trash in the receptacles just a few feet away. **10.** Some of the local Community College students have decided to address the poseidon city council about this problem when they meet on April Sixth at the neptune auditorium. **11.** Finally, a problem that has become apparent, especially during the 3 Summer months, is the behavior of our Lifeguards. **12.** I asked Captain Jorge Sanchez, the Head of the lifeguards, why his guards had to flirt with every Cindy, Bob, or Karen instead of paying attention to the Adults and children in the water. **13.** For example, the last time I was at puma beach, which has a wicked undertow, the 2 lifeguards hardly ever looked at the water because they were distracted by the young men and women on the beach. **14.** In fact, a recent article titled lazy lifeguards in the newspaper "poseidon weekly news" reported that five out of every ten water incidents at our beaches could be avoided if our lifeguards were better trained. **15.** Perhaps our City Leaders need to discuss Mr. Sanchez's effectiveness at their next meeting. **16.** Although these may not be the most important problems we have in Poseidon, they do need to be solved before our once beautiful, safe beaches become too unpleasant to visit.

Sentence Practice: Sentence Variety

Writing is challenging. As we have pointed out a number of times already, writing is a process that requires constant and countless choices. Much head scratching and crossing out go on between the beginning and the end of composing a paragraph. Each sentence can be framed in numerous ways, each version changing—subtly or dramatically—the relationships among the ideas.

Sometimes a short sentence is best. Look at the one that begins this paragraph and the one that begins the paragraph above. At other times you will need longer sentences to get just the right meaning and feeling. Sentence combining exercises give you an opportunity to practice how to express ideas in various ways by encouraging you to move around words, phrases, and clauses to achieve different effects.

When you construct a sentence, you should be aware not only of how it expresses your ideas but also of how it affects the other sentences in the paragraph. Consider the following paragraph as an example. It is the opening paragraph of Rachel Carson's book *The Edge of the Sea*.

> The edge of the sea is a strange and beautiful place. All through the long history of the earth it has been an area of unrest where waves have broken heavily against the land, where the tides have pressed forward over the continents, receded, and then returned. For no two successive days is the shoreline precisely the same. Not only do the tides advance and retreat in their eternal rhythms, but the level of the sea itself is never at rest. It rises or falls as the glaciers melt or grow, as the floor of the deep ocean basins shifts under its increasing load of sediments, or as the earth's crust along the continental margins warps up or down in adjustment to strain and tension. Today a little more land may belong to the sea, tomorrow a little less. Always the edge of the sea remains an elusive and indefinable boundary.

As you can see, Rachel Carson opens her paragraph with a short, simple sentence. Then she writes a sentence that is much longer and more complicated because it begins to explain the general ideas in the first one. It even seems to capture the rhythm of the sea against the land. She follows that one with another short, simple sentence. As the paragraph continues, she varies the length and complexity of her sentences according to what she needs to say. Notice how she ends the paragraph with another simple statement that matches her opening sentence.

Sentence Combining Exercises

In the following sentence combining exercises, you will practice writing sentences so that some are short and concise and others are lengthier and more complex.

 EXAMPLE   Combine the following sentences into three sentences. Experiment with which sounds best.

  a. Sometimes a very simple idea can make a person wealthy.
  b. It was 1873.
  c. A fifteen-year-old boy was uncomfortable in the harsh Maine weather.
  d. He asked his mother to make him a pair of "ear flaps."
  e. All of his neighbors wanted pairs of their own.
  f. His family patented the idea.
  g. They soon became rich.
  h. They called their new product Ear Muffs.

Sometimes a very simple idea can make a person wealthy. In 1873, a fifteen-year-old boy was uncomfortable in the harsh Maine winter, so he asked his mother to make him a pair of "ear flaps." When all of his neighbors wanted pairs of their own, his family patented the idea and soon became rich, calling their new product Ear Muffs.

1. Combine the following sentences into two or three sentences.

  a. It was 1866.
  b. General Placido Vega of Mexico sent four of his men to San Francisco.
  c. They were to buy arms and ammunition.
  d. One man died before they reached San Francisco.
  e. That man was the only one who had the authority to approve any purchase.
  f. The other three men buried the six bags.
  g. The bags were full of gold and heirloom jewelry.
  h. The gold and jewelry were worth $200,000.
  i. They buried the bags in the hills outside of San Bruno.

_____

_____

_____

_____

Sentence Combining Exercises

continued

2. Combine the following sentences into two or three sentences.

    a. There was a shepherd named Diego Moreno.
    b. He saw the men bury the treasure.
    c. The men rode away.
    d. Diego unearthed the six bundles.
    e. He found gold and jewelry.
    f. It was enough to allow him to return to his home.
    g. His home was in Sonora, Mexico.
    h. He would be rich man.

    _____

    _____

    _____

    _____

3. Combine the following sentences into two sentences.

    a. Diego was on his way home.
    b. He feared he was about to be robbed.
    c. He buried the treasure beneath a tree.
    d. The tree was in the Cahuenga Pass.
    e. The Cahuenga Pass is just north of present-day Hollywood.
    f. Diego rode on to Los Angeles.

    _____

    _____

    _____

    _____

Sentence Combining Exercises

continued

4. Combine the following sentences into three sentences.

    a. In Los Angeles Diego Moreno became ill.
    b. There was a wealthy rancho owner.
    c. He was named Jesus Martinez.
    d. He took Diego into his home.
    e. He cared for Diego.
    f. Diego Moreno was grateful.
    g. Diego told Don Jesus about the treasure.
    h. He promised to share it with Don Jesus.
    i. It was as soon as the promise had left his lips.
    j. Diego went into convulsions and died.

_____

_____

_____

_____

5. Combine the following sentences into three sentences.

    a. Jesus Martinez traveled to the Cahuenga Pass.
    b. His stepson Gumisindo Correa traveled with him.
    c. They went to find the treasure.
    d. They found the tree.
    e. It was the tree Diego Moreno had told them about.
    f. They began to dig beneath the tree.
    g. At that very moment Don Jesus had a seizure and died.
    h. His stepson fled from the area.
    i. He vowed never to return.

_____

_____

_____

_____

Sentence Combining Exercises

continued

6. Combine the following sentences into three sentences.

   a. General Vega's three agents returned to San Bruno Hills.
   b. They intended to retrieve the treasure they had buried.
   c. They discovered it had been stolen.
   d. Two of the men were suspicious of each other.
   e. They began to argue.
   f. They drew their pistols.
   g. They killed each other.
   h. The third agent was murdered a few years later.
   i. He was in a mining dispute in Arizona.

   _____

   _____

   _____

7. Combine the following sentences into three sentences.

   a. It was 1886.
   b. A Basque shepherd found his dog digging.
   c. It was digging beneath a tree in the Cahuenga Pass.
   d. He looked at where the dog was digging.
   e. He found an old bag.
   f. The bag was full of gold coins and jewelry.
   g. The shepherd believed the treasure was a sign from God.
   h. The sign was to return to his home in Spain.

   _____

   _____

   _____

   _____

Sentence Combining Exercises

continued

8. Combine the following sentences into two sentences.

   a. The shepherd wanted to hide the treasure from robbers.
   b. He sewed the coins and jewelry into the lining of his poncho.
   c. He was wearing the poncho on a dock.
   d. The dock was in Barcelona Harbor.
   e. He lost his balance.
   f. He fell into the water.
   g. He drowned.

   _____

   _____

   _____

   _____

9. Combine the following sentences into three sentences.

   a. The rest of the treasure remained hidden.
   b. It was 1892.
   c. It was twenty-six years after the treasure was first buried.
   d. Gumisindo Correa heard the story about the single bag of treasure.
   e. It was the bag of treasure discovered by the Basque shepherd.
   f. Correa knew that six bags had been buried.
   g. He decided to return to the Cahuenga Pass.
   h. He wanted to find the other five bags.

   _____

   _____

   _____

   _____

continued

10. Combine the following sentences into two sentences.

    a. It was the day Correa planned to leave Los Angeles for the Cahuenga Pass.

    b. He was killed by an unknown assailant.

    c. To this day, no one has ever discovered the Cahuenga Pass treasure.

    d. It lies beneath some unmarked tree.

    e. The tree is between Hollywood and the San Fernando Valley.

Essay and Paragraph Practice: Expressing an Opinion

Assignment

You have now written narrative and descriptive papers (in Chapters One and Two) and expository papers (in Chapters Three and Four). Your final writing assignment will be to state and support an **opinion.** As in earlier chapters, Exercises 1C (page 299), 2C (page 311), and 3C (page 324) in this chapter have been designed as paragraph models of this assignment. Exercise 1C argues that college students could help defray the cost of their educations by doing volunteer work in their communities; Exercise 2C expresses the opinion that self-directed completion can be valuable; and Exercise 3C claims that the beaches in Poseidon, Oregon, have problems that need correction.

Note that each of these paragraphs includes a topic sentence that expresses an opinion supported by details and examples drawn from the writer's personal knowledge or experience. For instance, the paragraph in Exercise 1C presents examples to support the writer's opinion that students can do different types of community service to help defray the costs of their public education. Your assignment is to write a paper in which you express an opinion that you support with examples and details drawn from your own experiences or observations.

Prewriting to Generate Ideas

Prewriting Application: Finding Your Topic

Use prewriting techniques to develop your thoughts about one of the following topics or a topic suggested by your instructor. Before you choose a topic, prewrite to develop a list of possible reasons and examples that you can use to support your opinion. Don't choose a topic if you do not have examples with which you can support it.

1. Choose a proverb and show why it is or is not good advice. Consider these:

   Don't count your chickens before they hatch.

   The early bird gets the worm.

   Look before you leap.

   If at first you don't succeed, try, try again.

   If you can't beat 'em, join 'em.

   Money can't buy happiness.

2. Support an opinion about the condition of your neighborhood, your college campus, your home, or some other place with which you are familiar.

3. Some people compete in nearly everything they do, whether it be participating in sports, working on the job, or studying in college classes. Other people find competition distracting and even offensive. Write a paragraph in which you support your opinion about competition.

4. Do you eat in fast-food restaurants? Write a paragraph in which you support your opinion about eating in such places.

5. Should parents spank children? Write a paper in which you support your opinion for or against such discipline.

6. Should high school students work at part-time jobs while going to school? Write a paper in which you support an opinion for or against their doing so.

7. Do you know couples who live together without marrying? Write a paper in which you support an opinion for or against such an arrangement.

8. Is peer pressure really a serious problem for people today? Write a paper in which you support an opinion about the seriousness of peer pressure.

9. Is racism, sexism, homophobia, or religious intolerance still a common problem in our society? Write a paper in which you support your opinion one way or the other.

10. Do general education requirements benefit college students? Write a paper in which you support your opinion about such classes.

Choosing and Narrowing the Topic

Once you have settled on several possible topics, consider these points as you make your final selection.

- Choose the more limited topic rather than the more general one.

- Choose the topic about which you could discuss several, not just one or two, reasons in support of your opinion.

- Choose the topic about which you have the most experience or knowledge.

- Choose the topic in which you have the most personal interest. Avoid topics about which you don't really care.

Writing a Thesis Statement or Topic Sentence

If your assignment is to write a single paragraph, you will open it with a topic sentence. If you are writing a complete essay, you will need a thesis statement at the end of your introductory paragraph. In either case, you will need a clear statement of the topic and central idea of your paper.

Prewriting Application: Working with Topic Sentences

Identify the topic sentences in Exercises 1C (page 299), 2C (page 311), and 3C (page 324). What are the topic and the central point in each topic sentence?

Prewriting Application: Evaluating Thesis Statements and Topic Sentences

Write "No" before each sentence that would not make an effective thesis statement or topic sentence *for this assignment*. Write "Yes" before each sentence that would make an effective one. Using ideas of your own, rewrite each ineffective sentence into one that might work.

_____   **1.** The intersection of Whitewood and Los Alamos is one of the most dangerous traffic spots in our city.

_____

_____

_____   **2.** Sometimes the old proverb "If at first you don't succeed, try, try again" is the worst advice that one can give a person.

_____

_____

_____   **3.** Racism has existed in our country for many years.

_____

_____

_____   **4.** My father and mother were married when they were still teenagers.

_____

_____

_____ 5. Not everyone needs to be married to have a strong relationship and a happy family.

_____

_____

_____ 6. Almost every young teenager could benefit from participating in competitive sports.

_____

_____

_____ 7. Many high school students today work at part-time jobs.

_____

_____

_____ 8. Body piercing can be a healthy, safe expression of one's individuality.

_____

_____

_____ 9. There are several good reasons why a person should never drink any carbonated soft drinks.

_____

_____

_____ 10. Most people's family values are going straight downhill.

_____

_____

Prewriting Application: Talking to Others

Form a group of three or four people and discuss the topics you have chosen. Your goal here is to help each other clarify your opinions and to determine if you have enough evidence to support them. Explain why you hold your opinion and what specific reasons and examples you will use to support it. As you listen to the others in your group, use the following questions to help them clarify their ideas.

1. Can the opinion be reasonably supported in a brief paper? Is its topic too general or broad?

2. What specific examples will the writer provide as support? Are they convincing?

3. What is the weakest reason or example? Why? Should it be made stronger or completely replaced?

4. Which reasons or examples are the strongest? Why?

5. Which reason or example should the paper open with? Which should it close with?

Organizing Opinion Papers

An **emphatic** organization, one that saves the strongest supporting material until last, is perhaps most common in opinion papers. If you have a list of three, four, or five good reasons in support of your opinion, consider arranging them so that you build up to the strongest, most convincing one.

Writing the Essay

If your assignment is to write a complete essay:

- Place your **thesis statement** (which should clearly state your opinion) at the end of the introductory paragraph.

- Write a separate **body paragraph** for each reason that supports your opinion.

- Open each body paragraph with a **topic sentence** that identifies the one reason the paragraph will discuss.

- Within each body paragraph, use specific **facts, examples,** and **details** to explain and support your reason.

Writing the Paragraph

If your assignment is to write a single paragraph:

- Open it with a **topic sentence** that clearly identifies your opinion.

- Use **clear transitions** to move from one reason in support of your opinion to the next.

- Use specific **facts, examples,** and **details** to explain and support your reasons.

Writing Application: Identifying Transitional Words, Phrases, and Sentences

Examine Exercises 1C (page 299), 2C (page 311), and 3C (page 324). Identify the transitions that introduce each new reason offered in support of the opinion. Then identify any other transitions that serve to connect ideas between sentences.

Rewriting and Improving the Paper

1. Revise your examples so they are specific and concrete. As much as possible, use actual names of people and places.

2. Add or revise transitions wherever doing so would help clarify movement from one idea to another.

3. Improve your preliminary thesis statement (if you are writing an essay) or your preliminary topic sentence (if you are writing a single paragraph) so that it more accurately states the central point of your paper.

4. Examine your draft for sentence variety. If many of your sentences tend to be of the same length, try varying their length and their structure by combining sentences using the techniques you have studied in the Sentence Practice sections of this text.

Rewriting Application: Responding to Paragraph Writing

Read the following paragraph. Then respond to the questions following it.

School Sports

Many of my relatives believe that playing sports in high school and college is a waste of time and energy, but I disagree. I believe that school sports can help a person stay out of trouble and can lead to bigger and better things. I know, for instance, that sports can help young people who are heading for trouble with the law. I have a close friend who grew up in a very hostile environment. His parents abused him, and he belonged to gangs ever since he was very young. He had been in and out of juvenile court several times when he discovered something special about himself. He discovered that he is a good athlete. He began to excel at baseball and football. He developed a love for both sports. After playing football at Escondido High School, he earned a full scholarship to the University of Nevada. Playing sports can also help people emotionally. For example, sports have helped me learn to control my anger. I am a very emotional person, and when I get angry I just want to hit someone—hard. Whenever I feel like that, I get out on the football field and get physical. By the end of a hard practice, I'm ready to go back and live my life. Football helps me when I'm stressed out or depressed, too. I can always count on my teammates to bring me back up when I'm down. Furthermore, playing sports encourages students to stay in school and motivates them to do well. I'm the kind of person who hates school, but through sports I have learned that the road to success includes an education. There have been many times when I have wanted to drop out of school, but always holding me back is my love for the game of football. I know that football is not always going to be there for me, but school sports have changed my life and have affected the lives of many others as well.

1. Identify the topic sentence. State its topic and central idea. Does it express a definite opinion?

2. How many supporting points are presented in this paper? Identify them.

3. Identify the transitional sentences that introduce each major supporting point. What other transitions are used between sentences?

4. Consider the organization of the paragraph. Would you change the order of the supporting material? Explain why or why not.

5. Consider the sentence variety. What sentences would you combine to improve the paragraph?

Rewriting Application: Responding to Essay Writing

Read the following essay. Then respond to the questions at the end of it.

City Life

Because my father was in the navy, our family moved many times when I was growing up. As a result, I have lived in many different sizes of cities and towns all across the United States, from a tiny farm town outside Sioux Falls, South Dakota, to San Diego, California, one of the largest cities in the United States. After all these moves, I have developed my own opinions about where I want to spend my life. I know that small-town life has its attractions for some people, but as far as I'm concerned large cities offer the kind of life I like to live.

One of the reasons I like living in large cities is that there is always so much to do. I can see plays and movies, attend cultural and sporting events, go shopping, or take walks in the park. For example, within a one-week period last month, I went with my parents to see *Phantom of the Opera*, I attended a Padres baseball game with some friends, I spent a day at the Del Mar Fair, and I went shopping at Horton Plaza Mall. I am sure I could not have had that kind of week in a small town. This weekend I plan to visit the San Diego Wild Animal Park, where condors have been saved from extinction and are now being released into the wild.

I also like large cities because I get the chance to meet people from so many different cultural and ethnic backgrounds. For instance, in one of my first college classes, I met a person from South Vietnam who has become one of my good friends. He and his family have been in the United States for ten years, and they have all sorts of terrifying stories to tell about how they fled their country to start a new life. I also have many Hispanic and African American friends, a natural result of growing up in an area that has a large mix of people.

Finally, I enjoy large cities for a very practical reason. Because there are so many different kinds of companies and industries where I live, I can be relatively sure that I will always be able to find a job somewhere. My goal is to become a software designer, and a large city is exactly the kind of place where I will find many job opportunities. San Diego is the home of many high-tech companies, like Qualcomm, Peregrine, and Oracle. Whether I end up working for one of these companies or starting my own software business, a large city like San Diego is the place to be.

    I suppose life in large cities is not for everybody, but it sure is for me. I cannot imagine spending my day watching the cows or listening to crows in some tiny rural town. Maybe someday I will want the peace and quiet of a place like that, but not today.

1. Identify the thesis statement. State its topic and central idea. Is it an effective thesis statement? Does it state a definite opinion?

2. Identify each topic sentence. State its topic and central idea. Does each topic sentence clearly state a reason in support of the thesis?

3. What transitional words introduce each new body paragraph?

4. Consider the organization of the body paragraphs. Would you change their order in any way? Why or why not?

5. Is each reason supported with specific facts, examples, and details? Identify where such specific support is used. Where would you improve the support?

Proofreading

When proofreading your paper, watch for the following errors:

Sentence fragments, comma splices, and fused sentences

Misplaced modifiers and dangling modifiers

Errors in subject–verb agreement

Errors in pronoun case, pronoun–antecedent agreement, or pronoun reference

Errors in comma use

Errors in the use of periods, question marks, exclamation points, colons, semicolons, and quotation marks

Errors in capitalization, titles, and numbers

Errors in the use of irregular verbs or in word choice

Misspelled words

Now prepare a clean final draft, following the format your instructor has asked for.

Chapter 5 Practice Test

I. Review of Chapters Two, Three, and Four

A. Correct any fragments, fused sentences, or comma splices in the following sentences. Do nothing if the sentence is correct.

1. The BMW Roadster following me.

2. Michelle is eager to see her new python, it is due from FedEx tomorrow.

3. When Thor began hurling lightning bolts toward earth.

4. In order to get a closer photo, Carl climbed into the lion enclosure he was not happy with the results.

5. Yoyo Ma remained completely calm during his performance, however, two of his cello strings broke in the middle of his solo.

B. Correct any dangling or misplaced modifiers in the following sentences. Do nothing if the sentence is correct.

6. Disgusted by the rodents, traps were placed in strategic areas throughout the house.

continued

7. Determined to get to the airport on time, Claudia only decided to pack one dress.

_____

_____

8. The convicts were captured by the guards climbing down a rope from the wall of the prison.

_____

_____

9. Hoping to make a good impression during the interview, a new suit was ordered.

_____

_____

10. Mrs. Turpin walked outside and looked at the hog acting superior to everyone else.

_____

_____

C. Correct any subject–verb agreement errors in the following sentences. Do nothing if the sentence is correct.

11. The mumps are a serious illness often discussed by the staff of the clinic.

12. Have the news reporter or her camera operator reached the fire yet?

13. After a long meeting, the directing team of the series *Homeland* have decided not to kill off the male lead.

14. Here is the polka-dotted bow tie and cummerbund that you ordered for the wedding.

15. Every one of the spectators in the top two rows want the home team to lose.

D. Correct any pronoun use errors in the following sentences. Do nothing if the sentence is correct.

16. Someone who I had met at yesterday's Mardi Gras parade showed up at my front door this morning.

continued

17. Mick and Keith threw themselves against the people who were blocking their way to the stage, but they were not hurt.

18. The coach trying to find a shortstop could not decide between Charlotte and I.

19. Kyla was smarter than her brother, but he was much funnier than her.

20. Naomi's brother was surprised to discover that in England you are supposed to drive on the left side of the road.

II. Chapter Five

A. Add commas to the following sentences where necessary. Do nothing if the sentence is correct.

1. Carlos will you attend the Georgia O'Keeffe show at the museum or will you fly to New Mexico?

2. The Episcopal church in Murky Springs Colorado has invited the Baptist church from Dusty Fields Oklahoma for a potluck on Monday.

3. The Wicked Witch of the West had misplaced her broom a couple of monkeys and the sunscreen for her nose.

4. The terrifying destructive hurricane was moving slowly toward the coast of Florida so people were boarding up their homes and businesses.

5. For her trip down the Amazon Jane Austen who preferred to wear pinafores and sunbonnets packed only two pairs of olive-green dungarees.

6. Jennifer Anniston finished her latest film and called Sandra Bullock for a lunch date.

7. Little Miss Muffet's new friend a harmless spider enjoyed her company but it politely refused any of her curds and whey.

8. John Coltrane who was one of the world's greatest saxophone players admired Benny Goodman a band director of the forties and fifties.

9. After the warm-ups for her first Olympic ski run Su Lin threw her dirty wet sweater into the closet and said "It's time to go home."

10. On the way to Chicago where Elena had been born we stopped in the town of Arbor which is the home of the biggest corncob in the world.

Chapter 5 Practice Test

continued

B. Add periods, exclamation points, question marks, quotation marks, semicolons, colons, and apostrophes (or *'s*) where necessary. Do not add or delete any commas.

11. Pinocchio wondered how Cyranos nose had become so long

12. Eve asked, How do you like my Macintosh

13. Winnies shopping list included the following supplies for the picnic a container for honey, some treats for Piglet, a steak for Tigger, and some good news for Eeyore

14. Babe Ruth yelled, Bring me a dozen hotdogs and a gallon of beer!

15. The years first heavy storm dropped two feet of snow in the local mountains however, we couldnt make it to the slopes because we had to study

16. Oscars girlfriend was disgusted at a number of his habits for instance, she hated the way he signaled for a left turn

17. Gatsby, do you have a quarter for the Coke machine? asked Nick Carroway

18. One of these people has damaged Charles new Volkswagen Miss Scarlet, Colonel Mustard, or Mr. Green

19. Ken asked, Would you introduce me to one of the Bratz girls?

20. SeaWorlds main attraction, Shamu, was acting listless it had contracted a virus common to killer whales

C. In the following sentences correct any errors in the use of titles, capitalization, and numbers. (Indicate the need for italics in a title by underlining it.) Do not add or delete any commas. Do nothing if the sentence is correct.

21. in my american literature 135 class, we are studying william faulkner's short story a rose for emily.

22. The next novel on my reading list, which is titled texting while talking, was published in the summer of two thousand and thirteen.

continued

23. The movie facebook encounters has been running at the bestlook theater for one hundred and twenty-five straight days.

24. 421 lemmings jumped over the cliff at the end of sunset boulevard near my house last friday night.

25. every year the lyceum theater in downtown san diego, california, performs the play a christmas carol by charles dickens.

26. To introduce his products, steve jobs always wore a black turtleneck pullover, a pair of levi's jeans, and gray new balance running shoes.

27. 67 people joined us on our backpacking trip to the sierra nevada mountains to test coleman pup tents.

28. after her biology class on wednesday, michelle walked to her english class, where they were studying robert browning's poem my last duchess.

29. my most embarrassing incident took place at a house on remington avenue, pasadena, but luckily only 5 people witnessed it.

30. By five forty-five in the morning, we had gathered our crucial supplies: ten pounds of marshmallows, 45 bottles of sunscreen, and one hundred sixty-seven copies of stephen king's new paperback.

Chapter 6

Readings for Writers

We hope the reading selections in this chapter will interest you as well as stimulate you to think about the ideas they present. In these selections you will find stories of youthful recklessness and insecurities, reflections on how we should live our lives, and arguments about current issues. If you read these selections thoughtfully, you will find many ideas for topics of your own.

The reading selections are divided into groups of three, with each group illustrating one type of writing assignment from Chapters 1 through 5. Read these selections carefully, as you would read any college reading assignment. To get the most out of each selection, use the following guidelines.

Strategies for Successful Reading

Establish Your Expectations

- *Before* you read, take a moment to think. Consider the title of the selection. Does it raise any questions in your mind? Does it suggest a topic or point that you should look for as you read? Consider any background information that accompanies the reading selection. What does it suggest about the author or the reading material?

- Thinking about these questions should take only a minute or two, but these few minutes are important. They will help you understand more of what you read because you are starting your reading with a focused, active attitude.

First Reading: Underline or Highlight as You Read

- With a pen, pencil, or highlighter in hand, read the material from start to finish, slowly and carefully. During the first reading, you're trying to get an overall sense of the main idea of the selection. Don't try to take notes yet. Instead, just underline or highlight whatever sentences seem important to you. If a sentence seems to state a significant idea, mark it. If an example or fact is particularly striking, mark it, too. If you come across words that you do not recognize, circle or mark them.

Second Reading: Make Notes in the Margins

- Reread the sentences you have underlined or highlighted. In just a few words, write your thoughts or reactions to what you have marked. If you disagree with an idea, say so in the margin. If you don't understand something, write a question mark next to it. Some of the passages you have underlined won't seem important to you anymore. So skip them.

- Completing this step will help you understand what you have read much better than if you merely read the selection through once. You might also begin to recognize both the main idea of the reading selection and the organization of its supporting material.

Find the Central and Supporting Ideas

- Each of the writing assignments in *Inside Writing* asks you to focus on one central idea. Really, everything you write or read has some sort of central idea—even a shopping list. (Its central idea would be "Buy these things!") As you read each of the following selections, watch for the idea it develops. Sometimes the central idea will be stated clearly and obviously. Other times you will need to figure it out without the writer stating it directly. In either case, write out the central idea *in your own words*. Try to express it in only one or two sentences.

- If the central idea expresses an opinion or requires explanation, the reading selection will also include supporting ideas. Identify the supporting ideas, either by marking them in the margin of the selection or by writing them out on a separate sheet of paper.

Respond to the Reading Material

- Your reaction to what you have read is important. Depending on the nature of the reading selection, you may find yourself identifying with the writer, beginning to look at an idea you had never examined before, or disagreeing with the writer altogether. If you have questions or objections or new ideas as or after you read, write them down before you have moved on to other reading material.

Sample Reading Selection

Kill Your Television

James A. Herrick

James A. Herrick, a professor of communication at Hope College in Holland, Michigan, wrote the following selection for the Scripps Howard News Service in 1994. In it he presents five reasons why he does not watch television.

Vocabulary Check

dilemma (2)	uncompensated (6)	noxious (11)
garnering (5)	vacuous (11)	inadvertently (12)

People sometimes ask why I, a professor of communication, do not have a television in my home. When I try to explain this apparent inconsistency, the usual response is something like: "I admire that decision, but I don't think it would work for me." **1**

*A dilemma
It wastes time but we are still attracted to it*

Television presents a dilemma: Many of us find that it does not represent a productive or enriching use of time, but we nevertheless find it attractive as a source of entertainment and information. **2**

So how can a thoroughly modern American choose to get rid of the tube without committing cultural suicide? **3**

Eliminating television from your life can be a perfectly reasonable decision. Here are some of my reasons for taking the cultural path less traveled. **4**

1st reason to stop—objects to the commercial system (What does he mean here?)

First, I object to the system that drives television. Commercial television in America today must be understood, not principally as a medium for delivering entertainment and information, but as an enormous industry centered on garnering viewers of commercials. Entertainment and information are bait in television's great fishing expedition for audiences. And television seeks audiences for only one reason—to sell those audiences to advertisers. Commercials are the point of *commercial* television, and programming is a means of securing attention to those commercials. **5**

When I watch television, I am investing uncompensated time as a "commercials viewer"—my time is being sold to an advertiser by a network. **6**

No, thanks. I've got better things to do. **7**

2nd—a gigantic waste of time 5–6 hours/day! Little reward

(Second,) television viewing is a gigantic waste of time. The typical American family has the television on for five or six hours each day, and in many households it's on considerably longer than that. The only other activities to which most of us devote that much time are work and sleep. Our reward for that investment of time is a meager one—a heavily edited view of world events through "news" programming and the shallow comedies and tragedies of prime time. Given the choice, I would rather spend that time reading, taking a walk, talking with a friend. Which brings me to my (third point.) **8**

3rd—robs relationships of time—true!

Television robs relationships of time. Relationships among friends and family members take time to develop—quantity time. Marriages, for example, are nurtured on communication, and this communication takes time—lots of time, regular time. Television steals the time it takes to build and enjoy real-life relationships, which are a lot more satisfying than sitcoms. **9**

Doesn't time spent watching television together build relationships? No. Television does not usually encourage communication, either while people are watching it or afterward. I am an advocate of conversation, and thus an opponent of television. **10**

4th—the shows are lousy

(Fourth,) let's face it: Television programming is mostly vacuous, noxious or both. Need I elaborate? Does television programming typically set a high standard for personal conduct? Does it ask me to think hard about what I ought to value, and why? Does it provide insights into the intricate issues that face any citizen of this increasingly complex and diverse society? **11**

Television seldom does any of these things. And even when it inadvertently does accomplish a worthwhile goal, there are any number of surer paths to these ends. Most of us need more, not less, incentive to live humanely, think broadly, and engage relationships emphatically. **12**

5th—an unexamined concept of entertainment

(My final) reason for turning off the tube is that involvement with it is often based on an unexamined concept of entertainment. Television is usually justified as a means of entertaining ourselves, of relaxing from **13** the demands of work. But many of us have accepted uncritically the Hollywood notion of entertainment as "amusement without boundaries," whether those boundaries are of time or subject matter. I am not arguing against the fatigued duo of sex and violence. Rather, I am asking: How much time should go to entertaining myself, and which activities are really relaxing? Maybe I'm missing something here, but I don't find television viewing relaxing at all.

Is TV really relaxing?

Finding better sources of entertainment, information and relaxation is not difficult. People freed from the tube find a lot of imaginative and satisfying ways to fill newly discovered time.

There are better things to do.

14

Each of us has precious little time to use as we wish. Why should so much of that time go to television?

15

Narrating an Event

Salvation

Langston Hughes

Langston Hughes is a distinguished twentieth-century American writer. An African American who is best known for his poetry, he also wrote stories, novels, essays, an autobiography, and plays. The following selection, drawn from his autobiography, tells of a crisis early in his life.

Vocabulary Check

revival (1) rounder (6)

dire (3) knickerbockered (11)

I was saved from sin when I was going on thirteen. But not really saved. It happened like this. There was a big revival at my Auntie Reed's church. Every night for weeks there had been much preaching, singing, praying, and shouting, and some very hardened sinners had been brought to Christ, and the membership of the church had grown by leaps and bounds. Then just before the revival ended, they had a special meeting for children, "to bring the young lambs to the fold." My aunt spoke of it for days ahead. That night I was escorted to the front row and placed on the mourners' bench with all the other young sinners, who had not yet been brought to Jesus.

My aunt told me that when you were saved you saw a light, and something happened to you inside! And Jesus came into your life! And God was with you from then on! She said you could see and hear and feel Jesus in your soul. I believed her. I had heard a great many old people say the same thing and it seemed to me they ought to know. So I sat there calmly in the hot, crowded church, waiting for Jesus to come to me.

The preacher preached a wonderful rhythmical sermon, all moans and shouts and lonely cries and dire pictures of hell, and then he sang a song about the ninety and nine safe in the fold, but one little lamb was left out in the cold. Then he said: "Won't you come? Won't you come to Jesus? Young lambs, won't you come?" And he held out his arms to all of us young sinners there on the mourners' bench. And the little girls cried. And some of them jumped up and went to Jesus right away. But most of us just sat there.

1

2

3

A great many old people came and knelt around us and prayed, old women with jet-black faces and braided hair, old men with work-gnarled hands. And the church sang a song about the lower lights are burning, some poor sinners to be saved. And the whole building rocked with prayer and song. 4

Still I kept waiting to *see* Jesus. 5

Finally all the young people had gone to the altar and were saved, but one boy and me. He was a rounder's son named Westley. Westley and I were surrounded by sisters and deacons praying. It was very hot in the church, and getting late now. Finally Westley said to me in a whisper: "God damn! I'm tired o' sitting here. Let's get up and be saved." So he got up and was saved. 6

Then I was left all alone on the mourners' bench. My aunt came and knelt at my knees and cried, while prayers and songs swirled all around me in the little church. The whole congregation prayed for me alone, in a mighty wail of moans and voices. And I kept waiting serenely for Jesus, waiting, waiting—but he didn't come. I wanted to see him, but nothing happened to me. Nothing! I wanted something to happen to me, but nothing happened. 7

I heard the songs and the minister saying: "Why don't you come? My dear child, why don't you come to Jesus? Jesus is waiting for you. He wants you. Why don't you come? Sister Reed, what is this child's name?" 8

"Langston," my aunt sobbed. 9

"Langston, why don't you come? Why don't you come and be saved? Oh, Lamb of God! Why don't you come?" 10

Now it was really getting late. I began to be ashamed of myself, holding everything up so long. I began to wonder what God thought about Westley who certainly hadn't seen Jesus either, but who was now sitting proudly on the platform, swinging his knickerbockered legs and grinning down at me, surrounded by deacons and old women on their knees praying. God had not struck Westley dead for taking his name in vain or for lying in the temple. So I decided that maybe to save further trouble, I'd better lie, too, and say that Jesus had come, and get up and be saved. 11

So I got up. 12

Suddenly the whole room broke into a sea of shouting, as they saw   13
me rise. Waves of rejoicing swept the place. Women leaped in the air.
My aunt threw her arms around me. The minister took me by the hand
and led me to the platform.

When things quieted down, in a hushed silence, punctuated by a   14
few ecstatic "Amens," all the new young lambs were blessed in the
name of God. Then joyous singing filled the room.

That night, for the last time in my life but one—for I was a big boy   15
twelve years old—I cried, in bed alone, and couldn't stop. I buried my
head under the quilts, but my aunt heard me. She woke up and told my
uncle I was crying because the Holy Ghost had come into my life, and
because I had seen Jesus. But I was really crying because I couldn't bear
to tell her that I had lied, that I had deceived everybody in the church,
that I hadn't seen Jesus, and that now I didn't believe there was a Jesus
any more, since he didn't come to help me.

QUESTIONS FOR DISCUSSION

1. What did the young Hughes expect would happen to him in the church? Why did he expect what he did?

2. Narratives often build in tension until they reach a turning point, after which everything is different, both in the story and in the narrator's life. Identify what you believe to be the turning point in this story, and explain why you think it is.

3. Why is Hughes crying at the end of the story? How has he changed? Do you consider the change that has occurred significant? Why or why not?

SUGGESTIONS FOR WRITING

1. In the middle of this event, Hughes is surrounded by people, all of them praying for him and calling out for him to step forward. Have you ever felt the kind of pressure he might be feeling? Have you ever done something you regretted or made some unfortunate decision because of pressure from other people? Write about such a situation, explaining what happened and why.

2. Many people have experienced some event that changed the way they think about life, other people, or themselves. If you have experienced such an event, write a paper telling what happened and in what way you changed.

As They Say, Drugs Kill

Laura Rowley

Laura Rowley graduated from the University of Illinois in 1987, where she was the city editor of the *Daily Illini*. Since then she has worked at the *United Nations Chronicle* in New York City and as a freelance writer. The following selection was first published in *Newsweek on Campus* in 1987.

Vocabulary Check

cardiac arrest (2)	chorus (16)	randomly (29)
ambivalence (2)	gnashing (21)	speculated (29)
stupefied (3)	irreverent (26)	

The fastest way to end a party is to have someone die in the middle of it. 1

At a party last fall I watched a 22-year-old die of cardiac arrest after he had used drugs. It was a painful, undignified way to die. And I would like to think that anyone who shared the experience would feel his or her ambivalence about substance abuse dissolving. 2

This victim won't be singled out like Len Bias as a bitter example for "troubled youth." He was just another ordinary guy celebrating with friends at a private house party, the kind where they roll in the keg first thing in the morning and get stupefied while watching the football games on cable all afternoon. The living room was littered with beer cans from last night's party—along with dirty socks and the stuffing from the secondhand couch. 3

And there were drugs, as at so many other college parties. The drug of choice this evening was psilocybin, hallucinogenic mushrooms. If you're cool you call them "'shrooms." 4

This wasn't a crowd huddled in the corner of a darkened room with a single red bulb, shooting needles in their arms. People played darts, made jokes, passed around a joint and listened to the Grateful Dead on the stereo. 5

Suddenly, a thin, tall, brown-haired young man began to gasp. His eyes rolled back in his head, and he hit the floor face first with a crash. Someone laughed, not appreciating the violence of his fall, thinking the afternoon's festivities had finally caught up with another guest. The 6 laugh lasted only a second, as the brown-haired guest began to convulse and choke. The sound of the stereo and laughter evaporated. Bystanders shouted frantic suggestions:

"It's an epileptic fit, put something in his mouth!" 7

"Roll him over on his stomach!" 8

"Call an ambulance; God, somebody breathe into his mouth." 9

A girl kneeling next to him began to sob his name, and he seemed to moan. 10

"Wait, he's semicoherent." Four people grabbed for the telephone, to find no dial tone, and ran to use a neighbor's. One slammed the dead phone against the wall in frustration—and miraculously produced a dial tone. 11

But the body was now motionless on the kitchen floor. "He has a pulse, he has a pulse." 12

"But he's not breathing!" 13

"Well, get away—give him some f——ing air!" The three or four guests gathered around his body unbuttoned his shirt. 14

"Wait—is he OK? Should I call the damn ambulance?" 15

A chorus of frightened voices shouted, "Yes, yes!" 16

"Come on, come on, breathe again. Breathe!" 17

Over muffled sobs came a sudden grating, desperate breath that passed through bloody lips and echoed through the kitchen and living room. 18

"He's had this reaction before—when he did acid at a concert last spring. But he recovered in 15 seconds . . . ," one friend confided. 19

The rest of the guests looked uncomfortably at the floor or paced purposelessly around the room. One or two whispered, "Oh, my God," over and over, like a prayer. A friend stood next to me, eyes fixed on the kitchen floor. He mumbled, just audibly, "I've seen this before. My dad died of a heart attack. He had the same look. . . ." I touched his shoulder and leaned against a wall, repeating reassurances to myself. People don't die at parties. People don't die at parties. 20

Eventually, no more horrible, gnashing sounds tore their way from the victim's lungs. I pushed my hands deep in my jeans pockets wondering how much it costs to pump a stomach and how someone could be so 21 careless if he had had this reaction with another drug. What would he tell his parents about the hospital bill?

Two uniformed paramedics finally arrived, lifted him onto a stretcher and quickly rolled him out. His face was grayish blue, his mouth hung open, rimmed with blood, and his eyes were rolled back with a yellowish color on the rims.

22

The paramedics could be seen moving rhythmically forward and back through the small windows of the ambulance, whose lights threw a red wash over the stunned watchers on the porch. The paramedics' hands were massaging his chest when someone said, "Did you tell them he took psilocybin? Did you tell them?"

23

"No, I . . . "

24

"My God, so tell them—do you want him to die?" Two people ran to tell the paramedics the student had eaten mushrooms five minutes before the attack.

25

It seemed irreverent to talk as the ambulance pulled away. My friend, who still saw his father's image, muttered, "That guy's dead." I put my arms around him half to comfort him, half to stop him from saying things I couldn't believe.

26

The next day, when I called someone who lived in the house, I found that my friend was right.

27

My hands began to shake and my eyes filled with tears for someone I didn't know. Weeks later the pain has dulled, but I still can't unravel the knot of emotion that has moved from my stomach to my head. When I told one friend what happened, she shook her head and spoke of the stupidity of filling your body with chemical substances. People who would do drugs after seeing that didn't value their lives too highly, she said.

28

But others refused to read any universal lessons from the incident. Many of those I spoke to about the event considered him the victim of a freak accident, randomly struck down by drugs as a pedestrian might be hit by a speeding taxi. They speculated that the student must have had special physical problems; what happened to him could not happen to them.

29

Couldn't it? Now when I hear people discussing drugs I'm haunted by the image of him lying on the floor, his body straining to rid itself of

30

substances he chose to take. Painful, undignified, unnecessary—like a wartime casualty. But in war, at least, lessons are supposed to be learned, so that old mistakes are not repeated. If this death cannot make people think and change, that will be an even greater tragedy.

QUESTIONS FOR DISCUSSION

1. Len Bias was a talented young basketball player who died of a drug overdose after signing with the Boston Celtics. Why does Rowley insist that the victim in her article is different from Bias, that he's "just another ordinary guy"?

2. Consider the effect of the opening paragraph. How did it affect you? Why did Rowley start a new paragraph with the second sentence?

3. Rowley suggests many reactions to the young man's death both as it happens and after, both from those present and from those who later heard about it. Identify the different reactions. Why does Rowley present so many?

SUGGESTIONS FOR WRITING

1. Narrative writing is often used to persuade readers to take or avoid action. Sometimes stories like the one Rowley tells us can engage a reader's emotions and convince him or her of a point more effectively than any argument. Describe one event from your own experience or observation that you hope will move some readers to change their behaviors. Consider an event that depicts some reality about drinking alcohol, smoking cigarettes, driving recklessly, or some other similar behavior.

2. Narrate an event that taught you some truth about life, such as the need for honesty in relationships, the importance of taking personal responsibility for one's actions, or the harm caused by stereotyping people.

"They Dropped Like Flies": The Great Flu Epidemic

Joseph R. Conlin

Joseph R. Conlin is an American historian who received his Ph.D. from the University of Wisconsin. He spent much of his teaching career at California State University, Chico. He has authored over ten books, among them *The American Past: A Survey of American History*. The following essay appears in the 10th edition of that book (2014), and it compares and contrasts the fates of the Central Pacific and Union Pacific railroad companies as they laid tracks across the United States.

Vocabulary Check

pandemic (1)	wretched (3)	afflictions (9)
prime (2)	unprecedented (4)	postulated (10)
trenches (3)	cataclysmic (5)	liaison (10)
curtailed (3)	appropriated (6)	plethora (11)

About 8 million soldiers died in Europe between 1914 and 1918. The "Spanish flu" pandemic of 1918–1919 was deadlier. In just 4 months, it killed 21 million people worldwide. The American army lost 49,000 soldiers in battle, 64,000 to disease, the majority to the flu; 548,452 civilians died of the disease. **1**

The flu first appeared at Fort Riley, Kansas, in March 1918. After a dust storm, 107 soldiers checked into the infirmary complaining of headaches, fever and chills, difficulty breathing, and aches and pains. The illness had hit them in an instant; one moment they were feeling fine, the next they could barely stand; some were dead. Within a week, Fort Riley had 522 cases and in a little more than a month, when the disease abruptly disappeared, 8000. About fifty of the men died. That was not a particularly disturbing figure in an era when a number of contagious diseases were deadly. Alert doctors noted a curious thing, however; most of the victims were in the prime of life and in excellent physical condition. **2**

The soldiers from Fort Riley were shipped to Europe in May and soon the deadly disease spread throughout the continent. In neutral Switzerland alone, 58,000 died of it in July. Flu was so devastating in the trenches that German General Erich Ludendorff curtailed his last ditch offensive. By June, the flu was sweeping Africa and India where **3** the mortality was "without parallel in the history of diseases." The catastrophe in India could be attributed to the wretched poverty of the subcontinent. But what of isolated and not particularly poor Western Samoa, where 7500 of the island's 38,000 people died?

Then the flu began a second world tour. The war had created ideal conditions for a pandemic (a worldwide epidemic). People were moving about in unprecedented numbers; 200,000 to 300,000 crossed the Atlantic to Europe each month, and almost as many crowded westbound steamships. The war also crowded people together. Conditions were perfect for the spread of an airborne virus. With so many hosts handy, the emergence of new viral strains was inevitable.

4

Which is apparently what happened in August, either in western Africa, France, or Spain (which got the blame: Americans called the disease the "Spanish flu"). The deadlier mutation returned to the United States where its effects were cataclysmic. In Boston, where the disease made its landfall, 202 people died on October 1, 1918. New York City reported 3100 cases in one day; 300 died. Later in the month, 851 New Yorkers died in a single day, the record for an American city, Philadelphia lost 289 on October 6; within a week, 5270 were dead. The city's death rate for the month was 700 times usual. Similar figures came in from every large city in the country. Just as worrisome, the flu found its way to the most isolated corners of the United States. An isolated winter logging camp in Michigan was hit. Oregon officials reported finding lone sheepherders dead by their flocks.

5

Public health officials responded as well as could be expected to a catastrophe that no one understood. Congress, many of its members laid low, appropriated money to hire physicians and nurses to set up clinics. Many cities closed theaters, schools, and churches and prohibited public gatherings such as parades and sporting events. Several cities required people to wear gauze masks and punished violators with fines of up to $100. Others, notably Kansas City, where the political boss said frankly that the economy was more important, carried on as usual and was not harder hit than cities that took extreme precautions.

6

Nationwide, about one person in five contracted the flu; the death rate was 3 percent. Philadelphia gathered the dead in carts, as had been

7

done during the "Black Death" of the Middle Ages. The A. F. Brill Company, a manufacturer of trolley cars, turned over its wood shop to coffin makers. Authorities in Washington, D.C., seized a train load of coffins headed for Pittsburgh.

Then, once again, the disease disappeared. There was a less lethal wave (another mutation?) in the spring of 1919 with President Wilson one of the victims. But the worst was over about the time that the First World War ended, allowing physicians to reflect on the character of the disease and to wonder what to do if it recurred.

There were some aspects of the disease upon which medical scientists reflected. The first was that the Spanish flu struck suddenly, giving no warning. Second, the disease went relatively easy on those people who are usually most vulnerable to respiratory disease—the elderly—and hardest on those who usually shook off such afflictions, healthy young people. In the United States, the death rate for white males between the ages of 25 and 34 was, during the 1910s, about 80 per 100,000. In a San Francisco maternity ward in October, 19 out of 42 women died of flue. In Washington, a college student telephoned a clinic to report that two of her three roommates were dead in bed and the third was seriously ill. The report of the police officer sent to investigate read "Four girls dead in apartment." Old people died too, of course, but the overall death rate among the elderly did not rise a single point during the epidemic! Finally, people who had grown up in the worst city slums were less likely to get the disease and, if they got it, less likely to die of it than were people who had grown up in rural environments.

In time, scientists concluded that the Spanish flu was a mutation of a common virus that caused a flu that was nothing more than an inconvenience. It was postulated, although never proved, that the deadly germ was the issue of an unholy liaison between a virus that affected humans and another that affected hogs. Spanish flu became known as "swine flu."

If the theory was true, it explained why poor city people, who were more likely to live with a plethora of minor diseases, had an immunity to the deadly virus that farm people had not. Because old people were more likely to be spared in 1918 and 1919, it may be that the flu was related to a less fatal virus that had caused an epidemic in 1889–1890. Having been exposed to that "bug," the elderly were immune to its descendant.

QUESTIONS FOR DISCUSSION

1. What distinguished the flu of 1918–1919 from other influenzas?

2. How did the flu pandemic spread? What was its geographic movement?

3. In what ways were conditions during World War I favorable for a pandemic?

SUGGESTIONS FOR WRITING

1. Since the 1918–1919 influenza, there have been a number of flu epidemics globally and locally but none as deadly. Still, the flu can still be a serious disease. Describe an instance when you, your family, or someone you know was stricken by the flu or another contagious disease and describe what happened and what the consequences of that illness were.

2. Diseases, of course, are not the only experiences that can cause pain and suffering. If your life has been affected by such an event, describe what happened and how it changed your life.

Describing a Place

Tinker Creek

Annie Dillard

Born in Pittsburgh in 1945, Annie Dillard has established a name for herself as a poet, essayist, and literary critic. Before she was thirty, she won a Pulitzer Prize for *Pilgrim at Tinker Creek*, which chronicles her scientific, spiritual, and philosophical reflections while living in the Roanoke Valley of Virginia. In this selection from *Pilgrim at Tinker Creek*, Dillard takes us from a windless summer evening on the bank of a creek to a vision of "stars, deep stars giving way to deeper stars, deeper stars bowing to deepest stars at the crown of an infinite cone."

Vocabulary Check

stalk (1)	unfathomable (2)	axis (4)
carp (1)	delta (2)	tarantella (4)
muskrat (1)	latitude (4)	

Where Tinker Creek flows under the sycamore log bridge to the tear-shaped island, it is slow and shallow, fringed thinly in cattail marsh. At this spot an astonishing bloom of life supports vast breeding populations of insects, fish, reptiles, birds, and mammals. On windless summer evenings I stalk along the creek bank or straddle the sycamore log in absolute stillness, watching for muskrats. The night I stayed too late I was hunched on the log staring spellbound at spreading, reflected stains of lilac on the water. A cloud in the sky suddenly lighted as if turned on by a switch; its reflection just as suddenly materialized on the water upstream, flat and floating, so that I couldn't see the creek bottom, or life in the water under the cloud. Downstream, away from the cloud on the water, water turtles smooth as beans were gliding down with the current in a series of easy, weightless push-offs, as men bound on the moon. I didn't know whether to trace the progress of one turtle I was sure of, risking sticking my face in one of the bridge's spider webs made invisible by the gathering dark, or take a chance on seeing the carp, or scan the mudbank in hope of seeing a muskrat, or follow the last of the swallows who caught at my heart and trailed it after them like

1

streamers as they appeared from directly below, under the log, flying upstream with their tails forked, so fast.

But shadows spread, and deepened, and stayed. After thousands of years we're still strangers to darkness, fearful aliens in an enemy camp with our arms crossed over our chests. I stirred. A land turtle on the bank, startled, hissed the air from its lungs and withdrew into its shell. An uneasy pink here, an unfathomable blue there, gave great suggestion of lurking beings. Things were going on. I couldn't see whether that sere rustle I heard was a distant rattlesnake, slit-eyed, or a nearby sparrow kicking in the dry flood debris slung at the foot of a willow. Tremendous action roiled the water everywhere I looked, big action, inexplicable. A tremor welled up beside a gaping muskrat burrow in the bank and I caught my breath, but no muskrat appeared. The ripples continued to fan upstream with a steady, powerful thrust. Night was knitting over my face an eyeless mask, and I still sat transfixed. A distant airplane, a delta wing out of a nightmare, made a gliding shadow on the creek's bottom that looked like a stingray cruising upstream. At once a black fin slit the pink cloud on the water, shearing it in two. The two halves merged together and seemed to dissolve before my eyes. Darkness pooled in the cleft of the creek and rose, as water collects in a well. Untamed, dreaming lights flickered over the sky. I saw hints of hulking underwater shadows, two pale splashes out of the water, and round ripples rolling close together from a blackened center. 2

At last I stared upstream where only the deepest violet remained of the cloud, a cloud so high its underbelly still glowed feeble color reflected from a hidden sky lighted in turn by a sun halfway to China. And out of that violet, a sudden enormous black body arced over the water. I saw only a cylindrical sleekness. Head and tail, if there was a head and tail, were both submerged in cloud. I saw only one ebony fling, a headlong dive to darkness; then the waters closed, and the lights went out. 3

I walked home in a shivering daze, up hill and down. Later I lay open-mouthed in bed, my arms flung wide at my sides to steady the whirling darkness. At this latitude I'm spinning 836 miles an hour round the earth's axis; I often fancy I feel my sweeping fall as a 4 breakneck arc like the dive of dolphins, and the hollow rushing of wind raises hair on my neck, and the side of my face. In orbit around the sun I'm moving 64,800 miles an hour. The solar system as a whole, like a merry-go-round unhinged, spins, bobs, and blinks at the speed of 43,200 miles an hour along a course set east of Hercules. Someone has piped, and we are dancing a tarantella until the sweat pours. I open my eyes and I see dark, muscled forms curl out of water, with flapping gills and flattened eyes. I close my eyes and I see stars, deep stars giving way to deeper stars, deeper stars bowing to deepest stars at the crown of an infinite cone.

QUESTIONS FOR DISCUSSION

1. How does Dillard respond to the scene? What seems to be her central impression, her emotional reaction? Point out any sentences that help you determine her reaction.

2. "After thousands of years we're still strangers to darkness, fearful aliens in an enemy camp with our arms crossed over our chests." What does Dillard mean? What prompts her to make such a statement?

3. Consider paragraph 4. In what way are Dillard's thoughts about the spinning earth connected to her observations of Tinker Creek?

SUGGESTIONS FOR WRITING

1. Consider any natural setting with which you are familiar and about which you have a strong feeling. Choose a specific place, one you remember well. If you can, revisit the place, paying particular attention to the specific sights, sounds, and smells that are there. Write a paper that conveys your central impression of the place as you describe it.

2. Tinker Creek causes Annie Dillard to reflect on her place in the universe full of stars as well as in a world of "dark, muscled forms . . . with flapping gills and flattened eyes." Has any place ever caused you to reflect on *who* you are or *why* you are? Write a paper describing such a place in detail and the effect it had on you.

In the Land of Coke-Cola

William Least Heat-Moon

William Least Heat-Moon is the pen name of William Trogdon, who traveled the off-roads of the United States in his van, Ghost Dancing. In 1986 these travels formed the basis of his best-selling work *Blue Highways*, a book named after his encounters on the secondary roads of America, those marked in blue on highway maps. "In the Land of Coke-Cola" presents one such encounter in a rural Georgia restaurant.

Vocabulary Check

artesian (1)	herbicide (2)	tepid (2)
coppice (1)	nematicide (2)	conglomerate (4)
tallow (2)	fumigant (2)	husbandry (6)
fungicide (2)	dehydrated (2)	chert (9)

In the land of "Coke-Cola" it was hot and dry. The artesian water was finished. Along route 72, an hour west of Ninety-Six, I tried not to look for a spring; I knew I wouldn't find one, but I kept looking. The Savannah River, dammed to an unnatural wideness, lay below, wet and cool. I'd come into Georgia. The sun seemed to press on the roadway, and inside the truck, hot light bounced off chrome, flickering like a torch. Then I saw what I was trying not look for: in a coppice, a long-handled pump. **1**

I stopped and took my bottles to the well. A small sign: WATER UNSAFE FOR DRINKING. I drooped like warm tallow. What fungicide, herbicide, nematicide, fumigant, or growth regulant—potions that rebuilt Southern agriculture—had seeped into the ground water? In the old movie Westerns there is commonly a scene where a dehydrated man, crossing the barren waste, at last comes to a water hole; he lies flat to drink the tepid stuff. Just as lips touch water, he sees on the other side a steer skull. I drove off thirsty but feeling a part of mythic history. **2**

The thirst subsided when hunger took over. I hadn't eaten since morning. Sunset arrived west of Oglesby, and the air cooled. Then a road sign: **3**

SWAMP GUINEA'S FISH LODGE

ALL YOU CAN EAT!

An arrow pointed down a county highway. I would gorge myself. A record would be set. They'd ask me to leave. An embarrassment to all.

The road through the orange earth of north Georgia passed an old, three-story house with a thin black child hanging out of every window like an illustration for "The Old Woman Who Lived in a Shoe"; on into hills and finally to Swamp Guinea's, a conglomerate of plywood and two-by-fours laid over with the smell of damp pine woods.

Inside, wherever an oddity or natural phenomenon could hang, one hung: stuffed rump of a deer, snowshoe, flintlock, hornet's nest. The place looked as if a Boy Scout Troop had decorated it. Thirty or so people, black and white, sat around tables almost foundering under piled platters of food. I took a seat by the reproduction of a seventeenth-century woodcut depicting some Rabelaisian banquet at the groaning board.

The diners were mostly Oglethorpe County red-shirt farmers. In Georgia tones they talked about their husbandry in terms of rain and nitrogen and hope. An immense woman with a glossy picture of a hooked bass leaping on the front of her shirt said, "I'm gonna be sick from how much I've ate."

I was watching everyone else and didn't see the waitress standing quietly by. Her voice was deep and soft like water moving in a cavern. I ordered the $4.50 special. In a few minutes she wheeled up a cart and began offloading dinner: ham and eggs, fried catfish, fried perch fingerlings, fried shrimp, chunks of barbecued beef, fried chicken, French fries, hush puppies, a broad bowl of cole slaw, another of lemon, a quart of ice tea, a quart of ice, and an entire loaf of factory-wrapped white bread. The table was covered.

"Call me if y'all want any more." She wasn't joking. I quenched the thirst and then—slowly—went to the eating. I had to stand to reach plates across the table, but I intended to do the supper in. It was all Southern fried and good, except the Southern-style sweetened ice tea; still I took care of a quart of it. As I ate, making up for meals lost, the Old-Woman-in-the-Shoe house flashed before me, lightning in darkness. I had no moral right to eat so much. But I did. Headline: STOMACH PUMP FAILS TO REVIVE TRAVELER.

The loaf of bread lay unopened when I finally abandoned the meal. At the register, I paid a man who looked as if he'd been chipped out of Georgia chert. The Swamp Guinea. I asked about the name. He spoke of himself in the third person like the Wizard of Oz. "The Swamp Guinea only tells regulars."

"I'd be one, Mr. Guinea, if I didn't live in Missouri." 10

"Y'all from the North? Here, I got somethin' for you." He went to the 11 office and returned with a 45 rpm record. "It's my daughter singin'. A little promotion we did. Take it along." Later, I heard a husky north Georgia voice let go a down-home lyric rendering of Swamp Guinea's menu:

> *That's all you can eat*
>
> *For a dollar fifty,*
>
> *Hey! The barbecue's nifty!*

And so on through the fried chicken and potatoes.

As I left, the Swamp Guinea, a former antique dealer whose name 12 was Rudell Burroughs, said, "The nickname don't mean anything. Just made it up. Tried to figure a good one so we can franchise someday."

The frogs, high and low, shrilled and bellowed from the trees and 13 ponds. It was cool going into Athens, a city suffering from a nasty case of the sprawls. On the University of Georgia campus, I tried to walk down Swamp Guinea's supper. Everywhere couples entwined like moonflower vines, each waiting for the blossom that opens only once.

QUESTIONS FOR DISCUSSION

1. Can you visualize the Swamp Guinea's Fish Lodge? List the details you remember and discuss what about them makes them memorable to you.

2. Why does Least Heat-Moon say the place "looked as if a Boy Scout troop had decorated it"? What is he responding to?

3. How many of the five senses are called into play in this selection? List all those you can find.

SUGGESTIONS FOR WRITING

1. Have you ever visited an out-of-the-way café, store, gas station, or any other place far off the main road? Describe it as thoroughly as you can, using specific and concrete details to convey your central impression of it.

2. The patrons in the Swamp Guinea's lodge, the waitress, and the Swamp Guinea himself can all be considered "details" that contribute to Least Heat-Moon's reaction to this place. Have you ever visited such a place, a place where the people themselves contribute to its unique atmosphere? If you have, describe it, using specific and concrete details to convey your central impression of it.

The Ecocity Concept in Curitiba, Brazil

G. Tyler Miller, Scott E. Spoolman

The following reading selection appears in the college textbook *Environmental Science* as a case study of one city's attempt to become more sustainable and livable. The authors describe an "ecocity" as "a people-oriented city, not a car-oriented city. Its residents are able to walk, bike, or use low-polluting mass transit. . . . Trees and plants adapted to the local climate and soil are planted throughout the city. . . . Small organic gardens and a variety of plants . . . often replace conventional grass lawns."

Vocabulary Check

ecological (1)	emissions (2)	capacity (7)
efficient (1)	surplus (5)	sustainability (8)

An example of an ecocity is Curitiba ("koor-i-TEE-ba"), a city of 3.2 million people, known as the "ecological capital" of Brazil. In 1969, planners in the city decided to focus on an inexpensive and efficient mass-transit system rather than on the car. Curitiba now has what some experts consider to be the world's best bus system, in which clean and modern buses transport about 72% of all commuters every day throughout the city using express lanes dedicated to buses. Only high-rise apartment buildings are allowed near major bus routes, and each building must devote its bottom two floors to stores—a practice that reduces the need for residents to travel. 1

Cars are banned from 49 blocks in the center of the downtown area, which has a network of pedestrian walkways connected to bus stations, parks, and bicycle paths running throughout most of the city. Consequently, Curitiba uses less energy per person and has lower emissions of greenhouse gases and air pollutants and less traffic congestion than do most comparable cities. 2

The city transformed flood-prone areas along its six rivers into a series of interconnected parks. Volunteers have planted more than 1.5 million trees throughout the city, none of which can be cut down without a permit, which also requires that two trees must be planted for each one that is cut down. 3

Curitiba recycles roughly 70% of its paper and 60% of its metal, glass, and plastic. Recovered materials are sold mostly to the city's more than 500 major industries, which must meet strict pollution standards. 4

The city's poor people receive free medical and dental care, child care, and job training, and 40 feeding centers are available for street children. Poor people who live in areas not served by garbage trucks 5 can collect garbage and exchange filled garbage bags for surplus food, bus tokens, and school supplies. The city uses old buses as roving classrooms to train its poor in basic job hunting skills and job training. Other retired buses have become health clinics, soup kitchens, and day care centers that are free to low-income parents.

About 95% of its adults have at least a high school education. All school children study ecology. Polls show that 99% of the city's inhabitants would not want to live anywhere else.   6

Curitiba now faces new challenges, as do all cities, mostly due to a fivefold increase in its population since 1965. Curitiba's once-clear streams are often overloaded with pollutants. The bus system is nearing capacity, and car ownership is on the rise. The city is considering building a light-rail system to relieve some of the pressure on the bus system.   7

This internationally acclaimed model of urban planning and sustainability is the brainchild of architect and former college professor Jaime Lerner, who has served as the city's mayor three times since 1969. In the face of new challenges, Lerner and other leaders in Curitiba argue that education is still a key to making cities more sustainable, and they want Curitiba to continue serving as an educational example for that great purpose.   8

QUESTIONS FOR DISCUSSION

1. Which paragraphs discuss Curitiba's approach to transportation? What details in these paragraphs do you find particularly striking?

2. Describe Curitiba's approach to caring for its poor. Do any of these approaches surprise you?

3. What percentage of Curitiba's citizens can read and write? Do you know—or can you find out—if that is higher or lower than the percentage of U.S. citizens who can read and write?

SUGGESTIONS FOR WRITING

1. Have you lived in a city, town, or neighborhood that you have found to be unique in some way? Perhaps its landscaping is quite beautiful (or quite horrible!). Perhaps its architecture is remarkable. Or perhaps the appearance of the single city block or acre of land or rural area where you were raised is still fresh in your memory. Describe that place, using specific and concrete details, to convey your overall impression of it.

2. Curitiba's efforts to care for its poor are described in the reading selection. Consider visiting a poorer section of the area in which you live. Look around. Describe that area, using specific and concrete details, to convey your overall impression of it.

Using Examples

My Way!

Margo Kaufman

Margo Kaufman has published essays in *Newsweek, USA Today, Cosmopolitan,* and *The Village Voice.* The following selection, taken from her first book *1-800-Am-I-Nuts* (1993), illustrates a personality type that we all participate in from time to time. See if you recognize yourself among the many examples she provides.

Vocabulary Check

atrophy (2)	scoffs (6)	hyperventilating (15)
compulsively (4)	compromised (7)	laissez-faire (16)

Is it my imagination, or is this the age of the control freak? I'm standing in front of the triceps machine at my gym. I've just set the weights, and I'm about to begin my exercise when a lightly muscled bully in turquoise spandex interrupts her chest presses to bark at me. "I'm using that," she growls as she leaps up from her slant board, darts over to the triceps machine, and resets the weights.   1

I'm tempted to point out that, while she may have been planning to use the machine, she was, in fact, on the opposite side of the room. And that her muscles won't atrophy if she waits for me to finish. Instead, I go to work on my biceps. Life's too short to fight over a Nautilus machine. Of course, *I'm* not a control freak.   2

Control freaks will fight over anything: a parking space, the room temperature, the last pair of marked-down Maude Frizon pumps, even whether you should barbecue with the top on or off the Weber kettle. Nothing is too insignificant. Everything has to be just so.   3

Just so *they* like it. "These people compulsively have to have their own way," says Los Angeles psychologist Gary Emery. "Their egos are based on being right," Emery says, "on proving they're the boss." (And it isn't enough for the control freak to win. Others have to lose.)   4

"Control freaks are overconcerned with the means, rather than the end," Emery says. "So it's more important that the string beans are the right kind than it is to just enjoy the meal."   5

"What do you mean just enjoy the meal?" scoffs my friend Marc. 6
"There's a right way to do things and then there's everything else."
It goes without saying that he, and only he, has access to that Big Right
Way in the Sky. And that Marc lives alone.

"I really hate to be in any situation where my control over what I'm 7
doing is compromised," he admits. "Like if somebody says, 'I'll handle
the cooking and you can shuck the corn or slice the zucchini,' I tell
them to do it without me."

A control freak's kitchen can be his or her castle. "Let me show you 8
the right way to make rice," said my husband the first time I made the
mistake of fixing dinner. By the time Duke had sharpened the knives,
rechopped the vegetables into two-inch squares, and chided me for
using the wrong size pan, I had decided to surrender all control of the
stove. (For the record, this wasn't a big sacrifice. I don't like to cook.)

"It's easier in a marriage when you both don't care about the same 9
things," says Milton Wolpin, a psychology professor at the University
of Southern California. "Otherwise, everything would be a battle."

And every automobile would be a battleground. There's nothing 10
worse than having two control freaks in the same car. "I prefer to
drive," my friend Claire says. "But no sooner do I pull out of the
driveway than Fred starts telling me what to do. He thinks that I'm an
idiot behind the wheel and that I make a lot of stupid mistakes."

She doesn't think he drives any better. "I think he goes really, really 11
fast, and I'm sure that someday he's going to kill us both," she says.
"And I complain about it constantly. But it's still a little easier for me to
take a back seat. I'd rather get to pick him apart than get picked on."

My friend Katie would withstand the abuse. "I like to control 12
everything," she says. "From where we're going to eat to what we're going
to eat to what movie we're going to see, what time we're going to see it,
where we're going to see it, where we're going to park. Everything!"

But you can't control everything. So much life is beyond our control. 13
And to me, that's what makes it interesting. But not to Katie. "I don't like
having my fate in someone else's hands," she says firmly. "If I take
charge, I know that whatever it is will get done and it will get done well."

I shuffle my feet guiltily. Not too long ago I invited Katie and a 14
bunch of friends out to dinner to celebrate my birthday. It was a control

freak's nightmare. Not only did I pick the restaurant and arrange to pick up the check, but Duke also called in advance and ordered an elaborate Chinese banquet. I thought Katie was going to lose her mind.

"What did you order? I have to know," she cried, seizing a menu. **15** "I'm a vegetarian. There are things I won't eat." Duke assured her that he had accounted for everybody's taste. Still, Katie didn't stop hyperventilating until the food arrived. "I was very pleasantly surprised," she confesses. "And I would trust Duke again."

"I'm sure there are areas where you're the control freak," says **16** Professor Wolpin, "areas where you're more concerned about things than your husband." *Me?* The champion of laissez-faire? "You get very upset if you find something visible to the naked eye on the kitchen counter," Duke reminds me. "And you think you know much better than me what the right shirt for me to wear is."

But I'm just particular. I'm not a control freak. **17**

"A control freak is just someone who cares about something more **18** than you do," Wolpin says.

So what's wrong with being a control freak? **19**

QUESTIONS FOR DISCUSSION

1. Consider the opening two paragraphs. Why does Kaufman present an example there rather than wait until later? What effect does the opening example have on the reader?

2. What does psychologist Gary Emery mean when he says, "Control freaks are overconcerned with the means, rather than the end"?

3. How many separate examples does Kaufman present in this essay? Identify them and discuss why they are or are not effective.

SUGGESTIONS FOR WRITING

1. "Control freaks" all have one personality trait in common—the need to be in control—although they may exhibit that need in different ways. Identify another personality trait that many people have in common, and write a paper in which you illustrate it with examples of your own.

2. Kaufman writes, "But you can't control everything. So much of life is beyond our control." What do you think of that observation? Is it a philosophy that you live by, or do you prefer to maintain control of life? Write a paper in which you use examples to illustrate the kind of person you are.

She's Your Basic L.O.L. in N.A.D.

Perri Klass

Perri Klass is a pediatrician, a mother of three children, and a writer of fiction as well as nonfiction. She has published essays, short stories, and novels. In the following selection she uses examples to illustrate her reactions to the language of medicine during her first three months working as a medical student in a hospital.

Vocabulary Check

jargon (2)	perennial (7)	pompous (15)
primeval (2)	syndromes (9)	locutions (15)

"Mrs. Tolstoy is your basic L.O.L. in N.A.D., admitted for a soft rule-out M.I.," the intern announces. I scribble that on my patient list. In other words Mrs. Tolstoy is a Little Old Lady in No Apparent Distress who is in the hospital to make sure she hasn't had a heart attack (rule out a myocardial infarction). And we think it's unlikely that she has had a heart attack (a *soft* rule-out). 1

If I learned nothing else during my first three months of working in the hospital as a medical student, I learned endless jargon and abbreviations. I started out in a state of primeval innocence, in which I didn't even know that "s̄ C.P., S.O.B., N/V" meant "without chest pain, shortness of breath, or nausea and vomiting." By the end I took the abbreviations so for granted that I would complain to my mother the English Professor, "And can you believe I had to put down three NG tubes last night?" 2

"You'll have to tell me what an NG tube is if you want me to sympathize properly," my mother said. NG, nasogastric—isn't it obvious? 3

I picked up not only the specific expressions but also the patterns of speech and the grammatical conventions; for example, you never say that a patient's blood pressure fell or that his cardiac enzymes rose. Instead, the patient is always the subject of the verb: "He dropped his pressure." "He bumped his enzymes." This sort of construction probably reflects that profound irritation of the intern when the nurses come in the middle of the night to say that Mr. Dickinson has disturbingly low blood pressure. "Oh, he's gonna hurt me bad tonight," the intern may say, inevitably angry at Mr. Dickinson for dropping his pressure and creating a problem. 4

When chemotherapy fails to cure Mrs. Bacon's cancer, what we say is, "Mrs. Bacon failed chemotherapy."   5

"Well, we've already had one hit today, and we're up next, but at least we've got mostly stable players on our team." This means that our team (group of doctors and medical students) has already gotten one new admission today, and it is our turn again, so we'll get whoever is next admitted in emergency, but at least most of the patients we already have are fairly stable, that is, unlikely to drop their pressures or in any other way get suddenly sicker and hurt us bad. Baseball metaphor is pervasive: a no-hitter is a night without any new admissions. A player is always a patient—a nitrate player is a patient on nitrates, a unit player is a patient in the intensive-care unit and so on, until you reach the terminal player.   6

It is interesting to consider what it means to be winning, or doing well, in this perennial baseball game. When the intern hangs up the phone and announces, "I got a hit," that is not cause for congratulations. The team is not scoring points; rather, it is getting hit, being bombarded with new patients. The object of the game from the point of view of the doctors, considering the players for whom they are already responsible, is to get as few new hits as possible.   7

These special languages contribute to a sense of closeness and professional spirit among people who are under a great deal of stress. As a medical student, it was exciting for me to discover that I'd finally cracked the code, that I could understand what doctors said and wrote and could use the same formulations myself. Some people seem to become enamored of the jargon for its own sake, perhaps because they are so deeply thrilled with the idea of medicine, with the idea of themselves as doctors.   8

I knew a medical student who was referred to by the interns on the team as Mr. Eponym because he was so infatuated with eponymous terminology, the more obscure the better. He never said "capillary pulsation" if he could say "Quincke's pulses." He would lovingly tell over the multinamed syndromes—Wolff-Parkinson-White, Lown-Ganong-Levine, Henoch-Schonlein—until the temptation to suggest Schleswig-Holstein or Stevenson-Kefauver or Baskin-Robbins became irresistible to his less reverent colleagues.   9

And there is the jargon that you don't ever want to hear yourself   **10**
using. You know that your training is changing you, but there are
certain changes you think would be going a little too far.

The resident was describing a man with devastating terminal   **11**
pancreatic cancer. "Basically he's C.T.D.," the resident concluded.
I reminded myself that I had resolved not to be shy about asking when
I didn't understand things, "C.T.D.?" I asked timidly.

The resident smirked at me. "Circling The Drain."   **12**

The images are vivid and terrible. "What happened to Mrs. Melville?"   **13**

"Oh, she boxed last night." To box is to die, of course.   **14**

Then there are the more pompous locutions that can make the   **15**
beginning medical student nervous about the effects of medical training.
A friend of mine was told by his resident, "A pregnant woman with
sickle-cell represents a failure of genetic counseling."

Mr. Eponym, who tried hard to talk like the doctors, once   **16**
explained to me, "An infant is basically a brainstem preparation." A
brainstem preparation, as used in neurological research, is an animal
whose higher brain functions have been destroyed so that only the most
primitive reflexes remain, like the sucking reflex, the startle reflex, and
the rooting reflex.

The more extreme forms aside, one most important function of   **17**
medical jargon is to help doctors maintain some distance from their
patients. By reformulating a patient's pain and problems into a language
that the patient doesn't even speak, I suppose we are in some sense
taking those pains and problems under our jurisdiction and also reducing
their emotional impact. This linguistic separation between doctors
and patients allows conversations to go on at the bedside that are
unintelligible to the patient. "Naturally, we're worried about adreno-C.A.,"
the intern can say to the medical student, and lung cancer need never
be mentioned.

I learned a new language this past summer. At times it thrills me to   **18**
hear myself using it. It enables me to understand my colleagues, to
communicate effectively in the hospital. Yet I am uncomfortably aware
that I will never again notice the peculiarities and even atrocities of
medical language as keenly as I did this summer. There may be specific
expressions I manage to avoid, but even as I remark them, promising

myself I will never use them, I find that this language is becoming my professional speech. It no longer sounds strange in my ears—or coming from my mouth. And I am afraid that as with any new language, to use it properly you must absorb not only the vocabulary but also the structure, the logic, the attitudes. At first you may notice these new alien assumptions every time you put together a sentence, but with time and increased fluency you stop being aware of them at all. And as you lose that awareness, for better or for worse, you move closer and closer to being a doctor instead of just talking like one.

QUESTIONS FOR DISCUSSION

1. Jargon is language unique to a specific profession. What is Klass's reaction to the medical jargon she discusses in this essay? Does she have one overall reaction or several different reactions? Refer to specific statements that reveal her attitude.

2. What is your reaction to the terminology in this selection? Do you find it offensive? Understandable? Dehumanizing? Humorous?

3. Klass writes, "And I am afraid that as with any new language, to use it properly you must absorb not only the vocabulary but also the structure, the logic, the attitudes." What does she mean by this statement? Why should she fear absorbing this new vocabulary?

SUGGESTIONS FOR WRITING

1. Klass discovers a new way of talking and thinking while working as a medical student. Consider your own experiences in new situations. Have you ever found yourself in a new environment, one that changed the way you thought, talked, or acted? Perhaps your first year as a college student introduced you to new ways of thinking or acting. Maybe a new job affected you the same way, or a new group of friends. Write a paper in which you use examples to illustrate how you changed for the better or the worse in a new environment.

2. Like doctors, many groups have their own unique ways of speaking that identify members of that group and exclude others. Write a paper examining the language of a group to which you belong. Give examples of that language, explaining not only what it means but also its purpose. Do certain terms create a bond among the speakers? Do they suggest an attitude toward others? Explain the purpose of each example as clearly as you can.

The Three Worst Nuclear Power Plant Accidents

G. Tyler Miller, Scott E. Spoolman

The following reading selection appears in the college textbook *Environmental Science* as a case study involving the advantages and disadvantages of using nuclear power. The authors present three examples of serious nuclear power plant accidents, discussing the causes and consequences of each one.

Vocabulary Check

mandatory (2)	tsunami (6)	optimistic (8)
inadequate (3)	radius (7)	preliminary (9)

The world has experienced three major nuclear power plant accidents— one in the United States, one in the former Soviet Union, and one in Japan. **1**

The first of these accidents involved the partial meltdown of a reactor core at the Three Mile Island nuclear plant in the U.S. state of Pennsylvania in 1979. No mandatory evacuation was ordered, but within a few days, 140,000 people had voluntarily left the areas. The accident caused no known deaths among plant workers or the general public. The cleanup cost the plant owners about $1 billion—about 2.5 times the cost of constructing the reactor. **2**

Several years of investigation revealed that the accident involved a loss of coolant water due to equipment failure stemming from a violation of a U.S. Nuclear Regulatory Commission (NRC) operating rule. Another problem was that the plant operators were not trained well enough to identify and understand what was happening. The accident led to a tightening of NRC regulations. However, critics say that some of the regulations and their enforcement are still inadequate especially for spent fuel rod storage. They also criticize the almost automatic 20-year extensions of the operating licenses that by 2010, had been granted for 63 aging U.S. nuclear reactors whose designs are now outdated, including 23 reactors like the ones involved in Japan's 2011 accident. **3**

The world's worst nuclear power plant accident occurred in 1986 at the Chernobyl nuclear power plant in Ukraine. Two explosions in one of the reactors blew the roof off of the reactor building and partially melted the reactor core. The resulting fires burned for 10 days and **4** released large amounts of radiation into the atmosphere that spread to several countries. Some 350,000 people living within a 19-mile radius of the plant were eventually evacuated from the area.

The Chernobyl death toll may never be known, but investigators have estimated that at least 6,000 workers and cleanup personnel died from exposure to radiation released by the accident. Projections of long-term deaths, mostly from cancers and other health effects caused by radiation exposure, range from 9,000 to 212,000. Investigations revealed that that accident was caused by a combination of poor reactor design, inadequate operating regulations, and human error. Fortunately, the reactor design is not used in most other countries.

The third major accident occurred on March 11, 2011, at the Fukushima Daiichi Nuclear Power Plant in northeast Japan. The accident, which damaged all six of the plant's reactors, was triggered by a major 8.9 offshore earthquake that caused a severe tsunami. A huge wave of seawater washed over the nuclear plant's protective seawalls and knocked out the circuits and backup generators of its emergency core cooling system. Then, explosions (presumably from the buildup of hydrogen gas) blew the roofs off of three of the reactor buildings and released radioactivity into the atmosphere and nearby coastal waters. Evidence indicates that these three reactors suffered partial meltdowns of their cores.

After some initial confusion and conflicting statements about the severity of the accident, the Japanese government implemented mandatory evacuation of all residents within a 10-kilometer (6-mile) radius of the plant. Later, as the severity of the accident became more apparent, this zone was extended to 31 kilometers (19 miles) and U.S. nuclear experts urged extending it to 80 kilometers (50 miles).

Experts have estimated that as many as 50 of the workers involved in dealing with the accident will die from excessive exposure to radioactivity. However, the reasonably quick evacuation of a fairly large zone around the plant should reduce numbers of deaths, cancers, and other health effects of radiation exposure among the public. In 2011, it was not known how long residents would be prevented from returning to their homes. Officials were projecting that it would take at least a year to

5

6

7

8

bring the reactors under control and to clean up the radioactivity in and around the plant, but some experts believed that to be overly optimistic.

After preliminary investigations in 2011, it seemed that one of the most important lessons to be learned from this accident was about the danger of storing intensely radioactive spent fuel rods. The Fukushima plant rods were stored in pools above the reactors, and the most serious radiation emissions probably resulted from the loss of water in these pools. Exposed to the air, the spent fuel rods caught fire and released clouds of radioactive materials.

9

QUESTIONS FOR DISCUSSION

1. Which of these three accidents do the authors describe as the worst? What makes it the worst?

2. The discussions of Three Mile Island and Fukushima both refer to spent fuel rods as an issue. What are spent fuel rods? What is the concern about them at the two sites?

3. Other than the issues discussed in this reading selection, what advantages or disadvantages of using nuclear power are you aware of?

SUGGESTIONS FOR WRITING

1. Accidents at nuclear power plants are dramatic and life-threatening, but many of us participate in activities that can be just as personally dangerous. Some people drive cars in reckless ways; some participate in violent sports; some snow ski or sky dive; even the walk to and from a parking lot can be a dangerous activity. Choose an activity that you participate in or are personally familiar with and illustrate how dangerous it can be with specific examples from your own experience or the experiences of people you know.

2. Unexpected and sometimes life-changing events can occur in anyone's life at any time. Such events do not have to be dramatic and overtly obvious. To the outside observer they might even seem trivial and unimportant, yet they are important to the person who experiences them. If you have had such experiences, write a paper in which you provide several examples of them drawn from your own life or the lives of people you know.

Comparing and Contrasting

Americanization Is Tough on Macho

Rose del Castillo Guilbault

Rose del Castillo Guilbault, the recipient of numerous awards in journalism, has written stories for newspapers, periodicals, radio, and television. In 1991 she was appointed to President George Bush's Advisory Commission on Educational Excellence for Hispanic Students. The following essay first appeared in 1989 in the *San Francisco Chronicle*. In it the author examines differing expectations of what it means to be *macho* in American and Hispanic cultures.

Vocabulary Check

connotations (2)	recalcitrant (10)	patriarchal (15)
disdain (4)	stoically (10)	chauvinistic (16)
quintessential (7)	menial (11)	semantics (16)
ambiguities (10)	indulgent (11)	prototype (16)

What is *macho*? That depends which side of the border you come from. 1

Although it's not unusual for words and expressions to lose their subtlety in translation, the negative connotations of *macho* in this country are troublesome to Hispanics. 2

Take the newspaper descriptions of alleged mass murderer Ramon Salcido. That an insensitive, insanely jealous, hard-drinking, violent Latin male is referred to as *macho* makes Hispanics cringe. 3

"*Es muy macho,*" the women in my family nod approvingly, describing a man they respect. But in the United States, when women say, "He's so macho," it's with disdain. 4

The Hispanic *macho* is manly, responsible, hardworking, a man in charge, a patriarch. A man who expresses strength through silence. What the Yiddish language would call a *mensch*. 5

The American *macho* is a chauvinist, a brute, uncouth, selfish, loud, abrasive, capable of inflicting pain, and sexually promiscuous. 6

Quintessential *macho* models in this country are Sylvester Stallone, Arnold Schwarzenegger, and Charles Bronson. In their movies, they exude toughness, independence, masculinity. But a closer look reveals their machismo is really violence masquerading as courage, sullenness disguised as silence, and irresponsibility camouflaged as independence. 7

If the Hispanic ideal of *macho* were translated to American screen roles, they might be Jimmy Stewart, Sean Connery, and Laurence Olivier. 8

In Spanish, *macho* ennobles Latin males. In English, it devalues them. This pattern seems consistent with the conflicts ethnic minority males experience in this country. Typically the cultural traits other societies value don't translate as desirable characteristics in America. 9

I watched my own father struggle with these cultural ambiguities. He worked on a farm for twenty years. He laid down miles of irrigation pipe, carefully plowed long, neat rows in fields, hacked away at recalcitrant weeds and drove tractors through whirlpools of dust. He stoically worked twenty-hour days during harvest season, accepting the long hours as part of agricultural work. When the boss complained or upbraided him for minor mistakes, he kept quiet, even when it was obvious the boss had erred. 10

He handled the most menial tasks with pride. At home he was a good provider, helped out my mother's family in Mexico without complaint, and was indulgent with me. Arguments between my mother and him generally had to do with money, or with his stubborn reluctance to share his troubles. He tried to work them out in his own silence. He didn't want to trouble my mother—of course that backfired, because the imagined is always worse than the reality. 11

Americans regarded my father as decidedly un-*macho*. His character was interpreted as nonassertive, his loyalty nonambition, and his quietness ignorance. I once overheard the boss's son blame him for plowing crooked rows in a field. My father merely smiled at the lie, knowing the boy had done it, but didn't refute it, confident his good work was well known. But the boss instead ridiculed him for being "stupid" and letting a kid get away with a lie. Seeing my embarrassment, my father dismissed the incident, saying, "They're the dumb ones. Imagine, me fighting with a kid." 12

I tried not to look at him with American eyes because sometimes the reflection hurt. 13

Listening to my aunts' clucks of approval, my vision focused on the qualities America overlooked. "He's such a hard worker. So serious, so responsible." My aunts would secretly compliment my mother. 14

The unspoken comparison was that he was not like some of their husbands, who drank and womanized. My uncles represented the darker side of *macho*.

In a patriarchal society, few challenge their roles. If men drink, it's 15 because it's the manly thing to do. If they gamble, it's because it's how men relax. And if they fool around, well, it's because a man simply can't hold back so much man! My aunts didn't exactly meekly sit back, but they put up with these transgressions because Mexican society dictated this was their lot in life.

In the United States, I believe it was the feminist movement of the 16 early seventies that changed *macho*'s meaning. Perhaps my generation of Latin women was in part responsible. I recall Chicanos complaining about the chauvinistic nature of Latin men and the notion they wanted their women barefoot, pregnant and in the kitchen. The generalization that Latin men embodied chauvinistic traits led to this interesting twist of semantics. Suddenly a word that represented something positive in one culture became a negative prototype in another.

The problem with the use of *macho* today is that it's become an 17 accepted stereotype of the Latin male. And like all stereotypes, it distorts truth.

The impact of language in our society is undeniable. And the misuse 18 of *macho* hints at a deeper cultural misunderstanding that extends beyond mere word definitions.

QUESTIONS FOR DISCUSSION

1. What do you mean when you describe someone as *macho*? Do you see it as a desirable or undesirable trait? Does your usage match up with the author's explanation of what it means in the United States?

2. Guilbault mentions Sylvester Stallone, Arnold Schwarzenegger, and Charles Bronson as examples of American macho, and she contrasts them with Jimmy Stewart, Sean Connery, and Laurence Olivier. How do the first three meet her definition of the word? Do you agree with her evaluation of them? What examples of other movie actors or of personalities in other fields can you give?

3. What point is the author making in her description of her father in paragraphs 10–15? To whom does she compare her father?

SUGGESTIONS FOR WRITING

1. Guilbault writes, "Typically the cultural traits other societies value don't translate as desirable characteristics in America." This statement expresses a truth about differences between groups within one society as well as between entire societies. Characteristics valued within one group or society are not valued in another. Write a paper in which you contrast the reactions of two different groups of people to the same behaviors, customs, or attitudes.

2. Guilbault writes that today the word *macho* suggests a stereotype and that all stereotypes distort truth. Write a paper in which you examine how one stereotype with which you are familiar distorts the truth. Contrast what that stereotype suggests with examples of real people. For instance, what is the stereotype of a police officer or of a young person dressed all in black, baggy clothing? Contrast the stereotypical characteristics associated with such people with real people you know.

The Just-Right Wife

Ellen Goodman

Ellen Goodman has worked as a nationally syndicated columnist and as assistant editor of the *Boston Globe*. She has published many collections of her popular newspaper columns and in 1980 won the Pulitzer Prize for Distinguished Commentary. In the following selection she considers the desire of the American male for the "just-right" wife.

Vocabulary Check

maliciously (8)	Neanderthal (10)
drudge (10)	siphon (12)

The upper-middle-class men of Arabia are looking for just the right kind of wife. Arabia's merchant class, reports the Associated Press, finds the women of Libya too backward, and the women of Lebanon too forward, and have therefore gone shopping for brides in Egypt. 1

Egyptian women are being married off at the rate of thirty a day—an astonishing increase, according to the Egyptian marriage bureau. It doesn't know whether to be pleased or alarmed at the popularity of its women. According to one recent Saudi Arabian groom, the Egyptian women are "just right." 2

"The Egyptian woman is the happy medium," says Aly Abdul el-Korrary of his bride, Wafaa Ibrahiv (the happy medium herself was not questioned). "She is not too inhibited as they are in conservative Moslem societies, and not too liberal like many Lebanese." 3

Is this beginning to sound familiar? Well, the upper-middle-class, middle-aged, merchant-professional-class man of America also wants a "happy medium" wife. He is confused. He, too, has a problem and he would like us to be more understanding. 4

If it is no longer chic for a sheik to marry a veiled woman, it is somehow no longer "modern" for a successful member of the liberal establishment to be married to what he used to call a "housewife" and what he now hears called a "household drudge." 5

As his father once wanted a wife who had at least started college, now he would like a wife who has a mind, and even a job, of her own. The younger men in his office these days wear their wives' occupations on their sleeves. He thinks he, too, would like a wife—especially for 6 social occasions—whose status would be his status symbol. A lady lawyer would be nice.

These men, you understand, now say (at least in private to younger working women in their office) that they are bored with women who "don't do anything." No matter how much some of them conspired in keeping them at home Back Then, many are now saying, in the best Moslem style, "I divorce thee." They are replacing them with more up-to-date models. A Ph.D. candidate would be nice.

7

The upper-middle-class, middle-aged man of today wants a wife who won't make him feel guilty. He doesn't want to worry if she's happy. He doesn't want to hear her complain about her dusty American history degree. He doesn't want to know if she's crying at the psychiatrist's office. He most definitely doesn't want to be blamed. He wants her to fulfill herself already! He doesn't mean that maliciously.

8

On the other hand, Lord knows, he doesn't want a wife who is too forward. The Saudi Arabian merchant believes that the Egyptian woman adapts more easily to his moods and needs. The American merchant also wants a woman who adapts herself to his moods and needs—his need for an independent woman and a traditional wife.

9

He doesn't want to live with a "household drudge," but it would be nice to have an orderly home and well-scrubbed children. Certainly he wouldn't want a wife who got high on folding socks—he is not a Neanderthal—but it would be nice if she arranged for these things to get done. Without talking about marriage contracts.

10

He wants a wife who agreed that "marriage is a matter of give and take, not a business deal and 50–50 chores." It would help if she had just enough conflict herself (for not being her mother) to feel more than half the guilt for a full ashtray.

11

Of course, he sincerely would like her to be involved in her own work and life. But on the other hand, he doesn't want it to siphon away her energy for him. He needs to be taken care of, nurtured. He would like her to enjoy her job, but be ready to move for his, if necessary (after, of course, a long discussion in which he feels awful about asking and she ends up comforting him and packing).

12

He wants a wife who is a sexually responsive and satisfied woman, 13
and he would even be pleased if she initiated sex with him. Sometimes.
Not too often, however, because then he would get anxious.

He is confused, but he does, in all sincerity (status symbols aside), 14
want a happy marriage to a happy wife. A happy medium. He is not
sure exactly what he means, but he, too, would like a wife who is "just
right."

The difference is that when the upper-middle-class, middle-aged 15
man of Arabia wants his wife he goes out and buys one. His American
"brother" can only offer himself as the prize.

QUESTIONS FOR DISCUSSION

1. What does Goodman see as the characteristics of an American "just-right"
   wife? Identify places in the selection where she provides those characteristics.

2. What is Goodman's attitude toward the American man who wants such a
   wife? How do you determine her attitude? Point out places in the selection
   that reveal what she thinks.

3. In what way does this selection reveal comparison/contrast techniques?
   Identify what is compared or contrasted with what in this selection.

SUGGESTIONS FOR WRITING

1. Many of us hold unreasonable expectations of other people, whether those
   people are parents, brothers or sisters, students, or teachers. We want other
   people to act in a way that will make us comfortable. Write a paper in
   which you contrast the unreasonable expectations we place on one type
   of person with the reality of what it might be reasonable to expect.

2. Goodman reveals many characteristics of the "just-right" wife. Is there
   also a "just-right" husband? Choose three characteristics of the "just-right"
   wife and compare and/or contrast them with characteristics of the
   "just-right" husband.

Building the Transcontinental

Joseph R. Conlin

Joseph R. Conlin is an American historian who received his Ph.D. from the University of Wisconsin. He spent much of his teaching career at California State University, Chico. He has authored over ten books, among them *The American Past: A Survey of American History*. The essay "Building the Transcontinental" appears in the 10th edition of that book (2014), and it compares and contrasts the fates of the Central Pacific and Union Pacific railroad companies as they laid tracks across the United States.

Vocabulary Check

sordid (1)	prohibitive (6)	coven (8)
trestles (4)	accommodate (8)	maximize (10)
perpendicular (4)	villainous (8)	feat (10)

The business history of the first transcontinental railroad is sordid. The story of its construction is heroic, an adventure of pathbreaking engineering, mighty labors, and superb organization of a massive undertaking. 1

The Central Pacific's starting point was just east of Sacramento. Except for timber, which was abundant in the Sierra Nevada, nearly all the materials needed to build a railroad had to be brought in by sea around Cape Horn, an 18,000-mile voyage taking ships up to 8 months. Even buying locomotives and rolling stock was difficult until the Civil War ended; during the war the federal government had first claim on both. Coordinating shipments so that materials arrived when they were needed remained a daunting job until the final spike was driven. Nor were there nearly enough unemployed men in California to fill the huge workforce the Central Pacific needed. 2

And so, by September 1865, the railroad reached only 54 miles east to Colfax, California, and those miles were in friendly terrain. Just ahead lay the Sierra Nevada where the CP had to climb to 8000 feet above sea level. Entering the mountains with an inadequate and undependable labor force, Charles Crocker, in charge of construction, experimented with Chinese laborers. He was astonished by their efficiency. Moreover, because they hired on in gangs recruited by Chinese contractors who provided their meals (and, like tyrants, regimented them), Crocker's job was reduced to little more than paying their wages which were far 3 less than white workers demanded. Soon, 80 percent of the CP's workforce was Chinese; there were as many as 7000 on the payroll at a time.

They built timber trestles up to 1600 feet long and, on nearly perpendicular cliffs, they carved out a platform for the trackbed. Men working with heavy hammers and iron miner's bits dangled in baskets lowered from above in order to drill holes for explosives. Dynamite was not yet available. It was patented in 1867 but was not immediately sold in the United States. Crocker first tried nitroglycerine to blast away the rock but, after several horrible accidents with the unstable compound, he forbade its use and switched to black powder. The workmen went through as many as 500 kegs of powder a day. Twice the CP exhausted California's entire supply of the explosive after driving up the price of a keg from $2.50 to $15.

The winter of 1866–1867 was a bad one in California. There were forty-four heavy snowfalls in the mountains; several blizzards each dropped 6 feet of snow. Luckily, eleven tunnels had been begun before the Sierra was buried. That winter, the Chinese workers "lived like moles," rarely seeing the sun. By spring it was obvious that train service in winter would be at best irregular. CP engineers solved the problem by designing snowsheds on the most vulnerable parts of the mountain route. For 34 miles, the CP literally ran indoors through tunnels and snaking timber sheds.

The Union Pacific, building westward from Omaha, Nebraska, faced no difficult mountain crossings. Its challenge was the endless distance of the prairie and plains. Supply was not a problem. Materials could be brought to the head of construction by locomotives. There was, however, no timber on the plains from which cross-ties could be hewn: Cottonwood proved too soft for the stress heavy trains would subject it to. So, the UP had to import its ties from the northwoods of Minnesota, Wisconsin, and Michigan. That distance was not prohibitive in the railway age, but it added cost to a material—lumber—that Americans were accustomed to thinking of as dirt cheap.

The UP had problems with Indians that the CP was spared. Survey and grading crews, working miles ahead of the large construction gangs, frequently exchanged gunfire with small bands of hunters. Most of all the tribes of the Great Plains, the railroaders feared the Cheyenne who had long combined raiding with hunting bison. In August 1867, Cheyenne warriors actually derailed a train bringing supplies to the work gangs and killed the crew.

The UP's laborers were recently discharged Civil War veterans and recent immigrants from Ireland. To accommodate them on the unpopulated plains, construction superintendent Jack Casement, who dressed like a Russian Cossack in winter, designed bunkhouses, kitchens, and dining halls on wheels so that the workers' "town" moved with them as their work progressed. UP camps were not orderly as the CP's Chinese camps were. At the winter headquarters of 1867–1868 at the site of present-day Cheyenne, Wyoming, "the principal pastimes were gambling, drinking villainous rotgut whiskey, and shooting"—and patronizing a mobile coven of resourceful prostitutes whose brothels were also mounted on rolling stock. "Sodom-at-the-end-of-the-line," a visitor called it. Casement was a no-nonsense hands-on disciplinarian as, indeed, he had to be. Although a short man, "sawed off" his employees said, he decked hulking, unruly workers. Firing them was a warning to others who might be thinking to stir up trouble.   8

On average, UP crews laid 2 miles of track a day. A newspaper reporter described their relentless pace: 9

> Track-laying is a science. A light car, drawn by a single horse, gallops up to the front with its load of rails. Two men seize the end of a [18- to 25-foot] rail and start forward, the rest of the gang taking hold by twos. They come forward at a run. At a word of command the rail is dropped in its place, less than thirty seconds to a rail for each gang, and so four rails go down to the minute.

Toward the end of the great project, when the CP and UP were racing to maximize their federal land grants by laying track as quickly as possible, the UP set the single-day record, more than 10 miles of more-or-less functional railroad. The feat involved bedding 31,000 ties and pounding 120,000 spikes.   10

QUESTIONS FOR DISCUSSION

1. What role did geography play in building the railroad for the Central Pacific and the Union Pacific?

2. How did the railroad crews for the two railroad companies differ?

3. Other than the terrain, what were the biggest challenges in laying track for the Central Pacific and the Union Pacific?

SUGGESTIONS FOR WRITING

1. "Building the Transcontinental" compares and contrasts the building of the Central Pacific and Union Pacific railroads. Consider your own experience accomplishing some difficult task. Have you ever found that one approach to the task worked much more effectively than another? Write a paper in which you compare and/or contrast two different ways to approach the same task.

2. The Central Pacific railroad had to cross snow-covered mountains. The Union Pacific crossed vast stretches of flat prairie. Consider areas of your own life where you have experienced the same activity in different locations. Perhaps you have biked in the mountains as well as in the desert. Perhaps you have skied in different locations or camped in very different locales. Choose one such activity and write a paper in which you compare and/or contrast performing that activity in two different locales.

Expressing an Opinion

Bullied to Death

Emma Teitel

Emma Teitel is a freelance writer and a nutrition and eating psychology coach. She has a background in women's studies, holistic health, and Eastern and Western psychology. In the following article, she argues that the dangers of cyberbullying could be prevented if parents monitored their children's use of the computer as closely as they monitored their activities outside the home. This article first appeared in *Maclean's* in 2012.

Vocabulary Check

albeit (2)	consensus (5)	ubiquitous (7)
mauling (4)	voyeurism (6)	pedophile (9)
angst (4)	vendetta (6)	

The Canadian public is mourning the loss of Amanda Todd, a 15-year-old   1
teenager from Port Coquitlam, B.C., whose social-media tormentors
dared her to take her own life, and rejoiced in cyberspace when she
eventually did. Todd died last Wednesday, one month after she posted a
heartbreaking eight-minute YouTube confessional about the events that
drove her into a severe depression. Over 100 Facebook walls have been
erected in Todd's memory since her death, and some anti-bullying
activists have called for Pink Shirt Day, a national anti-bullying initiative,
to honour Todd's memory. NDP MP Dany Morin introduced a
motion in the House of Commons that proposes increased funding
for anti-bullying organizations as well as an in-depth study of bullying
in Canada.

This is all great news. It confirms we're a well-meaning country: we   2
take care of our own—albeit too late in this case. But it also confirms that
Amanda Todd is now an official martyr of the anti-bullying movement,
a movement bent on proving that bullying is a social construct, and
that perhaps if we all love each other a little more and hug each other
a little longer, it will one day disappear.

I'm of the belief that bullying will always exist because so will   3
bullying's parents—discord and cruelty. But I'm equally uncomfortable

with the increasingly common assertion that bullying is a rite of passage; that kids will be kids, and bullies will be bullies. After all, just because something exists, doesn't mean that we can't limit its presence. The question is, how do we go about doing that? Unlike Mark Steyn—and anyone else with a crippling fear of political correctness—I don't think Pink Shirt Day is a scourge, but I do think it's largely ineffective. Why? Because nobody can see your anti-bullying T-shirt on the Internet, where Amanda Todd was arguably bullied to death.

I came of age on the Internet. Like 43 per cent of kids today, I was a victim of cyberbullying—though I didn't really think of it as such because the term hadn't been invented yet. I was also, undoubtedly, a cyberbully. My parents—God bless them—had no idea what I was doing on MSN Messenger and ICQ (precursors to Facebook and Formspring, today's most popular cyberbullying destinations). When I was eleven, I saw middle-aged men masturbating on webcam. I saw a video of two raccoons mauling each other to death. I saw two boys from my homeroom class strip for me in an online chat room. And I returned the favour. In fact, this was a weekly afternoon ritual for my girlfriends and me. While mom and dad were upstairs watching *Frasier,* we would be in the basement "exploring" the Internet. Sure, our parents checked in every once in a while (the sound of their footsteps leaving us more than enough time to close the page and delete the history) but it was when we went out, to the movies or a party, that they checked in with greater frequency and angst. "When will you be home?" they'd ask again and again, when what they probably should have been asking was, "Why do you clear the browser history every time you use the computer?" Or "What exactly are you doing down there in the basement?"

The public consensus about Amanda Todd is that she made a mistake by exposing her breasts on the Internet. What isn't being said, however, and what should be said, is that Todd's mistake is an extremely common one, one I made several times at her age—and one for which I am extremely lucky to have never paid the price.

And I'm not unique. A recent study by Plymouth University found that 80 per cent of respondents aged 16–24 "used a smartphone or the web for sexual purposes." In an investigative piece for the *Telegraph* in July called "Let's Talk about (teen) Sex," journalist Clover Stroud writes that half the teenagers she interviewed had "some experience with cybersex." One subject, an 18-year-old girl named Amber, illustrates this point perfectly. "When we were younger," she tells Stroud, "we quite often used chatrooms or MSN to flirt with guys. Occasionally this went a bit further, with people taking their tops off on a webcam, for example." What's more interesting, however, is what she says next. "I think this kind of stuff, like cybersex, happens more as a young teen between 13 and 15," she says. "I'd be surprised if this was something my [18-year-old] friends were doing." Webcam voyeurism, then, is the "truth or dare" of my generation—and, I suspect, will be for every wired generation to come. And the cyberbullying that often accompanies it is this generation's version of the schoolyard vendetta, only magnified by the breadth of the cyberworld and protected by its anonymity. A recent comprehensive study determined that one out of every five adolescents has at some point cyberbullied someone else. Yet parents are usually shocked to hear that their own kids are preying on the weakest, piling on the vulnerable.

A lot has changed since I was a teenager on the Internet. Photography   7
and photosharing are now completely ubiquitous. (Today's teens need only look at their own parents' online behaviour for proof.) Yet one thing remains the same: despite Internet parental controls, and increased awareness, most parents still do not monitor their kids as closely online as they do offline. If they did, cyberbullying would not be so endemic.

A recent study by *Consumer Reports* found that 7.5 million children   8
with Facebook accounts were younger than 13, and that the vast majority of those accounts were unsupervised by the users' parents. Another study found that 87 per cent of kids surf the Internet without parental rules.

What happened to Amanda Todd was a tragedy that should never   9
happen to another young person again. But the solution to cyberbullying and lewd photo-sharing isn't outreach. It's supervision. Where are the parents when these kids are sitting upstairs in their own bedrooms posing topless? Or posting hateful messages on the Facebook page of a girl who was bullied to death? There is nothing at all old-fashioned about parents monitoring their kids. After all, Todd's biggest bully

wasn't really a bully at all, but a pedophile: if online hacktivist group Anonymous is correct in its findings, then the stranger who pressured Todd to expose herself online and who circulated a topless photo of her wasn't a fellow teen from her high school, but a 32-year-old man living in Vancouver. Parents need to understand that for the first time in history, their kids are more likely to get into trouble in the presumed safety of their own homes than they are in the outside world.

QUESTIONS FOR DISCUSSION

1. What is Emma Teitel's attitude toward the idea that "bullying is a social construct, and that perhaps if we all love each other a little more and hug each other a little longer, it will one day disappear" (paragraph 2).

2. What is Teitel's solution for online bullying? Where do you find it expressed?

3. In paragraph 4 Teitel provides several examples of her own experiences with cybersex and cyberbullying. What is the purpose of these examples? In what way do they strengthen or weaken her argument?

SUGGESTIONS FOR WRITING

1. Consider your own experience with the Internet or social media. What dangers do you see, especially for youth, in those areas? Choose one particular area and write a paper expressing your opinion of that danger. Support your opinion with specific examples.

2. Teitel writes, "A recent comprehensive study determined that one out of every five adolescents has at some point cyberbullied someone else. Yet parents are usually shocked to hear that their own kids are preying on the weakest, piling on the vulnerable." Have you found her assertion to be accurate? Is cyberbullying or a similar behavior common among high school students? Write a paper expressing an opinion on this matter, supporting your opinion with specific examples.

The Media's Image of Arabs

Jack C. Shaheen

In the following selection, Jack Shaheen asks us to consider the damage done by the media's persistently negative portrayal of Arab Americans. He makes it clear that all such stereotypes "blur our vision and corrupt the imagination." This selection first appeared in *Newsweek* in 1988.

Vocabulary Check

stereotype (1)	cliché (2)	whipping boy (7)
caricatures (1)	humane (5)	swarthy (8)

America's bogeyman is the Arab. Until the nightly news brought us TV pictures of Palestinian boys being punched and beaten, almost all portraits of Arabs seen in America were dangerously threatening. Arabs were either billionaires or bombers—rarely victims. They were hardly ever seen as ordinary people practicing law, driving taxis, singing lullabies or healing the sick. Though TV news may portray them more sympathetically now, the absence of positive media images nurtures suspicion and stereotype. As an Arab-American, I have found that ugly caricatures have had an enduring impact on my family.   1

I was sheltered from prejudicial portraits at first. My parents came from Lebanon in the 1920s; they met and married in America. Our home in the steel city of Clairton, Pa., was a center for ethnic sharing—black, white, Jew and gentile. There was only one major source of media images then, at the State movie theater where I was lucky enough to get a part-time job as an usher. But in the late 1940s, Westerns and war movies were popular, not Middle Eastern dramas. Memories of World War II were fresh, and the screen heavies were the Japanese and the Germans. True to the cliché of the times, the only good Indian was a dead Indian. But when I mimicked or mocked the bad guys, my mother cautioned me. She explained that stereotypes blur our vision and corrupt the imagination. "Have compassion for all people, Jackie," she said. "This way, you'll learn to experience the joy of accepting people as they are, and not as they appear in films. Stereotypes hurt."   2

Mother was right. I can remember the Saturday afternoon when my son Michael, who was seven, and my daughter Michele, six, suddenly called out: "Daddy, Daddy, they've got some bad Arabs on TV." They   3 were watching that great American morality play, TV wrestling. Akbar the Great, who liked to hear the cracking of bones, and Abdullah the Butcher, a dirty fighter who liked to inflict pain, were pinning their foes with "camel locks." From that day on, I knew I had to try to neutralize the media caricatures.

It hasn't been easy. With my children, I have watched animated heroes Heckle and Jeckle pull the rug from under "Ali Boo-Boo, the Desert Rat," and Laverne and Shirley stop "Sheik Ha-Mean-Ie" from conquering "the U.S. and the world." I have read comic books like the "Fantastic Four" and "G.I. Combat" whose characters have sketched Arabs as "lowlifes" and "human hyenas." Negative stereotypes were everywhere. A dictionary informed my youngsters that an Arab is a "vagabond, drifter, hobo and vagrant." Whatever happened, my wife wondered, to Aladdin's good genie?

To a child, the world is simple: good versus evil. But my children and others with Arab roots grew up without ever having seen a humane Arab on the silver screen, someone to pattern their lives after. Is it easier for a camel to go through the eye of a needle than for a screen Arab to appear as a genuine human being?

Hollywood producers must have an instant Ali Baba kit that contains scimitars, veils, sunglasses and such Arab clothing as *chadors* and *kufiyahs*. In the mythical "Ay-rabland," oil wells, tents, mosques, goats and shepherds prevail. Between the sand dunes, the camera focuses on a mock-up of a palace from "Arabian Nights"—or a military air base. Recent movies suggest that Americans are at war with Arabs, forgetting the fact that out of 21 Arab nations, America is friendly with 19 of them. And in "Wanted Dead or Alive," a movie that starred Gene Simmons, the leader of the rock group Kiss, the war comes home when an Arab terrorist comes to the United States dressed as a rabbi and, among other things, conspires with Arab-Americans to poison the people of Los Angeles. The movie was released last year.

The Arab remains American culture's favorite whipping boy. In his memoirs, Terrel Bell, Ronald Reagan's first secretary of education, writes about an "apparent bias among mid-level, right-wing staffers at the White House" who dismissed Arabs as "sand niggers." Sadly, the racial slurs continue. At a recent teacher's conference, I met a woman from Sioux Falls, S.D., who told me about the persistence of discrimination. She was in the process of adopting a baby when an agency staffer warned her that the infant had a problem. When she asked whether the child was mentally ill, or physically handicapped, there was silence. Finally, the worker said: "The baby is Jordanian."

To me, the Arab demon of today is much like the Jewish demon of   8
yesterday. We deplore the false portrait of Jews as a swarthy menace. Yet a similar portrait has been accepted and transferred to another group of Semites—the Arabs. Print and broadcast journalists have started to challenge this stereotype. They are now revealing more humane images of Palestinian Arabs, a people who traditionally suffered from the myth that Palestinian equals terrorist. Others could follow that lead and retire the stereotypical Arab to media Valhalla.

It would be a step in the right direction if movie and TV producers   9
developed characters modeled after real-life Arab-Americans. We could then see a White House correspondent like Helen Thomas, whose father came from Lebanon, in "The Golden Girls," a heart surgeon patterned after Dr. Michael DeBakey on "St. Elsewhere," or a Syrian-American playing tournament chess like Yasser Seirawan, the Seattle grandmaster.

Politicians, too, should speak out against the cardboard caricatures.   10
They should refer to Arabs as friends, not just as moderates. And religious leaders could state that Islam like Christianity and Judaism maintains that all mankind is one family in the care of God. When all imagemakers rightfully begin to treat Arabs and all other minorities with respect and dignity, we may begin to unlearn our prejudices.

QUESTIONS FOR DISCUSSION

1. What does Shaheen mean when he writes that "the Arab demon of today is much like the Jewish demon of yesterday"?

2. What examples does Shaheen use to support his contention that "America's bogeyman is the Arab"? Do you find his examples convincing? Why or why not?

3. Why does Shaheen tell us what his mother said when he "mimicked or mocked the bad guys" (paragraph 2)?

SUGGESTIONS FOR WRITING

1. Consider the media's handling of other ethnic and racial groups—blacks, Hispanics, Native Americans, Chinese, Italians, or any other group. Write a paper expressing an opinion about how one such group is portrayed by the media and support your opinion with specific examples.

2. Do the media portray any other group of people in an unfair way? Consider the media's portrayal of homemakers, women with careers outside the home, homosexuals, athletes, husbands, or any other group. Write a paper expressing your opinion regarding the media's portrayal of one such group and support your opinion with specific examples.

Why Should We Protect Sharks?

G. Tyler Miller, Scott E. Spoolman

The following reading selection appears in the college textbook *Environmental Science* as a case study involving the importance of protecting "the variety of the earth's species, the genes they contain, [and] the ecosystems in which they live."

Vocabulary Check

phytoplankton (2)	extinction (5)	teeming (6)
exaggerates (3)	scalloped (5)	biodiversity (8)
pharmaceutical (4)	ecosystem (6)	

More than 400 known species of sharks inhabit the world's oceans. They vary widely in size and behavior, from the goldfish-sized dwarf dog shark to the whale shark, which can grow to a length roughly equal to that of a typical city bus and weigh as much as two full-grown African elephants.   1

Many people, influenced by movies, popular novels, and widespread media coverage of shark attacks, think of sharks as people-eating monsters. In reality, the three largest species—the whale shark, basking shark, and megamouth shark—are gentle giants. These plant-eating sharks swim through the water with their mouths open, filtering out and swallowing huge quantities of phytoplankton.   2

Media coverage of shark attacks greatly exaggerates the danger from sharks. Every year, members of a few species such as the great white, bull, tiger, oceanic whitetip, and hammerhead sharks injure 60–75 people worldwide, with the majority of the attacks occurring in U.S. waters. Between 1998 and 2009, there were of six deaths per year, on average, from such attacks. Some of these sharks feed on sea lions and other marine mammals and sometimes mistake swimmers, surfers, and scuba divers for their usual prey. Despite the publicity and fear, sharks caused only 49 known deaths in U.S. waters during the 339 years between 1670 and 2009, according to the International Shark Attack File.   3

However, *for every shark that injures or kills a person every year, people kill at least 1 million sharks. This amounts to 73–97 million shark deaths each year,* according to Australia's Shark Research Institute.   4

Many sharks are caught for their fins and then thrown back alive into the water, fins removed, to bleed to death or drown because they can no longer swim. This practice is called *finning*. The fins are widely used in Asia as an ingredient in shark fin soup and as a pharmaceutical cure-all. According to the World Wildlife Fund, shark fin soup can cost as much as $100 a bowl in Hong Kong, which imports about half of the world's shark fins. We also kill sharks for their livers, hides, and jaws, and because we fear them. And the long fishing lines and massive nets used by fishing fleets trap and kill some sharks.

According to a 2009 study by the International Union for Conservation of Nature (IUCN), about 32% of the world's open-ocean shark species are threatened or nearly threatened with extinction. One of the most endangered species is the scalloped hammerhead shark. Sharks are especially vulnerable to population declines because they grow slowly, take a long time to reach sexual maturity, and have only a few offspring per generation. Today, they are among the earth's most vulnerable and least protected animals. 5

Sharks have been around for more than 400 million years. As *keystone species,* some shark species play crucial roles in helping to keep their ecosystems functioning. Feeding at or near the tops of food webs, they remove injured and sick animals from the ocean. Without this ecosystem service provided by sharks, the oceans would be teeming with dead and dying fish and marine mammals. 6

In addition to playing their important ecological roles, sharks could help to save human lives. If we can learn why they almost never get cancer, we could possibly use this information to fight cancer in our own species. Scientists are also studying sharks' highly effective immune systems, which allow their wounds to heal without becoming infected. 7

Some argue that we should protect sharks simply because they, like any other species, have a right to exist. Another reason is that some sharks are keystone species, which means that we and other species need the free ecosystem services they provide. In this chapter we explore the keystone species' role and other special roles played by species in the story of the earth's vital biodiversity. 8

QUESTIONS FOR DISCUSSION

1. In the first paragraph, the authors choose to describe the length and weight of the whale shark in terms of a city bus and two full-grown African elephants. Why? Why don't they just give the actual length and weight ranges instead?

2. Take a closer look at paragraph 3. What is the main point of that paragraph? In what way does it support the larger point of the entire essay?

3. Explain what the authors mean by a "keystone species" in paragraph 6.

SUGGESTIONS FOR WRITING

1. Are you aware of other species or breeds of animal that are endangered or misunderstood by humans? If you are, write a paper expressing an opinion regarding that misperception or misunderstanding and support your opinion with specific examples.

2. Have you noticed that some people dislike or are repelled by animals that you find beautiful, attractive, or unique? If there is a particular animal about which you have a strong opinion (positive or negative), write a paper in which you state your opinion and support it with specific examples.

Practice Final Examination

I. Chapter One

A. Underline all subjects once and all verbs twice.

1. Have you located your iPad?

2. The Democrats and Republicans do not agree on the budget.

3. Emily Dickinson asked her sister to burn her poems, but luckily her sister saved them.

4. Icarus followed the bees to their hive because he wanted some wax.

5. Up the mountain climbed Sir Hillary and his team.

B. In the space provided, indicate whether the underlined word is a noun (N), pronoun (Pro), verb (V), adjective (Adj), adverb (Adv), preposition (Prep), or conjunction (Conj).

_____ 6. Vincent <u>seldom</u> used just a brush on his paintings.

_____ 7. The <u>eccentric</u> painter often put on paint with a palette knife.

_____ 8. Frodo feared the dark woods, <u>yet</u> he continued on the path.

_____ 9. Ms. Havisham will <u>invite</u> Pip to tea.

_____ 10. Ichabod asked <u>everyone</u> to be on the lookout for the headless horseman.

C. In the following sentences, place all prepositional phrases in parentheses.

11. The whole world was sad at the news of Nelson Mandela's death.

12. After sunset an eerie silence settled over the battlefield.

13. Nicola's piercings in her nose and in her tongue pleased her.

14. Through the night Browning thought about the many ways that he loved Elizabeth.

15. Many Visigoths were on their way to Rome.

continued

D. In the following sentences, correct any errors in the use of adjectives or adverbs (or the use of *then* and *than*) by crossing out any incorrect words and writing the correct words above them.

16. I thought the second Bonnie and Clyde film was more better than the recent one,

    which was real boring.

17. Of the two heirs, Agnes was richest, but Juanita was happiest.

18. Although the storm approached slow, we still headed for a shelter quick.

19. Miles felt badly about the dent in his trumpet because the cost to repair it was

    worse then he expected.

20. Who is the better novelist—John Updike, Toni Morrison, or John Steinbeck?

continued
II. Chapter Two

A. Correct all fragments, comma splices, and fused sentences. If the sentence is correct, do nothing to it.

21. Singing "Your Cheating Heart."

_____

_____

22. Terence was disappointed that Sara chose the sushi restaurant, he distrusted raw fish.

_____

_____

23. Writing late into the night, Shakespeare finally finished *Romeo and Juliet*.

_____

_____

24. Odysseus walked up to his home then his dog recognized him.

_____

_____

25. Theo van Gogh went to all the cafés in town he could sell none of Vincent's work.

_____

_____

26. After considering both the BMW and the Mercedes.

_____

_____

27. John told Ringo to speed up the rhythm, Paul disagreed with John.

_____

_____

continued

28. Charlie Parker's nickname was "Bird" it was short for "Yardbird."

_____

_____

29. Never look a grizzly bear in the eyes.

_____

_____

30. Trying to remain nonchalant yet wishing to impress Rhett.

_____

_____

B. In the spaces provided, identify the following sentences as simple, compound, complex, or compound-complex.

31. While Pooh was napping, Tigger stole his honey jar.   _____

32. Penelope kept working on her weaving; however, her suitors were becoming more and more impatient.   _____

33. With sightseeing boats in pursuit, the gray whales headed south toward Mexico.   _____

34. When Nelson Mandela died, South Africa designated ten days for mourning, and dignitaries from all over the world came to pay their respects.   _____

35. Christian Bale seemed embarrassed by his appearance as he played the role of Batman.   _____

continued

C. Compose simple, compound, complex, and compound-complex sentences according to the instructions.

36. Write a simple sentence that begins with a prepositional phrase.

_____

_____

37. Write a compound sentence. Use the coordinating conjunctions *but*, *so*, or *yet* to join the clauses.

_____

_____

38. Write a compound sentence. Use a transitional word like *however* or *therefore* and appropriate punctuation to join the clauses.

_____

_____

39. Write a complex sentence. Use the subordinators *if* or *while*.

_____

_____

40. Write a compound-complex sentence. Use the subordinator *when*.

_____

_____

continued
III. Chapter Three

A. Correct any misplaced or dangling modifiers in the following sentences. If the sentence is correct, do nothing to it.

41. Changing his planned route, Dan's car exited onto rural roads.

_____

_____

42. Sorrenta gave the white terrier to her uncle attached to a red leash.

_____

_____

43. Fearing the fugitive would escape, the house was surrounded by the police.

_____

_____

44. Cleopatra only became afraid when she saw the asp.

_____

_____

45. Flying lazy circles in the sky, the hawk's eye focused on a field mouse.

_____

_____

46. Paul wanted to give the gift to his wife that he had bought at a pet store.

_____

_____

47. The woman speaking into the phone quietly reached for a gun in her purse.

_____

_____

Practice Final Examination

continued

48. Hoping to stop the stone from rolling back down the hill, Sisyphus added spikes to his sandals.

_____

_____

49. The convict was trying to escape the posse trailing drops of blood.

_____

_____

50. Josefina almost spent five hours practicing on her cello.

_____

_____

B. In the following sentences, underline any infinitive phrases, participial phrases, adjective clauses, or appositive phrases and circle the words that they modify.

51. Nathaniel Hale had but one life to give for his country.

52. Reaching into a cave for a lobster, Neal was bitten by a moray eel.

53. The man who stood at the defense table smiled broadly.

54. We took our dogs, Pokey and Diablo, for a long walk.

55. Answering the question in his usual way, Yogi Berra caused a lot of laughter.

C. Add phrases or clauses to the following sentences according to the instructions. Be sure to punctuate correctly.

56. Add a verbal phrase. Use the verb *wander*.

The hikers soon became lost.

_____

_____

57. Add an adjective clause.

Alice rescued the Cheshire cat from the top of the tree.

_____

_____

continued

58. Add a participial phrase to the beginning of this sentence. Use the verb *drive*.

Suzette found herself stuck behind two huge trucks.

_____

_____

59. Add an appositive phrase.

His present delighted Jacobo, so he hugged his wife.

_____

_____

60. Add an infinitive verbal phrase. Use the verb *prepare*.

Antonio drank lots of coffee and stayed up all night.

_____

_____

Practice Final Examination

continued
IV. Chapter Four

A. Correct any subject–verb agreement errors in the following sentences by crossing out the incorrect verb form and writing the correct form above it. If the sentence is correct, do nothing to it.

61. Every dog in the fifteen dog carriers were inspected for fleas before being allowed aboard the planes.

62. A carefully picked group of Secret Service agents accompany the president wherever he goes.

63. Has the bridesmaids or the mother of the bride been told that the groom has been taken to the hospital?

64. The sergeant with his weary marines were late arriving at the base in Pakistan.

65. Everyone attending one of Celine's concerts receive a bright red rose.

66. Twenty pounds of ice cream are not enough for the ice-cream-eating contest.

67. Either my brother's dog Cerberus or one of his three children greets us when we arrive for Christmas dinner.

68. Someone in the upper rows of the balcony were using a cell phone at the concert last night.

69. Here is the jailhouse key and the ball and chain that we will present to Judge Kindless when he retires.

70. The team from a small town in the mountains have won the tournament.

continued

B. Correct any pronoun use errors in the following sentences by crossing out the incorrect pronoun and writing in the correct one above it. In some cases you may have to rewrite part of the sentence. If the sentence is correct, do nothing to it.

71. My brother and myself are planning to hike part of the John Muir Trail this spring.

72. If a truffle gatherer wants to have success, you should bring a pig along.

73. An interpretation of a passage from the *Book of Mormon* caused the argument

    between Jessica and he.

74. When she won a blind date with one of the Norse gods, Aphrodite told Diana the

    good news.

75. My professor locked the classroom door right on the hour so that anyone coming late

    would miss their chance to take the final.

76. A group of people crowded around the Venus de Milo; this bothered the guide.

77. When he saw the bear, Davy Crockett knew that his friend and hisself were in trouble.

78. Reggie's girlfriend pouted when he gave her a two-carat ring, which seemed odd to me.

79. When us delegates protested the way the votes were counted, the chairperson refused

    to listen.

80. The lieutenant asked Norman and him to take charge of the scouting party.

continued
V. Chapter Five

A. Add commas to the following sentences where necessary. If the sentence is correct, do nothing to it.

81. Yes George Washington did not tell a lie and Abe Lincoln walked miles to school in the winter.

82. On December 4 2013 President Obama shook hands with the dictator of Cuba and some people were shocked.

83. The bag contained several curious items: an ancient peace pipe a silver feather some rare coins two retractable garlic presses and a Smurf doll.

84. From the pile of soggy dirty clothes muddy footprints led toward the bathroom.

85. Do you know for example which English word ends in "mt"?

86. Mickey Mouse didn't like the way many people used his name because it hurt his dignity.

87. Mrs. Lincoln who was the First Lady of the United States would let her son sit with General Grant but she wouldn't let any other military person near him.

88. When the people of Jericho learned of the nuclear attack they were of course panic-stricken.

89. Unfortunately the snow started to melt in the spring weather so our ski trip was ruined.

90. Dismayed by the patient's action Sigmund was at a loss for words but he did not stay silent for long.

Practice Final Examination

continued

B. Correct any errors in the use of periods, exclamation points, question marks, semicolons, colons, quotation marks, or apostrophes (or *'s*) in the following sentences. If the sentence is correct, do nothing to it. Do not add or delete any commas.

91. My chemistry professor said, If you apply a blowtorch to Pepto-Bismol, you will end up with a hunk of metal

92. It was my mothers favorite dish when I was a child she was a good cook, too, answered Rebecca

93. When did the patriot say, Give me liberty or give me death

94. When Batman saw the run in his tights, he looked down and shouted, Oh no

95. Here is Alices list teacups, deck of cards, rabbit food, hedgehog food, and caterpillar food.

C. Correct any errors in the use of capitalization, titles, or numbers in the following sentences. If the sentence is correct, do nothing to it. (Indicate the need for italics in a title by underlining it.)

96. The los angeles times newspaper ran a story with the headline election postponed because no worthy candidates found.

97. In the Spring I started the diet called lose weight now, but it's already Summer, and I've gained 15 pounds.

98. Mr. McAlister brought one hundred ten ribbons for the students in his sophomore class to distribute for breast cancer awareness month.

99. One of my favorite poems by billy collins, the former poet laureate of the united states, is called shoveling snow with buddha.

100. Last semester in communications 101 class, we read the time magazine article titled boys won't be boys, concerning sweden's attempt at gender neutrality.

Appendix: Working with ESL Issues

If English is your second language, you know the confusion and frustration that can sometimes result when you try to apply the many different grammar rules and usage patterns of English. Of course, you are not alone. Anyone who has ever tried to speak or write a second language has encountered the same problem. This appendix is meant to review some of the more common issues that ESL writers face.

Count and Noncount Nouns

- **Count nouns** refer to nouns that exist as separate items that can be counted. They usually have singular and plural forms: *one bottle, two bottles; one thought, two thoughts, one teacher, two teachers*.

- **Noncount nouns** refer to nouns that cannot be counted and usually do not take plural forms. Here are some common noncount nouns:

EXAMPLES

Food and drink:	*meat, bacon, spinach, celery, water, milk, wine*
Nonfood material:	*equipment, furniture, luggage, rain, silver, gasoline*
Abstractions:	*anger, beauty, happiness, honesty, courage*

Note that noncount nouns stay in their singular form. It would be incorrect to say *bacons, furnitures,* or *courages*.

- Some nouns can be either count or noncount, depending on whether you use them as specific, countable items or as a substance or general concept.

EXAMPLES

Noncount:	The *fruit* on the table looks delicious.
Count:	Eat as many *fruits* and vegetables as you can each day.
Noncount:	Supposedly, nothing can travel faster than the speed of *light*.
Count:	The *lights* in the house were all on when we arrived home.

PRACTICE   If the underlined word is a count noun, write its plural form in the blank. If it is a noncount noun, write *noncount* in the blank.

1. Maria exuded <u>happiness</u> as she walked through the door.   *noncount*

2. Yesterday, my co-workers prepared a <u>surprise</u> for me.   _____

3. Enrique had forgotten the <u>name</u> of the man who saved his life.   _____

4. He felt an overwhelming <u>emotion</u> when he finally saw his

   cat again.   _____

5. When the <u>laughter</u> had finally subsided, Cecilia

   started to cry.   _____

6. Pluto may not be a planet, but it is still part of our solar

   <u>system</u>.   _____

7. The werewolf was convinced that the price of <u>silver</u>

   would skyrocket.   _____

8. Whatever <u>situation</u> arises, you can depend on

   Chenxi to solve it.   _____

9. At least once every <u>week</u>, I have to eat a noodle soup.   _____

10. One needs more than a little bit of <u>luck</u> to win at the casino.   _____

Articles with Count and Noncount Nouns

Indefinite Articles

 EXAMPLES

- The indefinite articles are *a* and *an*. They are used with *singular count nouns* that are *general* or *nonspecific*. Usually, the noun is being introduced for the first time.

Yesterday I saw a car with two teenagers in it.

An apple fell from the tree and rolled into the pool.

In these sentences, *car* and *apple* are general count nouns that could refer to any car or any apple at all, so the articles *a* and *an* are used with them.

- Do not use indefinite articles with noncount nouns.

 EXAMPLES

(incorrect)	She suffers from an insomnia.
(correct)	She suffers from insomnia.
(incorrect)	Americans value a freedom and an independence.
(correct)	Americans value freedom and independence.

 PRACTICE

Correct the following sentences by crossing out any unnecessary use of *a* or *an* or by adding *a* or *an* where needed. If a sentence is correct, do nothing to it.

1. I am very hungry, but I still do not want to eat ʌ*an* apple.

2. When cows are thirsty, they do not drink a milk.

3. That sad man does not believe in a happiness.

4. Nawal hired plumber to fix the clogged sink.

5. An envy makes people speak and act unpleasantly.

Definite Articles

The word *the* is a definite article. It is used with *specific nouns*, both *count* and *noncount*. You can usually tell if a noun is specific by its context. In some cases, other words in a sentence make it clear that the noun refers to a specific thing or things. In other instances, the noun has been mentioned in a previous sentence, so the second reference to it is specific.

 EXAMPLES

(This singular count noun refers to a *specific* table, the one in the hallway.)

I bumped into *the table* in the hallway.

(This singular count noun refers to a *specific* car, the one in the previous sentence.)

A car and a motorcycle roared down the street. *The car* sounded as if it had no muffler.

(This plural count noun refers to *specific* men, the ones who robbed the bank.)

The men who robbed the bank looked young.

(This noncount noun refers to the *specific* courage of one man.)

The courage that he demonstrated impressed me.

 PRACTICE

Correct the following sentences by crossing out any unnecessary use of *the* or by adding *the* where needed. If a sentence is correct, do nothing to it.

1. She did not see _∧ car that almost hit her.
the

2. The impatience causes many people to act prematurely.

3. Charles told his therapist about anxiety he had felt all month.

4. Because he really liked her, Jean Paul gave pineapple to Simone.

5. If someone would give him a little bit of the attention, he would calm down.

Articles with Proper Nouns

- Use *the* with plural proper nouns (*the United States, the Smiths*).

- Do not use *the* with most singular proper nouns (*John, San Diego, Germany*). There are, however, many exceptions.

- Use *the* with some singular proper nouns, including names of oceans, seas, and rivers (*the Mississippi River, the Atlantic Ocean*), names using *of* (*the Republic of China, the University of Colorado*), and names of large regions, deserts, and peninsulas (*the Mideast, the Sahara Desert, the Iberian Peninsula*).

No Articles

Noncount nouns and plural nouns are often used without an article to make general statements. (Remember that *all* singular count nouns require an article, whether they are specific or general.)

 EXAMPLE   *Racism* and *prejudice* should worry *parents* and *teachers.*

In this sentence, the noncount nouns *racism* and *prejudice* as well as the plural count nouns *parents* and *teachers* do not use articles because they are general, referring to *any* racism or prejudice and *any* parent or teacher.

PRACTICE   In the spaces provided, write the appropriate article (*a, an,* or *the*) wherever one is needed. If no article is needed, leave the space blank.

1. Arnold had never seen __*a*__ koala before he traveled to _____ Australia.

2. Serena thanked _____ man who had sold her _____ last concert ticket.

3. Her admission of _____ guilt made _____ conversation between them

   much easier.

4. Every time Josefina goes to _____ flamenco performance, she buys _____

   new CD.

5. _____ zebra that crossed _____ street together with the Beatles was

   barely noticed.

6. _____ joy was only one of the emotions they experienced as they

   approached _____ city.

7. Before he left home for _____ last time, Oscar knew he needed _____ good

   education.

8. _____ owner of the restaurant asked _____ cook to make an especially nice

   rice pudding for his favorite customer.

9. Many poor countries need _____ doctors and nurses to help fight _____

   disease and malnutrition.

10. Fred wants to gain _____ weight, so he bought five pounds of _____ turkey tail.

Subjects

- English, unlike some other languages, requires a *stated* subject in nearly every sentence. (Commands are an exception. See Chapter One.) Subjects are required in all subordinate clauses as well as in all main clauses.

 EXAMPLES

(incorrect)   Is hot in Las Vegas in August.

(correct)   *It* is hot in Las Vegas in August.

(incorrect)   My brother yelled with delight when hit a home run.

(correct)   My brother yelled with delight when *he* hit a home run.

- Although some languages immediately follow a subject with a pronoun that refers to the subject, it is incorrect to do so in English.

 EXAMPLES

(incorrect)   The cashier *she* gave me the wrong amount of change.

(correct)   The cashier gave me the wrong amount of change.

- If a subject follows the verb, a "dummy" subject is used before the verb.

 EXAMPLES

(incorrect)   Are some suspicious men at the door.

(correct)   *There* are some suspicious men at the door.

PRACTICE   Correct any errors in the following sentences by crossing out subjects that are not needed or by adding subjects that are missing.

1. *There* ∧Was no car in the driveway when we left.

2. Cyrano he had a very big nose.

3. Innocencia invited us all because had just been paid.

4. When we drove to Michoacan, the engine it had some trouble.

5. According to a news website, will be cold in Novosibirsk tomorrow.

6. Although Yulina loved her family, wanted to study abroad.

7. Mala's parents they stared at me all night long.

8. Is plenty of time to register for classes.

9. After the dog it stopped barking, we all were able to sleep.

10. Sancho Panza admired Don Quixote, so stayed with him all day.

Helping Verbs and Main Verbs

Choosing the right combination of helping verbs and main verbs can be difficult if English is your second language. To make the correct choices, you must first understand a few things about main verbs and helping verbs. (See Chapter One for a thorough discussion of this topic.)

- If the verb consists of one word, it is a main verb (MV).

 EXAMPLE

                        MV
The older server stared at the table.

- If the verb consists of two or more words, the last word of the verb is the main verb (MV). The earlier words are helping verbs (HV).

 EXAMPLES

              HV MV
The older server is staring at the table.

              HV MV
The older server must leave soon.

Helping Verbs

There are only twenty-three helping verbs in English, so it is not difficult to become familiar with them. Nine of the helping verbs are called *modals*. They are always helping verbs. The other fourteen words sometimes function as helping verbs and sometimes as main verbs. Here are the twenty-three helping verbs:

Modals:	can	will	shall	may
	could	would	should	might
				must

Forms of *do*:	do, does, did
Forms of *have*:	have, has, had
Forms of *be*:	am, is, are, was, were, be, being, been

Main Verbs

To use helping verbs and main verbs correctly, you need to know the forms that main verbs can take. All main verbs use five forms (except for *be*, which uses eight).

Base Form	-S Form	Past Tense	Past Participle	Present Participle
walk	walks	walked	walked	walking
call	calls	called	called	calling
eat	eats	ate	eaten	eating
give	gives	gave	given	giving
ring	rings	rang	rung	ringing

Notice that the past tense and the past participle of *call* and *walk* are spelled the same way, by adding *-ed*. They are called regular verbs. However, the past tense and past participle of *eat* and *ring* change spelling dramatically. These are irregular verbs. If you are unsure how to spell any form of a verb, use your dictionary. The spelling of each form is listed there.

Combining Helping Verbs and Main Verbs

When combining helping verbs and main verbs, pay careful attention to the verb forms that you use.

- **Modal + base form.** After one of the nine modals (*can, could, will, would, shall, should, may, might, must*), use the base form of a verb.

 EXAMPLES

(incorrect)	He will leaving soon.
(correct)	He will leave soon.

- *Do, does, did* **+ base form.** When forms of *do* are used as helping verbs, use the base form after them.

 EXAMPLES

(incorrect)	Did your daughter asked you for a present?
(correct)	Did your daughter ask you for a present?

- *Have, has, had* **+ past participle.** Use the past participle form after *have, has,* or *had*. Check a dictionary if you are not sure how to spell the past participle.

EXAMPLES

(incorrect)	The monkey has eating all of the fruit.
(correct)	The monkey has eaten all of the fruit.
(incorrect)	We had walk ten miles before noon.
(correct)	We had walked ten miles before noon.

- **Forms of *be* + present participle.** To show continuous action, use the present participle (the *-ing* form) after a form of *be* (*am, is, are, was, were, be, been*).

 EXAMPLES

| (incorrect) | I reading the book. |
| (correct) | I am reading the book. |

- **Forms of *be* + past participle.** To express passive voice (the subject receives the action rather than performs it), use a form of *be* followed by the past participle form.

 EXAMPLES

| (incorrect) | The football was threw by the quarterback. |
| (correct) | The football was thrown by the quarterback. |

 PRACTICE   Correct any errors in the use of helping verbs and main verbs.

1. During dinner my mother will ~~telling~~ *tell* you the whole story.

2. The plumber has not sending me the bill yet.

3. The woman who was hiding in the doorway has taking your sandwich.

4. The movie was finish long before I woke up.

5. Did the man in the red suit talked all night?

6. Rafiki showed them that he has not lose his keys.

7. Her little cousin is too frighten to enter the haunted house.

8. My parents do needs some help mowing their lawn.

9. Hiroko has turned off the music because she is prepare for a test.

10. For the pill to work, you must drinking three glasses of water.

Two-Word Verbs

Many verbs in English consist of a verb with a preposition. Together, the verb and its paired word create an *idiom*, which has a meaning you cannot know simply by learning the meaning of the verb or its paired word. For example, both *up* and *out* can be used with the verb *stay*, but they have very different meanings. *To stay up* means to remain awake. *To stay out* means to remain out of the house or out of a discussion.

When a verb is joined to a preposition introducing a prepositional phrase, the two words will not usually be separated.

 EXAMPLES

(correct)	Danny and Jenna *argued about* the proposed law.
(incorrect)	Danny and Jenna *argued* the proposed law *about*.

However, sometimes a verb is joined to a word *not* introducing a prepositional phrase, even though the word itself seems to be a preposition. (The words *off, on, up, down,* and *out* commonly do not introduce prepositional phrases after a verb.) In such cases, the verb and its paired word are sometimes separated.

EXAMPLES

(correct)	Hector decided to *try on* the blue tuxedo before he left.
(correct)	Hector decided to *try* the blue tuxedo *on* before he left.

Here are some common two-word verbs:

ask out	Fabiana hoped that Nick would not *ask* her *out*.
approve of	Her mother did not *approve of* the gown she chose for her prom.
call off	When it started to rain, we *called off* the game.
call on	Because he was in the neighborhood, Farbod decided to *call on* his aunt.
come across	While shopping at Macy's, we *came across* my biology instructor.
drop by	Lester does not appreciate it when people *drop by* (or *in*) unexpectedly.
drop off	Will you *drop* me *off* at the dentist's office?
figure out	After much discussion, we finally *figured out* what to do.
find out	Did you ever *find out* where he lives?
interfere with	It is not wise to *interfere with* a police officer on duty.
look over	Irene wanted to *look* the place *over* before they rented it.
look up	Please *look up* his phone number in your address book.
look after	Will Rachel *look after* our cockatiel while we are gone?

make up	Waldo loves to *make up* stories about his childhood.
object to	Does anyone here *object to* the smell of cigarette smoke?
pick out	Shauna was unable to *pick out* the man who robbed her.
reason with	It is difficult to *reason with* an angry two-year-old.
show up	We were all surprised when the mayor *showed up* at the party.
think over	Give me a few minutes while I *think* it *over*.
try on	The shoes looked too small, but he *tried* them *on* anyway.
turn up	Cathy was certain the lost hamster would *turn up* somewhere.
wait for	Isabel listened to music while she *waited for* the train.
wait on	The server who *waited on* us asked if we had enjoyed the food.

PRACTICE Create sentences of your own using the following two-word verbs. Use the sentences above as models. If you are uncertain of the meaning of a verb, consult a dictionary.

1. turn up   *If my lost keys don't turn up soon, we'll have to call a cab.*

2. come across   _____

3. look over   _____

4. call off   _____

5. reason with   _____

6. approve of _____

_____

7. ask out _____

_____

8. object to _____

_____

9. try on _____

_____

10. drop by _____

_____

Adjectives in the Correct Order

Adjectives usually precede the nouns that they modify. When one or more adjectives precede a noun, follow these guidelines.

- In a series of adjectives, place determiners first. (Determiners consist of articles, possessives, limiting and quantity words, and numerals.) Examples of determiners: _the_ old car, _Jim's_ empty wallet, _her_ sad face, _this_ heavy box, _some_ scattered coins, _three_ dead trees.

- If one of the modifiers is a noun, place it directly before the word it modifies: the boring _basketball_ game, the rusty _trash_ can.

- Evaluative adjectives (_beautiful, interesting, courageous_) usually come before descriptive adjectives (_small, round, red, wooden_): the _beautiful red_ rose, an _interesting wooden_ cabinet.

- Descriptive adjectives indicating size usually appear before other descriptive adjectives (but they appear after evaluative adjectives): my _huge_ leather sofa, a strange _little_ old man.

In general, avoid long strings of adjectives. More than two or three adjectives in a row will usually sound awkward to the native English speaker.

PRACTICE   Arrange the following groups of adjectives in the correct order.

1. (green, the, beautiful) parrot

the beautiful green parrot

2. (cotton, fresh, my) blouse

_____

3. (ripe, four, large) oranges

_____

4. (West African, a, busy) market

_____

5. (rusty, blue, that) Buick

_____

6. (worst, brother's, family, his) memory

_____

7. (jazz, two, popular) drummers

_____

8. (leather, hiking, old, that) boot

_____

9. (soccer, several, talented) players

_____

10. (mustard, seven, those, black) seeds

_____

Answers to Practices

Chapter One

Page 3:

2. Hester, letter, dress
3. Narcissus, reflection, pond

4. story, George Washington, tree, myth
5. Homer, holes, stories, writers

Page 4:

2. Siddhartha, home, world
3. Homer, lips, thought, plate, Spam
4. Scheherazade, story, mind, blank
5. suggestion, agnostic, back, church
6. depression, sense, meaninglessness, king

7. misanthrope, party, sigh, relief
8. philosophy, life, ideas, acceptance, willingness
9. courage, determination, lion, wizard
10. graduation, coyote, roadrunner, stage

Pages 5–6:

2. nouns: piggy, market
   pronouns: Each, us, which
3. nouns: Ankara, capital, Turkey, Istanbul, city
   pronouns: its
4. nouns: P.T. Barnum, suckers
   pronouns: you, what
5. nouns: court, law
   pronouns: Anything, you, you
6. nouns: explanation, fractals
   pronouns: anyone, her

7. nouns: Super Bowl, advertisements, brother
   pronouns: its, my, them
8. nouns: archeologists, fragments, period
   pronouns: that, many, they
9. nouns: collection, books, Herman Melville,
   Paul Lawrence Dunbar
   pronouns: My, anything
10. nouns: poetry, Emily Dickinson, description, hummingbird
   pronouns: anyone, who, her

Page 6:

Answers will vary. Here are some possible ones.
2. <u>You</u> should ask <u>him</u> to sing a <u>song</u> for <u>us</u>.
3. <u>One</u> of the <u>participants</u> asked for a <u>day</u>
   of <u>silence</u>.

4. <u>Who</u> took the <u>key</u> that belongs to <u>me</u>?
5. After <u>Elisa</u> cooked <u>her</u> <u>dinner</u>, <u>she</u> asked <u>her</u>
   <u>brother</u> to watch the <u>movie</u> with <u>her</u>.

Page 7:

2. burned
3. wear

4. searched
5. talked

Page 8:

2. is
3. felt

4. seem
5. are

Page 9:

2. verb: wanted
   tense: past
3. verb: will sit
   tense: future

4. verb: killed
   tense: past
5. verb: plays
   tense: present

Page 11:

2. HV
3. HV
4. MV
5. HV
6. MV

7. HV
8. MV
9. MV
10. HV

Pages 11–12:

A.

2. HV: have
   MV: caused
3. HV: was
   MV: swinging

4. HV: Should
   MV: go
5. HV: should have
   MV: exerted

B. Answers will vary. Here are some possible ones.

7. The huge meteor <u>raced</u> across the sky and <u>headed</u> directly for Palomar College.
8. Kwame <u>did</u> not <u>enjoy</u> the egusi soup that I <u>cooked</u> for him.

9. A spider <u>was</u> slowly <u>crawling</u> along the wall behind my sister.
10. You <u>should</u> never <u>have put</u> your hand in the garbage disposal when it <u>was running</u>.

Page 13:

2. HV: could
   MV: defeat
   Verbal: Playing
3. HV: will
   MV: describe
   Verbal: To illustrate

4. HV: had
   MV: taken
   Verbal: attending
5. HV: might
   MV: agree
   Verbal: stirring, to give

Page 13:

2. HV: were
   MV: waving
   Verbal: circling
3. HV: Did
   MV: enjoy
4. MV: has
   Verbal: to ask
5. HV: have been
   MV: protesting
   Verbal: to replace
6. HV: has
   MV: agreed
   Verbal: to please, to play

7. HV: should have
   MV: accepted
   Verbal: To tell
8. HV: did
   MV: nominate
   Verbal: Surprising
9. HV: was
   MV: used
   Verbal: to symbolize
10. HV: Does
    MV: recognize
    Verbal: attacking

Page 14:

2. S: Zeus
   MV: was
3. S: Zeus
   MV: divided

4. S: Poseidon
   MV: became
5. S: Zeus
   MV: gave

Page 15:

2. S: Biscotti
HV: were
MV: offered

3. S: game
HV: did
MV: attract

4. S: teacher
HV: might
MV: enter

5. S: men
MV: faced

Page 16:

2. S: dish, spoon
MV: ran

3. S: John Glenn, assistants
MV: prepared, ate

4. S: Eighteenth Amendment
HV: was
MV: ratified
S: it
HV: was
MV: repealed

5. S: Mrs. Johnson
MV: expressed
S: rifles, weapons
HV: should be
MV: banned

Page 17:

2. MV: was
S: President Franklin D. Roosevelt

3. HV: Could
S: John Philip Sousa
HV: have
MV: used

4. MV: is
S: elephant

5. S: you (understood)
MV: Forget

Pages 17–18:

2. subject: wildfires
verb: must have been

3. subject: Don Quixote
verb: will forget

4. subject: elbow
verb: had begun

5. subject: *Life of Pi*
verb: did win

6. subject: knight
verb: could remove

7. subject: You (understood)
verb: Give

8. subject: Bobby Zimmerman
verb: had loved
subject: he
verb: bought

9. subject: zebras, chipmunk
verb: were

10. subject: Charlie
verb: described, drew

Pages 18–19:

Answers will vary. Here are some possible ones.

2. <u>Sonia walked</u> into the restaurant and <u>started</u> to sing.

3. The <u>man</u> in the black trench coat <u>has left</u> the building.

4. <u>Are</u> <u>you</u> happy today?

5. <u>Empty</u> all of the ashtrays.

6. There <u>goes</u> the <u>winner</u> of last night's lottery.

7. The <u>man</u> from Seville and his famous <u>wife arrived</u> at the airport and then <u>took</u> a limousine to their hotel.

8. The <u>dog barked</u> at the cat when <u>it hissed</u> at him.

9. The <u>Padres might win</u> the World Series this year, or <u>they might lose</u> every game.

10. <u>Jason is working</u> in California because <u>his brother offered</u> him a job there.

Page 27:

2. *Hot* and *crispy* modify *fries*.
3. *Usually* modifies *eats*.

4. *tedious* and *short* modify *movie*, and *mercifully* modifies *short*.
5. *Tiny* modifies *animals*, and *continually* modifies *ran*.

Page 28:

A.

2. We attended an (unusual) concert (last) Saturday.

3. (Five) (gray) pelicans glided above the (busy) beach.

4. (Those) (rickety) (old) bleachers might collapse if (our) (entire) (marching) band tries to sit in them.

5. (Next) October Homer will spend (his) (vacation) time in (his) (redecorated) barn making

   a (new) (Spam) costume for the (Halloween) party.

B. Answers will vary. Here are some possible ones.

7. An *inattentive* aardvark wandered into our *back* yard and looked for ants.

8. The *old* hermit lived in a *log* cabin in the woods.

9. The dog in the street avoided the *red* car and the *pickup* truck.

10. Officials tried to blame the *unsightly* mess on the birds that lived near the *stagnant* pond.

Page 30:

A.

2. The happy couple (always) said that they were (extremely) lucky.

3. The black widow (sometimes) (gleefully) destroys her mate.

4. As Ichabod Crane rode (swiftly) down the lane, he was (already) beginning to worry about the headless horseman.

5. Dido was (excruciatingly) sad as she stood on the (rather) sheer cliff.

B. Answers will vary. Here are some possible ones.

7. The exuberant school children ran *quickly* across the schoolyard.

8. Elmo *carefully* opened the garbage can and looked for the puppet.

9. The dune buggy *just* missed the cactus but smashed into the tree.

10. The ship escaped many perils and *finally* reached its destination.

Page 32:

2. clearer, clearest

3. funnier, funniest

4. more joyful, most joyful

5. more suddenly, most suddenly

6. uglier, ugliest

7. more comfortable, most comfortable

8. farther, farthest

9. more quickly, most quickly

10. more powerful, most powerful

Pages 33–34:

2. The **worst** mistake he made was deciding to buy the **most expensive** car on the lot.

3. Although Abraham Lincoln was one of our greatest presidents, some say he was the **ugliest** one.

4. Karl Marx was very (or really) intelligent though his theory of economics did not work very well.

5. Of the two, who was the **more** beautiful, Marie Antoinette or Anne Boleyn?

6. Russell Crowe, who is from Australia, is the **best** actor on the screen today.

7. Robert de Niro felt bad when he forgot his lines during rehearsal.

8. The Trojans were **better** prepared than the Greeks, but the Greeks were **trickier.**

9. Halle Berry said that the interviews are **worse than** the filming.

10. Sofia always drives **safely**, even when she has to get somewhere as **quickly** as possible.

Pages 41–42:

A.

2. subject: you
   verb: Do know
   subject: Meryl Streep
   verb: won
   coordinating conjunctions: and

3. subject: Miriam
   verb: experienced
   subject: musical
   verb: would last
   coordinating conjunction: yet

4. subject: Sam
   verb: did like
   subject: he
   verb: did care
   coordinating conjunction: nor

5. subject: sink
   verb: was draining
   subject: we
   verb: called
   coordinating conjunction: so

B.

7. but *or* yet

8. and

9. for

10. so

Page 43:

2. Without, from
3. During, on
4. near, for
5. from, to

Pages 44–45:

A.

2. Prep   Obj
of the first female journalists
Prep   Obj
in the United States

3. Prep Obj
for weeks
Prep Obj
with him

4. Prep   Obj
in the Potomac River
Prep   Obj
of this habit

5. Prep   Obj
to the riverbank
Prep   Obj
into the cold water

6. Prep   Obj
near the shore
Prep   Obj
on his clothes

7. Prep   Obj
toward the bank
Prep   Obj
for an interview

8. Prep   Obj
In spite of his pleas
Prep Obj
to her

9. Prep   Obj
in the water
Prep   Obj
by the determined reporter

10. Prep   Obj
After this incident
Prep   Obj
of Anne Royall's close friends

Page 55:

1. The farmer waited in front of the bank.
2. The **old** farmer waited in front of the bank.
3. The old farmer **in overalls** waited in front of the bank.
4. The old farmer in **faded** overalls waited in front of the bank.
5. The old farmer in faded overalls waited **patiently** in front of the bank.

Chapter Two

Pages 83–84:

2. MC
3. MC
4. N
5. SC
6. N

7. MC
8. SC
9. MC
10. N

Page 84:

2. PP

3. PP

4. PP

5. SC

6. SC

7. PP

8. PP

9. SC

10. PP

Pages 84–85:

2. After their fight, Ali shook Joe's hand.

3. Shamu splashed the people (who) were sitting by the tank.

4. (If) the creek does not rise, Mr. Murdoch will buy the newspaper.

5. The government cannot operate effectively (until) both political parties agree to compromise.

6. The dinner was delicious (although) some people became sick from the shrimp.

7. The student loved Emily Dickinson, (whose) poem she was reading.

8. The DJ played hip-hop music (while) the crowd danced.

9. Stonewall stared at the mountain (where) the Yankees were loading their cannons.

10. Maria and Jackson listened to the wind (that) blew through the trees.

Page 86:

2. (When) General Lee left his tent, Traveller was waiting for him.

3. Miley was hurt (because) Elton John called her a "meltdown waiting to happen."

4. (Before) Admiral Nelson could make a choice, he consulted his wife.

5. Someone threw a water balloon (as) the senator started to speak.

Page 86:

Answers will vary. Here are possible ones.

2. When he paid the check, Howard forgot to leave a tip.

3. Vincent moved to France as summer changed to autumn.

4. While he slept, Delilah cut Samson's hair.

5. The children threw their Brussels sprouts under the table as soon as their parents looked away.

Page 87:

2. A saxophone player (whom) we all like was the first act.

3. A drummer (who) lives next door to us played with her.

4. The Billie Holiday Special, (which) is my favorite, is a bagel in the shape of a gardenia.

5. A Dalmatian (that) everyone calls Thelonious greets people at the door.

Page 88:

Answers will vary. Here are some possible ones.
2. Joshua, <u>who was holding</u> a <u>trumpet</u>, looked up at the walls of Jericho.
3. Nathaniel showed his new house to Herman, <u>who admired its seven gables.</u>
4. The princes were kept in the tower <u>that looked out over the city.</u>
5. One of the fiercest battles of the Civil War was the Battle of Antietam, <u>which resulted in over 22,000 dead,</u> <u>wounded, and missing.</u>

Page 88:

2. Ophelia asked Hamlet <u>if he still loved her</u>. (Adv)
3. Stephanie liked to play the Bob Dylan songs <u>that are on her iPhone.</u> (Adj)
4. My mother plays croquet <u>whenever she can</u>. (Adv)
5. Darby liked to run in Brady Park, <u>which is near my home.</u> (Adj)

Page 89:

Answers will vary. Here are some possible ones.
2. Sheila, <u>who was looking forward to her vacation</u>, loaded her skis onto her car. (Adj)
3. <u>Because we frightened it,</u> the snake crawled under the house. (Adv)
4. Meredith refused to go to classes <u>that bored her.</u> (Adj)
5. The candle at the edge of the table began to flicker <u>whenever the wind blew.</u> (Adv)

Pages 97–98:

Answers will vary. Here are some possible ones.
2. The small dog ran into the street.
3. There are three white mice behind the refrigerator.
4. Near the traffic light a man in a black parka stepped into the street.
5. Send us your car payment immediately!

Page 99:

Answers will vary. Here are some possible ones.
2. The heat wave has lasted for two weeks; however, we should see some rain soon.
3. Miranda received her third ticket for speeding; as a result, she lost her license.
4. The play was about to begin, yet we could not find our seats.
5. The table was unstable; therefore, Bill's coffee cup fell to the floor.

Page 100:

2. simple:	S: He	V: was stationed, flew
3. compound:	S: mountains	V: were
	S: flights	V: were
4. compound:	S: mountains	V: were called
	S: pilots	V: were known
5. simple:	S: pilots	V: lost
6. compound:	S: Captain Bush	V: lived
	S: he	V: found
7. compound:	S: mongoose	V: had made
	S: he	V: allowed
8. compound:	S: mother	V: would send
	S: he	V: would share
9. simple:	S: he	V: noticed
10. compound:	S: mongoose	V: can kill
	S: hut	V: was

Page 101:

Answers will vary. Here are some possible ones.

2. When the telephone rang, Justin ran from the room.

3. The spider that crawled into Marcia's handbag was black with orange dots.

4. Amy passed the class with a high grade even though she had done almost no homework.

5. Rita offered her last sweet roll to Mr. Jenkins, who had forgotten to bring his lunch.

Pages 102–103:

Answers will vary. Here are some possible ones.

2. A man who was wearing a red hat ran into the intersection; luckily, there were few cars on the road at the time.

3. Clara's new Ferrari, which she bought last week, has an automatic transmission; in addition, it has leather seats and a convertible top.

4. Miles will play "Autumn Leaves," or he will sit down and smoke a cigarette after he finishes his last set.

5. Apple introduced "iTunes Radio" this fall, and it has become quite popular because it has many attractive features.

Page 103:

2. simple:	S: story	V: concerns
3. complex:	S: King Minos	V: ordered
	S: who	V: were
4. simple:	S: Theseus	V: accompanied
5. compound:	S: Ariadne	V: was
	S: she	V: fell
6. simple:	S: Ariadne	V: gave
7. compound-complex:	S: Theseus	V: took
	S: he	V: unraveled
	S: he	V: went
8. compound-complex:	S: He	V: planned
	S: he	V: wanted
	S: he	V: would follow
9. compound:	S: Theseus	V: listened
	S: he	V: found
10. complex:	S: he	V: reached
	S: he	V: killed, led

Pages 113–114:

Answers will vary. Here are some possible ones.

2. *fragment:* The man who helped rescue the kidnapped woman.
   possible correction: The man who helped rescue the kidnapped woman was given an award.
3. *fragment:* While Persephone was in Hades. That she might never see her again.
   possible correction: While Persephone was in Hades, her mother was worried that she might never see her again.
4. *fragment:* To ensure that you get a good seat.
   possible correction: Arrive early at the theater to ensure that you get a good seat.
5. *fragment:* When John F. Kennedy was assassinated in Dallas.
   possible correction: When John F. Kennedy was assassinated in Dallas, it seemed as if the whole country grieved.
6. *fragment:* If he wanted to live on his own.
   possible correction: If he wanted to live on his own, Arnie needed to find a job.
7. *fragment:* Even as Craig was dashing across the street. Begging for him to let him in.
   possible correction: The Chocolate Shoppe owner was locking the door even as Craig was dashing across the street, begging for him to let him in.
8. *fragment:* Although he would always be ashamed of his actions.
   possible correction: Odysseus continued to love his daughters, although he would always be ashamed of his actions.
9. *fragment:* To join his parents at the theater to see *Les Miserables*.
   possible correction: Chris planned to join his parents at the theater to see *Les Miserables*.
10. *fragment:* Even though U2 had canceled the Saturday concert.
    possible correction: Deborah and Carlton headed for Arrowhead Pond, even though U2 had canceled the Saturday concert.

Pages 117–118:

Answers may vary. Here are some possible ones.

2. F   Bottom went peacefully to sleep, and then he awoke with the head of an ass.
3. Correct
4. CS   The series *Bones* is about police forensics; therefore, viewers are exposed to many gory scenes involving dead bodies.
5. CS   Doc Ford opened the door to his laboratory; all of his crabs were on the floor.
6. CS   Siddhartha was raised in a royal household; eventually, he left home and sought enlightenment.
7. F   You can cut off your cat's tail, but it will not grow back again.
8. CS   Adrian was happy because *Justified* still had five segments to go.
9. Correct
10. F   All of the Dracula-themed films and series are becoming boring, so I am not going to watch them anymore.

Chapter Three

Pages 155–156:

2. The server apologized to the customers sitting by the front door.

3. Leaping gracefully, the gazelle crossed the valley.

4. Dancing across the stage, Bill gave his best performance ever.

5. Because she is a responsible citizen of the world, Amina does not buy any jewelry produced by child labor.

6. The (mockingbird) perching on the telephone pole imitated the blue jay in the pine tree.

7. Blaise wanted to meet the (woman) giving the lecture on South Africa.

8. Hurt by her remark, (Chris) slowly turned red.

9. Wondering about the trustworthiness of Napoleon, (Toussaint) walked out of his house in Port-au-Prince.

10. (Antonia), threatened by the pitbull for the fifth time, called the police.

Page 157:

2. Staring at their history book, (they) realized they could not celebrate Columbus Day any longer.

3. Most of the shoppers were (glad) to buy the Girl Scout cookies from Tomasita.

4. Overwhelmed by its beauty, (Narcissus) stared at the image in the pond.

5. Peter's (determination) to find customers for his herbal supplement business irritated many of his friends.

6. Pandora could not resist her (desire) to open the box.

7. Reading her travel guide, (Alicia) eagerly researched Tokyo's jazz scene.

8. Frustrated by the recipe, (Sarah) simply added ten more cloves of garlic.

9. Wallace stood and stared at the (man) playing the blue guitar.

10. Reading *Heart of Darkness*, (Chinua Achebe) became more and more enraged.

Page 165:

2. (Walden), which was written by Henry David Thoreau, condenses his two-year stay at Walden Pond into one year.

3. (Everyone) who entered the contest was asked to proceed to the exit.

4. Only twenty minutes from (Las Vegas), which is famous for its noisy casinos, one can visit (Red Rock Canyon), which is an oasis of tranquility.

5. Caesarean section is a surgical procedure named after (Julius Caesar), who was supposedly born by that method.

6. The (crocodile) that followed our rowboat made a strange ticking sound and even seemed to smile at us.

7. Oscar told us the story of the (day) when Leticia proposed to him.

8. She asked him to pass her the fish (sauce) that was on the table to his left.

9. (Mongolia), which is a country adjacent to China, was the home of (Genghis Khan), who was the founder of the Mongol Empire.

10. Luisa was raised in (Mexico City) where she learned to speak both English and Spanish.

Pages 166–167:

2. (Jay Gatsby,) a wealthy but lonely man, stared at the green light at the end of the dock.

3. Jerome and Geena wanted to enroll in an (MOOC), a massive open online course.

4. (Martin), an opponent of online courses, counseled them to go to a real college.

5. One of the key figures of the American Revolution was (Benjamin Franklin), the famous author, inventor, and diplomat.

6. (Twitter) a medium through which one can let other people know that one has just sneezed, is now on the stock market.

7. High school (teachers), an underpaid and stressed-out group of professionals, refuse to be blamed for all the problems of society.

8. Christopher picked up his favorite (instrument), a handcrafted classical guitar, and began to play.

9. The recent storms damaged two of Esther's favorite (trees), the eucalyptus in her front yard and the cypress right next to it.

10. (Ophelia), an ophthalmologist practicing in Oman, offered her services to the oligarch.

Pages 167–168:

Answers will vary. Here are some possible ones.

2. Marie Antoinette had no idea that there was going to be a revolution that was to be her undoing.
3. Hosni Mubarak, the former president of Egypt, was equally surprised by the Arab Spring.
4. Ichabod Crane, a character invented by Washington Irving, listened fearfully to the story about the strange rider.
5. Bombay, which is also known as Mumbai, is a city with a very large film industry.
6. The pilot flew fearlessly into the Bermuda Triangle, which is famous for the many ships and planes that have disappeared in it.
7. She was torn between the beef empanadas and the lamb kebab, a dish her mother often made on Sundays.
8. The librarian hopped into his car and drove to his fishing spot, Loch Ness.
9. Poseidon, the Greek god of the sea, looked confused when the sailors started to call him Neptune.
10. Octavio Paz was listening to an old recording by Celia Cruz, the famous Cuban singer.

Page 177:

2. The poet standing at the curb <u>sadly</u> stared at the rejection letter in his hand.
   The poet standing at the curb stared sadly at the rejection letter in his hand. (Other correct placements are possible.)
3. After the battle, Tecumseh wished only that his Shawnee be left in peace.
   Correct.
4. The two men who had been arguing <u>quietly</u> reached a compromise.
   The two men who had been quietly arguing reached a compromise. (Other correct placements are possible.)
5. By the time he had <u>almost</u> fallen ten thousand feet, the skydiver was wondering if he should open his chute.
   By the time he had fallen almost ten thousand feet, the skydiver was wondering if he should open his chute.
6. Peyton Farquhar <u>nearly</u> crept to the edge of the trees before he saw the Union soldiers.
   Peyton Farquhar crept nearly to the edge of the trees before he saw the Union soldiers.
7. Because she had eaten a large lunch, Araceli <u>just</u> decided to order a small dinner salad.
   Because she had eaten a large lunch, Araceli decided to order just a small dinner salad.
8. The counselor advised Fred frequently to attend the meetings.
   The counselor advised Fred to attend the meetings frequently. (Other correct placements are possible.)

9. Richard and Keisha were surprised that the trendy restaurant only offered two vegan dishes.
   Richard and Keisha were surprised that the trendy restaurant offered only two vegan dishes.

10. The sportswriter criticized the game even though he <u>nearly</u> had missed the <del>entire</del> second half.
    The sportswriter criticized the game even though he had missed nearly the entire second half.

Pages 179–180:

2. Vera gave a cake to her boyfriend <u>soaked in rum</u>.
   Vera gave a cake soaked in rum to her boyfriend.

3. Artemis shot the arrow at the frightened stag <u>using her strong bow</u>.
   Using her strong bow, Artemis shot the arrow at the frightened stag.

4. Lester set his suitcase next to the flight attendant <u>that held his collection of dead watch batteries.</u>
   Lester set his suitcase that held his collection of dead watch batteries next to the flight attendant.

5. My German shepherd lunged at the skunk, <u>which sleeps at the foot of my bed</u>, when it entered our garage.
   My German shepherd, which sleeps at the foot of my bed, lunged at the skunk when it entered our garage.

6. *Full Metal Jacket* has become a classic film about the Vietnam War <u>directed by Stanley Kubrick</u>.
   Full Metal Jacket, directed by Stanley Kubrick, has become a classic film about the Vietnam War.

7. *To Live,* an excellent movie by Zhang Yimou, depicts life during the Cultural Revolution in China, <u>who is a famous Chinese director.</u>
   To Live, an excellent movie by Zhang Yimou, who is a famous Chinese director, depicts life during the Cultural Revolution in China.

8. Gong Li plays the lead role in that movie, <u>who stars in many of Zhang Yimou's early films</u>.
   Gong Li, who stars in many of Zhang Yimou's early films, plays the lead role in that movie.

9. The monkeys in the cage looked out at the tourists <u>hanging from limbs by their tails</u>.
   The monkeys hanging from limbs by their tails in the cage looked out at the tourists.

10. Amber showed the koi to her kindergarten class, <u>which had bright orange and black markings</u>.
    Amber showed the koi, which had bright orange and black markings, to her kindergarten class.

Page 181:

2. D

3. C

4. D

5. D

Pages 182–184:

2. <u>Waiting for the game to begin</u>, Michael's stomach was upset.
   Waiting for the game to begin, Michael felt nauseated. (Other correct answers are possible.)

3. <u>After drinking the magic potion</u>, his disappointment was obvious.
   After he drank the magic potion, his disappointment was obvious. (Other correct answers are possible.)

4. Determined to die with dignity, the philosopher drank the cup of hemlock.
   Correct

5. <u>After running swiftly up the hill</u>, the flag was raised by the warrior.
   After running swiftly up the hill, the warrior raised the flag. (Other correct answers are possible.)

6. <u>Concerned about her students' dangling modifiers,</u> Leanne's new lesson plan began to take shape.
   Concerned about her students' dangling modifiers, Leanne shaped a new lesson plan. (Other correct answers are possible.)

7. <u>To watch the solar eclipse</u>, sunglasses will protect your eyes.
   To watch the solar eclipse, you will need to wear sunglasses to protect your eyes. (Other correct answers are possible.)

8. <u>Breathing hard,</u> the Eiffel Tower seemed to have too many stairs.
   Breathing hard, Martin insisted that the Eiffel Tower had too many stairs. (Other correct answers are possible.)

9. <u>Startled by the sudden explosion</u>, the summer sky was filled with cranes and egrets.
   Startled by the sudden explosion, cranes and egrets filled the summer sky. (Other correct answers are possible.)

10. <u>To be certain,</u> the test results were checked a third time.
    To be certain, she checked the test results a third time. (Other correct answers are possible.)

Chapter Four

Pages 220–221:

2. The **mattresses inflate** easily.
3. Every Christmas my **sister decorates** the tree.
4. In the field, the **worker was** raising the pole for the circus tent.
5. My neighbors' **cars make** too much noise.

Pages 222–223:

                S
2. The weathered cross with its peeling paint (give <u>gives</u>) visitors to the church a bad impression.
         S   S
3. Each demerit and low grade (cause <u>causes</u>) a cadet to receive punishment.
      S   S
4. Forgiveness and compassion (seems <u>seem</u>) to be personal qualities worth cultivating.
     S
5. Some of the citizens of Rome (believes <u>believe</u>) the Visigoths are nomadic, peaceful people.
                              S
6. At the summit of the mountain, everyone who arrives (sign <u>signs</u>) a logbook.
                  S
7. Each winter, the churches in our town (<u>provide</u> provides) shelter for homeless people.
         S   S
8. The murder of a king and the appearance of his ghost (<u>create</u> creates) interest from the first scene of the play.
    S
9. A few of the clues for the crime (<u>lead</u> leads) back to the housekeeper.
    S
10. Marie, as well as her traveling companions, (<u>is</u> are) unwilling to face the troll.

Pages 224–225:

     S
2. A pack of wolves (<u>has</u> have) made a den in our foothills.
          S   S
3. Either Sandy or her daughters (<u>leave</u> leaves) some fruit at our backdoor each week.
               S   S
4. Neither my best friend nor my worst enemy (<u>was</u> were) involved in the prank played on the principal.
         S   S
5. Her trip to Disneyland or her vacation to Nepal (<u>is</u> are) all Amanda thinks about.
                  S
6. In that society a jury of one's peers (<u>makes</u> make) the decision.
    S   S
7. Don is my only friend who still (<u>eats</u> eat) a sirloin steak three times a week.
                  S   S
8. (<u>Has</u> Have) Mr. Ed or Private Francis said anything to you?
    S
9. A troop of Boy Scouts (meet <u>meets</u>) at our church on Thursdays.
    S   S
10. Van Gogh is one of the impressionist painters who (is <u>are</u>) currently featured at the Getty Museum.

Page 226:

2. Thirty-six inches of two-by-four boarding (<u>is</u> are) required for the job.
   ^S

3. The manager's main concern (<u>was</u> were) the players who chewed tobacco during the game.
   ^S   ^S

4. Carlos has found that mathematics (<u>confuses</u> confuse) him, especially if he doesn't study the textbook.
   ^S   ^S   ^S

5. (<u>Has</u> Have) economics caused people to avoid talking about the issue?
   ^S

6. Ten miles of a tortuous trail (<u>winds</u> wind) up that mountain.
   ^S

7. (Does <u>Do</u>) some of the users seem unable to install Apple's new operating system?
   ^S

8. There, next to the St. Bernard, (sits <u>sit</u>) a hamster and a gecko.
   ^S   ^S

9. The main topic at Anthony's table (<u>was</u> were) the mosquitos that seemed to be everywhere.
   ^S   ^S

10. Here (<u>goes</u> go) my first attempt to cook a dark chocolate cake.
    ^S

Page 232:

2. Many people today are worried about their weight, so **they** watch those diet ads on television.

3. When a person signs up for one of those miracle diets, **he or she needs** to check the cost of it carefully.

4. Nevertheless, people can find diets that will effectively cause **them** to lose some weight.

5. A prospective dieter should be aware that an exercise program is also needed to help **him or her** lose weight in a healthful way.

Page 234:

2. Anyone starting a car should not forget to check **his or her** (**or the**) rear view mirror.

3. When parents read a story by the Brothers Grimm, **they** might scare **their** children.

4. The team from Atlanta was surprised when a fan objected to **its** (**or the**) "tomahawk chop."

5. Each police officer and sheriff has turned on **his or her** siren.

6. Correct

7. After a patient sees that doctor a few times, **he or she** might consider changing clinics.

8. Wolf Blitzer asked the camera operator to quit popping **his** (**or her**) gum.

9. When people drive on our street, **they** need to watch out for children.

10. Neither Juanita nor Donna wanted to get **her** flu shot.

Pages 236–237:

Answers will vary. Here are some possible ones.

2. General Eisenhower and Field Marshall Montgomery met to discuss their plans for the invasion.

3. No matter how many times Sheila tried talk to her mother, her mother always cried.

4. The children spoke rudely to their mother and then gave her their report cards; later, she discussed the children with her husband.

5. Susie received a kitten from her aunt and a puppy from her mother at Christmas, but she refused to play with the puppy.

Page 238:

Answers will vary. Here are some possible ones.

2. Bertha's uncle was unhappy that she disliked visiting him. (Other correct answers are possible.)
3. Randy said he wasn't worried about the tar getting all over his motorcycle nor about its cracked windshield. (Other correct answers are possible.)
4. Dr. Freud daydreamed as he smoked his cigar, and this daydreaming worried him. (Other correct answers are possible.)
5. Southern California has beaches for summer surfing and mountains for winter skiing, and these features are why I want to move there. (Other correct answers are possible.)

Page 240:

2. Paris and **I** chose the apple to give to the most beautiful goddess.
3. We argued among **ourselves** about what choice Paris would make.
4. The Republicans and **he** could not agree on the budget.
5. The principal gave the awards to the third graders and **me.**

Pages 240–241:

2. As finals approached, Burt and **I** started drinking many bottles of those energy drinks a day.
3. Many astrologers were bothered because the stars were aligned in never-before-seen formations and because **Pluto** was no longer considered a planet. (Other correct answers are possible.)
4. Katrina asked Paula to go rock climbing with Stephanie and her even though Paula doesn't really like **Stephanie (or Katrina).**
5. Dickson himself stood up and told Sandra that All Night Fitness would be the best choice. (Correct)
6. Terry wanted to play reggae music for his pool party, but he couldn't get **his sound system** to work.
7. The instructor **bored the entire class as he** droned on for two hours about unclear pronouns. (Other correct answers are possible.)
8. Oprah and the people in her audience agreed among **themselves** that Dr. Phil had not been very wise for a change.
9. When Ken bought a new car and then a new GPS system, Barbie decided to buy **a new car (or a new GPS system)** for herself.
10. Although **Sam (or Leon)** was ill with the flu and most likely contagious, Sam shook hands with Leon.

Page 248:

2. Obj
3. Sub
4. Obj
5. Obj
6. Sub
7. Sub
8. Obj
9. Sub
10. Obj

Page 250:

2. me
3. her
4. he
5. them
6. him
7. me
8. he
9. I
10. her

Page 251:

2. who

3. whom

4. whoever

5. whomever

Pages 251–252:

2. me

3. they

4. me

5. she

Page 252:

2. me

3. he

4. her

5. I

Page 253:

2. he

3. I

4. she

5. whoever

6. me

7. her

8. she

9. whom

10. he, him

Chapter Five

Page 285:

2. Bonnie Parker loved Clyde Barrow, but all he cared about was robbing banks.

3. Romeo loved Juliet and did not care what his family thought.

4. Penelope loved Odysseus, so she kept on fighting off other suitors.

5. Rhett loved Scarlett for her passion and for her strength and independence.

Page 286:

2. We studied the gods of the Greeks, the goddesses of Norse mythology, and the heroes of the Native Americans in our mythology class.

3. Spiderman sewed a tear in his suit, repaired his webcaster, and went to look for someone who needed help.

4. The server brought us a delightful, delicious chablis.

5. The professor could see that the wrinkled, sloppy paper had been carefully researched, but the quality of its writing was atrocious.

6. Delilah sharpened her shears for two hours, and then she began cutting.

7. Gatsby was generous with his money but careless about his moral behavior.

8. Carlos Santana might arrive an hour early for his performance, or he could be two hours late.

9. LaVere bought some flowers, visited her sick friend, caught the trolley, and went to work.

10. The rancid, bitter honey disappointed Pooh.

Page 288:

2. Taking Cheetah by the hand, Tarzan kissed Jane goodbye.
3. Teetering dangerously at the top of the hill, the large stone might have rolled down and crushed Sisyphus.
4. Before they left for the trip to the space station, the crew of the shuttle emailed their families.
5. Yes, I have always wanted to have a wisdom tooth pulled without any anesthetic.
6. Pledging his undying devotion, Popeye asked Olive Oyl to marry him.
7. As Hester walked through town, Pearl was always beside her.
8. After Jack Reacher thought long and hard, he decided to pull the trigger.
9. For instance, my mother had never heard of the Kardashians.
10. To impress Daisy, Jay Gatsby threw his beautiful shirts onto the table.

Page 289:

2. During World War I, for instance, more men died of influenza than from bullets or artillery.
3. Dexter felt bad about stealing money; however, he did it anyway.
4. Maria agreed to attend, I think, because she admires you so much.
5. Ms. Mendoza's main fear, moreover, is that an airplane will crash into her house.

Pages 290–291:

2. Penelope, who was a very faithful wife, kept finding ways to delay her decision.
3. Tranquility Base, which was the name of the first lunar landing site, was established in 1969.
4. Correct
5. "Stopping by Woods on a Snowy Evening," which was written by Robert Frost, is one of the most well-known American poems.

Page 291:

2. The cute boy standing on the right in the photograph is my grandson. (Correct)
3. Leonard Cohen, trying not to show his despair, kept singing in front of the three beautiful women in black.
4. Roxanne, trained always to be polite, tried not to giggle at the sight of such a large nose.
5. Howard, attempting to stifle his yawns, fell asleep while watching the home movies.

Page 292:

2. Mercutio, one of the most interesting characters in *Romeo and Juliet,* is killed early in the play.
3. Gary, an avid hiker, did not mind being called a tree hugger.
4. We were married on July 19, a day before the first man stepped onto the moon.
5. The Australian shepherd, an intelligent dog, was introduced into Australia to herd sheep.

Page 293:

2. Lee Harvey Oswald changed the course of history on November 22, 1963, when he pulled the trigger.
3. Michelle, what is your favorite breed of dog?
4. Send this order of trout to Harbor House, 2978 South First Street, Seattle, Washington, by noon tomorrow.
5. Tell Adam that I am grateful, Katie.

Page 294:

2. Edgar Allan Poe sat down at the table and said, "Sister, we have got to quit meeting like this."
3. *Dracula,* a novel by Bram Stoker, has scared many readers and has been the subject of many movies.
4. Ahab, how do you like my new wide-wale corduroy pants?
5. The events of June 28, 1914, started World War I.
6. At Hiroshima, Japan, and Nagasaki, Japan, tragic events took place on August 6, 1945.
7. Our famous performing arts center, designed by Frank Lloyd Wright, recently underwent a renovation.
8. Bill has watched *Big Night,* his favorite film, at least fifteen times.
9. Samson, of course, didn't wake up while his hair was being cut.
10. Gawain, give this note to Guinevere, who will hide it from Arthur.

Pages 301–302:

2. Who is on first?
3. The kitchen's on fire!
4. Brent wondered whether a boa constrictor could swallow a mature tiger.
5. Does Roscoe want to visit the Liberace Museum?
6. How does Dante get out of hell?
7. Stop it immediately!
8. Rosemary studied for her Ph.D. at Yale.
9. Has Dr. Payne agreed to treat you?
10. Hamlet asked why it all had to end this way.

Page 303:

2. Homer bought the following items: bag balm, cow chip hardener, and an okra peeler.
3. Nessie was seldom seen in the loch; however, today would be an exception.
4. This summer Beauregard is going to visit Gettysburg, Shilo, and Manassas. (Correct)
5. Every night Wilbur had the same dream: he saw himself flying through the air in some strange machine.

Pages 304–305:

2. "It was the best of times, it was the worst of times" are the opening lines of what novel by Charles Dickens?
3. Starbuck looked at Ishmael and said, "Pass the half and half"; however, Ishmael refused.
4. Paul kept repeating the following words to himself: "One if by land, and two if by sea."
5. Clint Eastwood spoke into his cell phone and said, "Play that dangerous song for me again."
6. "Would you like to hear a riddle?" asked the Sphinx.
7. The San Diego Chargers fan got up at halftime and started to leave, shouting, "Never again!"
8. When Sisyphus rolled the stone to the top of the hill, why did he say, "Please don't roll back down"?
9. Ambrose Bierce said, "A bore is someone who talks when you wish him to listen."
10. Marc Antony said, "I come to bury Caesar, not to praise him"; however, he really had much more to say.

Pages 306–307:

2. James's idea was to write a modern novel based on the *Odyssey*.

3. Didn't you enjoy Jennifer Lawrence's performance in *The Hunger Games*?

4. When I quit, I was given a month's salary.

5. Charles's son couldn't believe how beautiful his sister's new baby was.

6. It's time for Persephone's return from Hades.

7. As he rode in the back of his manager's car, the boxer said, "I could've been a contender!"

8. My sister-in-law's children will have only three weeks' vacation this year.

9. Roy Lee's eating habits disgusted his parents and in-laws.

10. It's a shame the bobcat's territory hasn't been protected.

Page 307:

Answers will vary. Here are some possible ones.

2. Deacon asked to borrow Louis's car.

3. My father-in-law's pet iguana can desalinate seawater.

4. The children's petting zoo included grizzly bears, coyotes, and caribous.

5. Mr. Andrews's daughter, a veterinary nurse, doesn't mind her snake slithering all over her apartment.

Page 313:

2. In Nathaniel Hawthorne's short story "Young Goodman Brown," the main character loses his faith in the goodness of people.

3. When I opened my mailbox, I found my current issue of *Time* and *The New Yorker* magazines.

4. Billy Collins's poem "Absence" uses the game of chess as a metaphor.

5. Two recent films, *Great Expectations* and *The Great Gatsby,* are based on classic novels.

Page 315:

2. *A Morning for Flamingos,* a novel by James Lee Burke, takes place in the South.

3. *Sierra* magazine always gives me good articles on traveling, like the one titled "Georgia's Len Foote Hike Inn."

4. In the old bar, John Prine's "Old Folks" was playing.

5. Several prominent citizens of Sioux Falls, South Dakota, are veterans of the war in Iraq.

6. Every New Year's Eve, which occurs on Tuesday this year, Juan volunteers to be the designated driver.

7. The people in the Philippines are suffering through the worst typhoon in history.

8. Every actor wants a chance to play the leading role in William Shakespeare's play *Hamlet*.

9. As Professor Kelber sat in the airliner, a flight attendant offered her copies of *Time, American Pilot,* and *The New Yorker* magazines.

10. The thrift store run by the Episcopal church on State Street has decided to move three blocks north this summer.

Page 317:

2. *The Secret Life of Walter Mitty* was showing at **12:00** and at 2:15.

3. For the class party, Suzette bought 10 boxes of plastic knives and forks, **145** paper plates of various sizes, 55 plastic cups, 110 paper coffee cups, and 350 paper napkins.

4. May 8, 1945, is commonly known as V-E Day.

5. Mr. Johnson told **five** of his students to read Act **1,** scene **4** of the play.

Appendix

Page 416:

2. surprises
3. names
4. emotions
5. noncount
6. systems

7. noncount
8. situations
9. weeks
10. noncount

Page 417:

2. When cows are thirsty, they do not drink milk.
3. That sad man does not believe in happiness.
4. Nawal hired a plumber to fix the clogged sink.
5. Envy makes people speak and act unpleasantly.

Page 418:

2. Impatience causes many people to act prematurely.
3. Charles told his therapist about the anxiety he had felt all month.
4. Because he really liked her, Jean Paul gave the pineapple to Simone.
5. If someone would give him a little bit of attention, he would calm down.

Page 419:

2. Serena thanked the man who had sold her the last concert ticket.
3. Her admission of guilt made the conversation between them much easier.
4. Every time Josefina goes to the flamenco performance, she buys a new CD.
5. The zebra that crossed the street together with the Beatles was barely noticed.
6. Joy was only one of the emotions they experienced as they approached the city.
7. Before he left home for the last time, Oscar knew he needed a good education.
8. The owner of the restaurant asked the cook to make an especially nice rice pudding for his favorite customer.
9. Many poor countries need doctors and nurses to help fight disease and malnutrition.
10. Fred wants to gain weight, so he bought five pounds of turkey tail.

Pages 420–421:

2. Cyrano had a very big nose.
3. Innocencia invited us all because she had just been paid.
4. When we drove to Michoacan, the engine had some trouble.
5. According to a news website, it will be cold in Novosibirsk tomorrow.
6. Although Yulina loved her family, she wanted to study abroad.
7. Mala's parents stared at me all night long.
8. There is plenty of time to register for classes.
9. After the dog stopped barking, we all were able to sleep.
10. Sancho Panza admired Don Quixote, so he stayed with him all day.

Page 423:

2. The plumber has not sent me the bill yet.
3. The woman who was hiding in the doorway has taken your sandwich.
4. The movie was finished long before I woke up.
5. Did the man in the red suit talk all night?
6. Rafiki showed them that he has not lost his keys.
7. Her little cousin is too frightened to enter the haunted house.
8. My parents do need some help mowing the lawn.
9. Hiroko has turned off the music because she is preparing for a test.
10. For the pill to work, you must drink three glasses of water.

Pages 425–426:

Answers will vary. Here are some possible sentences.

2. If you come across my keys sometime today, will you let me know?
3. Would you look over this manuscript for me?
4. The umpire called off the game because it had started to rain.
5. No matter how much logic I use, I am unable to reason with my brother.
6. My mother doesn't approve of the man I met at the club last night.
7. I wonder what she would say if I asked her out on a date.
8. Do you think the officer would object to my offering her a bribe?
9. I will not leave the store until I have a chance to try on this sport coat.
10. If you have some extra time this afternoon, drop by for a bite to eat.

Page 427:

2. my fresh cotton blouse
3. four large ripe oranges
4. a busy West African market
5. that rusty blue Buick
6. his brother's worst family memory
7. two popular jazz drummers
8. that old leather hiking boot
9. several talented soccer players
10. those seven black mustard seeds

Credits for Readings, Chapter 6

Index